DISRUPTING COLONIAL PEDAGOGIES

TRANSFORMATIONS: WOMANIST, FEMINIST,
AND INDIGENOUS STUDIES

Edited by AnaLouise Keating

A list of books in the series appears at the end of this book.

DISRUPTING COLONIAL PEDAGOGIES

Theories and Transgressions

Edited by
JILLIAN FORD
AND
NATHALIA E. JARAMILLO

UNIVERSITY OF ILLINOIS PRESS
Urbana, Chicago, and Springfield

© 2023 by the Board of Trustees
of the University of Illinois
All rights reserved
1 2 3 4 5 C P 5 4 3 2 1
♾ This book is printed on acid-free paper.

Publication was supported by a grant from the
Howard D. and Marjorie L. Brooks
Fund for Progressive Thought.

Library of Congress Cataloging-in-Publication Data
Names: Ford, Jillian, editor. | Jaramillo, Nathalia E., editor.
Title: Disrupting colonial pedagogies : theories and
     transgressions / edited by Jillian Ford and Nathalia E.
     Jaramillo.
Description: Urbana : University of Illinois Press, [2023]
     | Series: Transformations: womanist, feminist, and
     indigenous studies | Includes bibliographical references
     and index.
Identifiers: LCCN 2023007871 (print) | LCCN 2023007872
     (ebook) | ISBN 9780252045370 (cloth) | ISBN
     9780252087493 (paperback) | ISBN 9780252054976
     (ebook)
Subjects: LCSH: Womanism. | Sex discrimination against
     women. | Male domination (Social structure) | Critical
     pedagogy.
Classification: LCC HQ1197 .D57 2023 (print) | LCC HQ1197
     (ebook) | DDC 305.42—dc23/eng/20230414
LC record available at https://lccn.loc.gov/2023007871
LC ebook record available at https://lccn.loc.gov/
     2023007872

*To the women who have inspired this anthology and who helped
shape our understandings of the truths we lay bare*

Contents

Foreword   ix
AnaLouise Keating

Acknowledgments   xi

Introduction   1
Nathalia E. Jaramillo and Jillian Ford

PART I: DISEMBODYING COLONIALITY

1   *Vivisection*: Decolonizing Media's Hidden Curriculum
of Black Female Subjectivity through a Mash-Up of Visual Arts
and Performance   13
Khalilah Ali

2   Breath, Spirit, and Energy Transmutation:
Womanist Praxes to Counter Coloniality   32
Jillian Ford

PART II: TRANSFORMING INTERVENTIONS

3   Discursive Colonialism of Hmong Women in Western Texts:
Education, Representation, and Subjectivity   51
Leena N. Her

4   A Spiritual Infusion: An Anti-Colonial Feminist Approach
to Academic Healing and Transformative Education   69
Angela Malone Cartwright

5   Healing the Soul—Curando el Alma—Na' Sanna'e Ini'e Collective:
A Feminist BIPOC Migrant Mixtec Serving Leadership
and Research Initiative   85
*Lorri J. Santamaría, Adriana Diego, Genevieve Flores-Haro, Silvia García
Aguilár, Luisa León Salazár, Claudia Lozáno, Liliana Manriquez, and
Alberta Salazár*

PART III: UNDOING COMMAND

6   #CrunkPublicHealth: Decolonial Feminist Praxes
of Cultivating Liberatory and Transdisciplinary Learning,
Research, and Action Spaces   115
LeConté J. Dill

7   Activating Space and Spirit: Meditations on Spiritually
Sustaining Pedagogies   134
Sameena Eidoo

8   Dear Doctoral Student of Color: Academic Advising
as Anti-Colonial Womanist Pedagogy and Theory   152
Patricia Krueger-Henney

Contributors   171

Index   177

Foreword

ANALOUISE KEATING

How does transformation happen, and what roles can scholarship play in effecting progressive change, at both individual and collective levels? How do we create books that do not simply replicate the status quo—the conventional academic disciplinary boundaries and approaches to pedagogy and knowledge production—but, instead, transform it? How do we reshape education into more inclusive, expansive, revolutionary forms? How do we take what we've learned in the academy out into our various communities? And what roles might Spirit (define it how you will) play in these transformations? What might Spirit-inflected pedagogies, epistemologies, ontologies, and methods look like?

The series, Transformations: Womanist, Feminist, and Indigenous Studies, emerged from these and related questions. Grounded in the belief that radical progressive change—on individual, collective, national, transnational, and planetary levels—is urgently needed and, in fact, possible (although not necessarily easy to achieve), this book series exists to invite radical change. It offers new venues for transdisciplinary scholarship informed by women-of-colors theories, decolonial perspectives, and post-oppositional knowledge creation. As I define it, post-oppositionality represents relational approaches to coalition building, theory making, identity formation, and social change. Post-oppositionality invites us to learn from, build on, and liberate ourselves from the dichotomous (us-against-them) theories and practices we generally employ. Post-oppositionality demands that we think differently, that we step beyond our conventional (colonial/colonizing) rules, that we take new risks.

Foreword

I describe this theory praxis as "post-oppositional" (rather than "nonoppositional") to underscore both its relationship to oppositional thought and its visionary invitation to move through (and, perhaps, beyond) it. Post-oppositionality does not entirely reject oppositional thought and action; instead, it uses context and self-reflection to borrow from and transform oppositionality itself (see my book *Transformation Now! Toward a Post-Oppositional Politics of Change* for more on post-oppositionality). Put differently: when we adopt a post-oppositional approach, we don't reject oppositionality (which, ironically, would be oppositional); instead, we draw from and build on oppositionality's lessons. (To borrow from this book's title: We *disrupt* oppositionality's dichotomous framework!) Although post-oppositionality can take many forms, these forms typically share several traits: the belief in our radical interconnectedness with all that exists; the acceptance of paradox, contradiction, and complexity; and the use of relational difference to foster radical inclusivity. These traits enable us to create complex commonalities and broad-based alliances for social change.

Nathalia E. Jaramillo and Jillian Ford's edited collection *Disrupting Colonial Pedagogies: Theories and Transgressions* beautifully illustrates these post-oppositional traits and others, as well. Look, for instance, at the editors' inclusivity: Contributors represent a wide range of academic fields and locate themselves both inside and outside academic institutions; they are professors, administrators, students, community healers, activists, othermothers, and more. This inclusivity is foundational to *Disrupting Colonial Pedagogies'* decolonial work. I greatly appreciate this collection's theoretical diversity; it reminds us that we need many radical perspectives and intertwined visions to facilitate progressive transformation.

Drawing on these diverse legacies, contributors offer much-needed disruptions to the academic status quo—the colonial foundations and Cartesian-based knowledge systems that stifle our growth, create disparate outcomes for students, and in other ways reinforce existing power systems. Through their words and bold examples, the authors encourage us to take our own risks. *Disrupting Colonial Pedagogies: Theories and Transgressions* offers an incredibly useful, highly complex, radically diverse tool kit filled with practices and perspectives designed to nourish our souls as we work to enact radical transformation in our classrooms and beyond. May *your* work be transformed through the words in this book.

January 2023
Denton, Texas
Unceded territories of the Comanche,
the Wichita, the Tawakani, and the Kiikaapoi

Acknowledgments

The editors acknowledge the sun(s), moon(s), stars, oceans, rivers, and all parts of the universe in which we live and those parts in which we do not live. We are humbled by the duality of our relative insignificance paired with the reality that who we are and what we do *matters*. We thank all plants and animals—past, present, and future—and recognize that as humans, we are no more or less important than any other living thing. We are grateful for AnaLouise Keating, the Transformations: Womanist, Feminist, and Indigenous Studies series editor, for her inspiration, guidance, and unwavering support. We honor our spiritual, familial, and academic ancestors and offer this project as a way to give thanks. We share deep gratitude for the chapter contributors for their wisdom, beautiful writing, trust, and patience as the process unfolded. Significantly, we are thankful for the deepened friendships and formations of sisterhood that have developed throughout the years it took to complete this volume.

Jillian's acknowledgments: Thank you to my parents; grandparents; siblings, Alison and Lewis; aunts; uncles; niece; nephews; and cousins for being my first examples of how to love. Thank you to my chosen fam, including Marcela, Melanie, Holiday, Strawberi, Ana, Tiffany, Janine, my Orlando family, my niblings, all members of the Pandemic Chat Crew, Las Mariposas, collaborators in #BlackTeachersMatter, comrades in Stronger Together, and my students who continue to challenge and inspire me. Thank you to my four-legged kids, Combahee, Next, and Jonquil, for helping me learn that love transcends species. Thank you to the vegetables that grow in our garden, for demonstrating graceful change: the art

Acknowledgments

of unfurling. And thank you to my late wife, Jamilah Johnson Singh—who transitioned in the middle of this project—for reorienting me toward the sun.

Nathalia's acknowledgments: Thank you to the women who have contributed to this collection and provided us with inspiration. To all women who have continuously challenged the patriarchal and colonial social order and demonstrated with their words and actions that another world is possible. I dedicate this collection to my mother, Gloria, for always instilling in me grace and strength to navigate the messy terrain of living in dual worlds. I also dedicate this collection to Adolfo Alvarez (my Uncle Al), a man of integrity, warmth, generosity, and brilliance who took me as his own and left this earth so suddenly as I worked on the final details of this volume. My dearest Uncle Al; he expressed womanist solidarity in heart, actions, and spirit. Thank you to our young artist Kenya Santamaría for gifting us a beautiful cover that captures the sentiment of this text. On the cover she included the New Zealand flower pohutakawa, which fills our hearts with aroha. Pohutakawa has deep spiritual meaning in Aotearoa, for connecting the beginning and ending of human life. A lone centuries-old pohutakawa tree sits cramped between boulders, jettisoning toward the meeting place of the Tasman Sea and the Pacific Ocean, at Cape Reinga on the North Island. Reinga, *Te Rerenga Wairua*, Leaping Off Place of Spirits. At that place of stillness, I acknowledge the sacredness of the women who inspired this volume. Thank you to my coeditor, Jillian, for her commitment to this project and for working with me over the years to bring this to fruition. And finally, special gratitude to the Interdisciplinary Studies Department, Kennesaw State University, for their financial assistance with the index and more importantly, for their collegiality and support.

Introduction

NATHALIA E. JARAMILLO AND JILLIAN FORD

Colonial pedagogies seek to control bodies and bodies of knowledge. Disrupting these pedagogies of control requires both an exposure of their mechanics and a rewriting of the aims, forms, functions, and locations of relational meaning-making, which offer emancipatory alternatives. One of the most entrenched legacies of colonialism in the United States is the ongoing harm inflicted on Indigenous, Black, Latino/a/as, Asian, and other students and communities of Color in schools. We offer *Disrupting Colonial Pedagogies: Theories and Transgressions* as an interepistemic project to engage readers with a wide range of feminist theories—especially Black and of Color—written by scholars and practitioners from several disciplines. Our aim is to add to the literature that shifts thinking about colonialism as a historical event in education to coloniality, which names the contemporary manifestations of power, hierarchy, and perceived human worth as they relate to pedagogies in and outside prekindergarten through twelfth grade (P–12) and higher education classrooms in the United States.

From the outset of this project, we hoped to bring together women who engage in socially transformative educational research and practice from the contextual specificity of their geographical, epistemic, and ontological locations. We aspired to enter into a multivocal conversation with the larger field of critical pedagogy from the "place" of women's engaged practice. As we read and reflected on the contributions submitted to our initial call for chapters, we noted that despite our varied histories and identities, we shared the lived experience of working and living within the echelons of a globalized, Western-centric educational apparatus that is structurally shaped by the histories of conquest and capitalist exploitation.

Introduction

Europeans created race as a heuristic to serve as the framework within which philosophical and material justifications were made for the conquest, genocide, and enslavement that constituted colonization (Quijano & Ennis, 2000). While colonialism refers to a specific political and economic relationship wherein one nation usurps control over another nation or people's sovereignty, coloniality refers to the structures that continue to govern subordination and power long after the colonized nation has won "independence." Coloniality of power exposes the ways that domination continues to organize the production and legitimization of knowledge in modern times (Maldonado-Torres, 2007; Richardson, 2012), which are crucial dimensions for analyzing what goes on in schools today. Contributors to this volume critique how popular culture influences perceptions of Black women, how mainstream textbooks represent Hmong women, and how "at-risk" discourses persist about Black and Brown youth in the field of public health. Others describe the value of community-generated research and knowledge, the role of spirituality in higher education, and the importance, difficulty, and beauty of supporting women and gender-expansive graduate students of Color as they enter into the violence of the academy. Due to its seemingly omnipresent nature, coloniality survives historical and ongoing attempts by Black, Indigenous, and other People of Color (BIPOC), to gain academic freedom. Nelson Maldonado-Torres explains,

> [Coloniality] is maintained alive in books, in the criteria for academic performance, in cultural patterns, in common sense, in the self-image of peoples, in aspirations of self, and so many other aspects of our modern experience. In a way, as modern subjects we breathe coloniality all the time and every day. (2007, p. 243)

In the United States and other (settler) colonial nation-states, the significance of race and labor is so integral to how society functions that children often learn them before learning *about* them. That is to say, two fundamental axes of power that define modernity, race and capitalism, do much of their work before children enter formal schooling. Structures of public schooling, including funding formulas, curriculum, and pedagogies, most often serve to maintain and accelerate those logics that shaper wider society. They were founded and maintained in the context of the "imperial attitude" (Maldonado-Torres, 2007, p. 246), which tags racialized people as disposable.

This work has been an intense labor of love, the kind of love that bell hooks references when she writes of love as "a combination of care, commitment, knowledge, responsibility, respect, and trust" (1994, p. 131). Through our labor of love, we ultimately hope to stimulate discussions over the legacy of conquest and colonization in pedagogical practice. In addition to offering a space for critical engagement with the legacy of coloniality in the diverse disciplines reflected in this collection, we found it imperative to center this body of work on how women activists, researchers, artists, and philosophers disrupt colonial pedagogies. On this point, we are reminded of the contributions by our foremothers who are centrally referenced throughout—Gloria Anzaldúa, Cherríe Moraga, Grace Lee Boggs, Cynthia Dillard, bell hooks, Patricia Hill Collins, Linda Tuhiwai Smith, Chandra Mohanty, the Combahee River Collective, and the Sangtin Writers Collective to name a few—all of whom were disruptive transgressors. Disruption, in this sense, is about transcending the boundaries that have situated us as outcasts to begin with. This edited collection builds upon a legacy of queer, Black, Latinx, Asian, feminist, womanist, materialist, anti-colonial, decolonizing, and decolonial writers, researchers, educators, and activists, creating generative experiences for our students and collaborators and infusing our disciplines with concepts and pedagogical practices that refute colonial domination.

Conquest, Colonization, and Pedagogy

The historical traditions of conquest and colonization reverberate in both subtle and overt ways. In the years following the American Revolution, the federal government created laws that gave stolen Indigenous lands to new states entering the union with a mandate that a portion of these lands be used to establish and maintain systems of public education. That is, schooling has been an instrument of genocide and dispossession since its inception. We only need to consider the famed assimilationist boarding schools of Native American children in the late nineteenth century in the United States that operated under the ethos "kill the Indian in him, save the man." Such schools intended to erase the "Indian"—by name, spirit, aesthetic, and ways of knowing—and replace it with the presumed nobility of White, male, Christian heteropatriarchy. Efforts to take the "Indian" out of the "man" were not limited to primary education alone. As Sandy Grande has so powerfully noted, several of the most revered universities in the country—Harvard University, the College of William and Mary, and Dartmouth College—had "all been established with the charge of 'civilizing' and 'Christianizing' Indians as an inherent part of their institutional missions" (2015, pp. 15–16), dating back to the mid-eighteenth century.

The so-called civilizing mission of education in the United States was formative and foundational to an evolving citizenry that grew to incorporate more women, Black people, Latino/a/s, Asians, and immigrants from other parts of world into formal education. The effects of this civilizing mission continue to impact education and operate as an interlocking system of gendered, sexual, racial, and economic oppression within the backdrop of the colonial enterprise. Further, formal education in the US functions as a site for the transmission of what Grande refers to as the "deep structures of colonialist consciousness" (2015, p. 99) or what others refer to as the modernist worldview (see Grosfoguel, 2013). Drawing on the work of Robert Dreeben (1968) and Linda Tuhiwai Smith (1992), Grande outlines five implications of these elements of colonialist consciousness on contemporary schooling:

- Students are expected to comport themselves individually; *student independence is rewarded* such that behaving well means acting as though one is alone, despite a classroom of other students.
- *Achievement is equated with self-worth*; standards of excellence pinpoint abstract measure of success. Students are socialized to understand school performance as a means to a (materially greater) end.
- *Students are taught that their actions alone determine their fate*; that secular humanism reveals truth. Enlightenment ideals of empiricism dictate that students can know everything there is to know through observation and rationality. This implication debases spiritual and religious knowledges.
- *Official knowledge is learned at schools*; students' familial and personal "funds of knowledge" are insufficient or invalid (Moll, Amanti, Neff, & Gonzalez, 1992).
- *Students are taught to understand themselves as distinct from nature.* They learn that consequential knowledge is transmitted inside a classroom, inside a school building.

Against the backdrop of colonialist consciousness, *Disrupting Colonial Pedagogies* embraces hooks's notion of education as the practice of freedom. As hooks explains,

> To educate as the practice of freedom is a way of teaching that anyone can learn. That learning process comes easiest to those of us who teach who also believe that there is an aspect of our vocation that is sacred; who believe that our work is not merely to share information but to share in the intellectual and spiritual growth of our students. (1994, p. 13)

"Engaged pedagogy," in hooks's terminology, emphasizes well-being for self-actualization. Self-actualization is a process of disinterring the values, beliefs, and remembrances that have led to a perceived state of self.

Readers of this collection will encounter hooks's words and contributions repeatedly, as she has opened the discourse on pedagogy to include thoughts on love, eros, transformation, and transcendence as part of the learning community's experience. Our work—whether in the classroom or through the other mediums in which we find ourselves—is about the intellectual and spiritual growth of ourselves, our students, and our communities. There is a spiritual dimension in this pedagogical approach, one that is also echoed when several contributors in this collection invoke Dillard—Nana Mansa II of Mpeasem's notion of endarkened feminist knowledges. Dillard's endarkened epistemologies is informed by her travels to Ghana, dating back to 1995. Her time in Ghana provided an opportunity for her to reunite with African ways of knowing and being as a student of the length and breadth of Black history from the continent of Africa through its diaspora (2020). Endarkened epistemologies center around the African concept of *ubuntu*, which translates to "I am because we are" (2020, p. 375). For Dillard, endarkened knowledges have provided her students with an opportunity to "(re) member themselves and their culture and histories from Africa to the US and back again" (2020, p. 376). She has taken many of her students to Ghana with her to study abroad. To truly study abroad requires the skill to develop openness and understanding, to "center Black women's ways of knowing and being," and to deepen one's own spirituality as the practice of bearing "witness" to an energy and responsibility greater than ourselves (2020, p. 376).

Dillard's endarkened epistemologies and hooks's engaged pedagogies echo through the pages of this text. They enter into conversation with the thoughts of other women, such as Grace Lee Boggs, who in her activism and philosophical thought called for a recognition of how much "spiritual and moral force is involved in the people who are struggling" (2017). Many of us have been struggling to understand our identity and place in this complicated and painful world; in our collective struggle, we invoke a womanist, feminist, and decolonial critique to *disrupt colonial pedagogies*.

Organization of Book

We begin with Part One: Disembodying Coloniality, a pair of essays that examine how womanist, Black feminist, and decolonial theorizing and creative activity offer an introspective space to look at the impact of conquest and colonization on perceptions of the Black female body and spirit. We take our bodies back from colonial violence, and in so doing, we leave coloniality devoid of the power to articulate who we are to be, how we are to be represented, or how we should define our spiritual well-being.

In Part Two: Transforming Interventions, the authors directly engage the tropes prescribed to female subjectivities. Through text, philosophy, and research methodologies, the authors challenge colonizing definitions of womanhood,

5

enlightenment, and ontological well-being. We transform interventions that were developed and created to either "fix" the ailments of colonized women or to assuage our desire to recuperate knowledge(s) from our motherlands, knowledges inherently spiritual in dimension and liberatory in purpose. Here, our titular play on words is intentional: we are transforming colonialist interventions using interventions that are, themselves, transformative.

We conclude this collection with Part Three, Undoing Command. In this section, the authors—womanish, willful, courageous, loving, and undeterred—reject normative conceptions of how to engage pedagogically. Rather than obeying or internalizing the colonial pedagogical project, the authors in this section undo it and, in that process, find reprieve from its chokehold and offer insights for generations that will follow. We do not claim to have comprehensive answers to the complex issues in the process of undoing command, but we do find ourselves in a continuous state of resistance, as we struggle and create in the difficult liberatory task of remembering and redefining our many selves.

Disembodying Coloniality

The volume begins with Khalilah Ali's chapter, "*Vivisection*: Decolonizing Media's Hidden Curriculum of Black Female Subjectivity through a Mash-Up of Visual Arts and Performance," which explores the self through a decolonizing lens that exposes how the Black female body continues to function as a site of colonial reproduction. Commenting on the fundamental essence of the colonial project, which is to harness control over the colonized, Ali offers a womanist worldview intended to promote balance through art. *Vivisection*, a collaboration between fine artist Fabian Williams and emcee scholar activist Ali, is a mash-up of performance and visual art. Ali confronts the hidden curriculum that casts Black women and girls as unrape-able, impervious to abuse, and disposable; she offers new protocols, methodologies, and theories for creative collaborations between artists and researchers informed by a womanist decolonial worldview.

Jillian Ford's "Breath, Spirit, and Energy Transmutation: Womanist Praxes to Counter Coloniality" offers ideas about pathways to wellness from within the colonialist structures of schooling in the United States. The chapter explains how Black feminism helped open the fissures exposed during a significant spiritual revelation wherein she felt a powerful light emanate from within during a deep yogic pose at a friend's studio. After discussing coloniality, schooling, and mental illness, Ford describes three embodied practices that help clear possible pathways back to that light. Ford emphasizes the descriptive nature of the chapter and discourages readers from interpreting it as prescriptive.

Introduction

Transforming Interventions

Leena N. Her in "Discursive Colonialism of Hmong Women in Western Texts: Education, Representation, and Subjectivity" critiques the representation of Hmong women in Western academic texts. Of particular concern to Her is the way that Eurocentric epistemologies cast Hmong women as "authentic," "refugee," or "assimilated." Similar to the Black female experience Ali discusses in chapter 1, Hmong women are assigned various archetypes to denote their relationship to the West. These archetypes function to control and dominate—extending the colonial worldview and imperialist narratives of war and conquest imposed upon many Southeast Asian nations.

Angela Malone Cartwright in "A Spiritual Infusion: An Anti-Colonial Feminist Approach to Academic Healing and Transformative Education" dissects the Enlightenment-based worldview that lies at the root of formal teaching and learning. Malone Cartwright unearths anti-colonial and feminist philosophy and calls for a spiritual infusion to transform educational spaces, making them spaces of healing for both students and educators. She challenges the academy's adherence to the Enlightenment project and calls for a radical realignment in the academy to create transformative, inclusive environments.

In "Healing the Soul—Curando el Alma—Na' Sanna'e Ini'e Collective: A Feminist BIPOC Migrant Mixtec Serving Leadership and Research Initiative," Lorri J. Santamaría, Adriana Diego, Genevieve Flores-Haro, Silvia García Aguilár, Luisa León Salazár, Claudia Lozáno, Liliana Manriquez, and Alberta Salazár detail their co-decolonizing approach to addressing mental health well-being among the Mixtec population in the South-Central Coast of California. Both professionally trained and organic researchers, they articulate the push-pull factors of simultaneously researching and providing healing alternatives for women while using the lens of feminist ideas and decolonizing research methodologies.

Transforming interventions is messy, and all three chapters demonstrate that to do so, we need to radically transform the approaches and tools within our disciplines, texts, and philosophies.

Undoing Command

LeConté J. Dill in "#CrunkPublicHealth: Decolonial Feminist Praxes of Cultivating Liberatory and Transdisciplinary Learning, Research, and Action Spaces" centers Black feminism as a decolonizing praxis in her work as a public health scholar. She unearths the colonialist narratives that frame Black communities as in a perpetual state of "risk" for illness and offers a Black feminist-decolonizing approach to her own teaching, mentoring, and research with a new generation of public health practitioners. Dill crunks deficit-based curricula in pursuit of healing methodologies that can offer communities respite from the overwhelming influence of health interventions focused on disease, disability, and death. #CrunkPublicHealth centers art as decolonial public health praxis and amplifies activism and activists as knowledge producers.

Sameena Eidoo's "Activating Space and Spirit: Meditations on Spiritually Sustaining Pedagogies" reintroduces spirituality into learning. The daughter of Muslim immigrants from India, Eidoo seeks to cultivate sacred life-affirming spaces for those who were not meant to survive. Specifically, Eidoo looks at the interstices of faith, race, ethnicity, and sexuality. She pursues various spiritual activations in conceptualization of programming to engage participants in questions of religion, faith, and spiritual life and (re)imagines possibilities for unsettling colonial curriculum with spiritually sustaining pedagogies in higher education.

In the final chapter, Patricia Krueger-Henney extends the critique of dominant curricular practices that superimpose identities and ways of being. Krueger-Henney's chapter takes the form of a letter, "Dear Doctoral Student of Color: Academic Advising as Anti-Colonial Womanist Pedagogy and Theory." In it, she names the many ways that academia works against the logics of collaboration, creativity, and generative relationship building and explains the precarious corners in which she finds herself. We see this as a broader letter to our readers: one that may serve doctoral students and pretenure faculty of color by articulating what many of us feel but can be difficult to name. Krueger-Henney argues for anti-colonial and womanist pedagogies in student advising as a way to detach from "standardized curricular instructions and rubrics and unfold in opposition to master, homogenized narratives about people's histories and lived experiences." By ending the volume with this chapter, we intend to draw readers into the dialogue and have them consider the ways their own contexts are shaped by coloniality, as well as the solidarity necessary to resist.

Closing Thoughts: Be Disruptive

We have worked to bring voices together that are often kept apart: theorists, practitioners, activists, and teachers. We hope this volume works to disrupt disciplinary silos. Every discipline has its spoken and unspoken pedagogy and praxis, whether that is in how knowledge or the representation of knowledge is deemed valid or how emerging scholars, particularly women of color, evolve as practitioners in their fields. Although the women of this edited collection write from several philosophical, theoretical, creative, artistic, anti-colonial, decolonial, womanist, and feminist perspectives, the overriding focus of pedagogical studies allows us to speak amongst one another given the sheer diversity of scholarship in the pages that follow. In our collective experiences, the contributors examine the overriding structures of society, which are unabashedly capitalist in form, with their accompanying colonial logic embedded within, that continue to reproduce and activate social, economic, political, institutional, spiritual, and land-based exclusions predicated on our racial, ethnic, and gendered histories and identities. We do not, however, assume a unitary or homogenous voice in the expression of our personal experiences and professional work. We are Black, Latinx, South Asian, Southeast Asian, Indigenous, mixed-blood, immigrant, queer, cisgender, neurodivergent, Muslim, interfaith, and spiritual women. We span across territories, our ancestries intersect and interblend through indigeneity, slavery, and forced migration due to the many vestiges of conquest and colonization.

Our identities are mixed, and our daily realities are constructed by the multiple cultures we embody and confront. Here, we are reminded of our foremother Anzaldúa, who has immensely shaped our understanding of identity and vision for transcending social injustice and colonial domination. We relate to her when she shares,

> Like all people, we perceive the version of reality that our culture communicates. Like others having or living in more than one culture, we receive multiple, often opposing messages. The coming together of two self-consistent but habitually incomparable frames of reference causes un choque, a cultural collision. (1987, p. 100)

For us, women engaged in decolonial, decolonizing, and womanist traditions, the *choque*/collision sets into motion an introspective experience where we begin to untangle how we have come to know ourselves and our work. Our movement is diverse and divergent. The authors in this collection traverse disciplinary boundaries and take the reader on a theoretical, philosophical, and creative odyssey to contemplate difference among varying communities. Our approach is intentionally eclectic and iterative. *Disrupting Colonial Pedagogies* is not intended to provide uniform answers to the profound questions of self and society that the authors engage. (Indeed, to offer uniform answers would replicate the colonial project we aspire to disrupt.) To decolonize is to acknowledge and pursue, in the words of the Zapatistas, a world in which many worlds fit. Our *ofrenda*/contribution comes in the form of this book, as we each walk unique paths within the labyrinth of conquest and colonization that has brought us together. We have experienced marginality, and we have shared our observations of the violent and oppressive systems in place that intimately affect us. Our expressions of what needs to be

Introduction

done to counteract the ongoing legacies of sexism, racism, and ethnocentrism, amongst other structural forms of oppression, may vary, but we can, however, convey one common message. Be disruptive.

References

Anzaldúa, Gloria. (1987). La conciencia de la mesiza: Towards a new consciousness. *Borderlands/LaFrontera: The new Mestiza*. San Francisco, CA: Aunt Lute.

Boggs, Grace Lee. (2017, June 15). An interview with Bill Moyers. *Bill Moyers Journal. PBS*, 2008. Retrieved from https://www.pbs.org/moyers/journal/06152007/watch3.html

Dillard, Cynthia, & Neal, Amber. (2020). I am because we are: (Re)membering Ubuntu in the pedagogy of Black women teachers from Africa to America and back again. *Theory into Practice 59*(4): 370–378.

Dreeben, Robert. (1968). *On what is learned in school*. Boston, MA: Addison-Wesley.

Grande, Sandy. (2015). *Red Pedagogy* (10th anniversary ed.). New York, NY: Rowman and Littlefield.

Grosfoguel, Ramón. (2013). The structure of knowledge in Westernized universities, epistemic racism/sexism and the four genocides/epistemicides of the long 16th century. *Human Architecture: Journal of the Sociology of Self-Knowledge 11*(1): 73–90.

hooks, bell. (1994). *Teaching to transgress*. London, England: Routledge.

Maldonado-Torres, Nelson. (2007). On the coloniality of being. *Cultural Studies 21*(2): 240–270.

Moll, Luis C., Amanti, Cathy, Neff, Deborah, & Gonzalez, Norma. (1992). Funds of knowledge for teaching: Using a qualitative approach to connect homes and classrooms. *Theory into Practice 31*(2): 132–141.

Quijano, Anibal, & Ennis, Michael. (2000). Coloniality of power, Eurocentrism, and Latin America. *Nepantla, Views from the South 1*(3): 533–580.

Richardson, Troy A. (2012). Disrupting the coloniality of being: Toward de-colonial ontologies. *Philosophy of Education 31* (2012): 539–551.

Smith, Linda Tuhiwai. (1992). Decolonizing methodologies. London: Zed.

PART I

Disembodying Coloniality

When they torture your mother
plant a tree
When they torture your father
plant a tree
When they torture your brother
and your sister
plant a tree
When they assassinate
your leaders
and lovers
plant a tree
Whey they torture you
too bad
to talk
plant a tree.
When they begin to torture
the trees
and cut down the forest
they have made
start another.

—Alice Walker, *Torture*

1

Vivisection

Decolonizing Media's Hidden Curriculum of Black Female Subjectivity through a Mash-Up of Visual Arts and Performance

KHALILAH ALI

After fully examining my feelings around the spectacles of Black death splashed across social media . . . Sandra Bland's cold stare . . . the battered bodies . . . in-memoriam images of Rekia Boyd . . . videos of a shotgun-armed Koryyn Gaines facing down guards in full military body armor . . . I realized my personal experiences around marginalization as a Black queer neurodivergent woman ran parallel with what I surmised from the videos and transcripts about the executions of Bland, Boyd, and Gaines.[1] Later, the conversations around their assault and slaughter, both inside and outside the Black community, allowed for strange justifications of the ways in which Gaines's and Bland's resistance, in some way, justified their slaughter. The conflicting imagery of aggressive, loud, and hypersexual Black women, invented by adherents to the hegemonic metanarrative, continued through these women, who in many ways were used as props to extend the archetypical trope of the Sapphire,[2] whose sassiness often justified a sound open-handed slap in the mouth. Fast girls, nasty women, women who do not know their place, aggressive, loud—womanish.

Although celebrating self-determinate Black women is an important way to challenge culture's sexually repressive notions of women's innate purity and innocence, such depictions of Black women and girls sadly work against us and only serve to emphasize the deviance of Black femininity. Through the media's hidden curricular depiction of Black women as irascible and unrape-able, the architects of this curriculum successfully use these depictions to justify our abuse. In this chapter, fine artist

Fabian Williams and I conceptualize, through the *Vivisection* exhibit (a mash-up of performance and visual art), a metonymic vivisection, to relate human dissection to the methods used by curricular architects to deny Black women humanity.[3]

Patricia Hill Collins (2000) argues that Black women are often entirely perceived via the archetypal images such as the mammy, jezebel, matriarch, hoochie, or welfare queen. These controlling images are devised to condone the marginalization of Black women. The central lines of inquiry in *Vivisection* are: What is the hidden curriculum or obscured values and lessons taught about Black women in discursive spaces, including music and social media spaces, and how can Black women challenge the images Collins describes? By illustrating the ways the state uses its disciplinarians, we theorize about the ways in which the Black female body is a site of colonial reproduction. Our project allows us to interrogate how police act as vivisectors and uphold the power of an immoral colonial authority. We anchor our work as a counternarrative to media's hidden curricula and use Black women's bodies, disembodied hands, and scalpels and speculums as motifs to rehumanize the metonym of America's colonial project—the Black female body. Through this colonial metanarrative, the Black female body has been used as a canvas upon which beliefs about race, class, and gender are sketched out. Through our art (the preliminary sketches and commentary are included here), we expose the messages embedded in the hidden curriculum about Black femininity.

Conceptualizing Vivisection

We are the children of those who chose to
survive.
—Daughters of the Dust

America says dark corpses are worth multimil-
lion-dollar settlements because bankrupting your
quaint hamlet is a small price to pay for pallid
idyllic landscape, man-made.
—*Vivisection*

I have been an emcee since the Penhale Elementary schoolyards in the rustbelt of Campbell, Ohio, in the late '80s. Although I'd fully embraced a hip-hop identity, I had not performed extensively because working-class motherhood consumed my time. I only released one project—a short collection of several songs in 2009. That mixtape was re-released in 2019 because I felt the depiction of women emcees was rather one-note throughout most of my career, and as artists such as Cardi-B, Gwen Bunn, Sa-Roc, Rapsody, and Lizzo began to challenge popular notions of Blackness and femininity, I thought I could add to the conversation. While writing and recording my very obscure *Ancient Immortals* mixtape, a recurring theme regarding the abuse, silencing, and rendering invisible of Black girls and women in hip-hop became apparent. I had scrawled in my notebook, because I am old school like that, the lines from what was intended to be an ode to hip-hop "I Used to Love H.I.M." (2017):

You can fuck me raw with no Vaseline/slaughter me
Denying me my humanness—"I Used to Love H.I.M."

In a poem leading into another song, "Lemonade Stand," I had written more specifically about the sexual abuse of Black women rather than a generalized oppressed monolithic Black underclass so deified in rap folklore:

We take communion with her nakedness
wash her cunt down in pimp cups
> I have not shredded my own clavicle bone, ventricle, artery or the
> tendons that suspend organs in hollow bodies with full metal jacketed
> lead cores often plated with gilding cupronickel, copper alloys, or steel;
> a thin layer of harder metal protects the softer lead that corrodes tissue,
> expands flesh erupts bone soft unprotected—A spectacle.

In the time since I had written these lyrics and all but abandoned rap as my aesthetic oeuvre, I have continued to examine my own experiences and those of other Black women while paying attention to the public personification of Black femaleness in popular and social-media discourses and discussed this with Fabian, who was instrumental in bringing the project to light (he designed the album cover). Black women's and girls' sexualized and racialized bodies continue to be at the center, especially in online and popular culture discursive spaces, in part, due to an almost taken for granted consensus that foregrounds our bodies as the canvasses to sketch out hierarchies. Black females and the bodies they inhabit are, thus, the ideological ground zero upon which adherents to and constructors of colonial projects define, articulate, and justify their interlocking systems of degradation and oppression. Fabian and my previous collaboration on *Ancient Immortals*, our discussions about how Black women's suffering is often ignored in the hip-hop and art communities in Atlanta, and his insistence that I return to hip-hop led to our staging of *Vivisection* as a collaborative performance and fine-art exhibit.

Vivisection: Artist and Scholar-Intellectuals' Collaborations as Artivism

The narrative around the deaths of Black folks, whether at the hands of police or white vigilantes who fancy themselves defenders of genteel citizenry, often conjures up images of young Black men. Indeed, the data suggests that men, of all races, are disproportionately murdered by state-sanctioned violence. Although most antiterror advocates insist the *collective* of Black citizens are being sieged upon, some of the same advocates still fail to address the equally startling figures regarding Black women. It seems Black women's assaults and murders by the hands of the state are, relative to the commonness of their occurrences, reported on, retweeted about, or marched for in a manner inconsistent with the occurrence of these incidents. Even sadder still, when images do flash across our screen of Black women murdered and brutalized, all too often the victims are villainized, called sassy, mouthy, or in some other way blamed for the violence inflicted on them. Both Bland and Gaines, two Black female victims of extrajudicial murder, were excoriated in the uglier realms of social media for failing to comply, being sassy, nondocile, confrontational, unfeminine women—Sapphires. The archetypes of Black women have been used as justification for the violence committed against them. From the public-lynching trading cards of old to the current Facebook live executions on a seemingly daily basis, social interactivity plays a crucial role in the spectacularism and sensationalism of Black death. Indeed, the media's colonial hidden curriculum is rooted in Black death.

To address pop culture's depiction of Black female death, I, along with artivist Fabian Williams, whose work often depicts police violence, conceptualized the *Vivisection* exhibit, a mash-up of performance and visual art, to relate human dissection to the methods used by curricular architects to deny Black women humanity. The collection was to consist of nine mixed-media (acrylic, aerosol, oil, fiberglass, and canvas or board) works, and performative aspects would accompany the visual art and included prose, poetry, performance, and music. The exhibit was conceived as a juxtaposition of the grotesque (paintings of vivisected women) and the beautiful (women subjects' faces rendered in an ethereal style). This chapter outlines the pedagogical framework that undergirds our work as a challenge to the hidden curriculum. Scholars can use our work to conceptualize the utility of an aesthetic artifact to affect change or promote conversations around social justice. These "usable" texts when consumed by viewers (Toni Cade Bambara as cited in Lewis, 2015, p. 202) permit analyses that delve into the complemental web of ideas spun when seemingly differing disciplines converge. Thus, by insisting on previously unexplored modes of expression, artist-intellectuals as researchers update our methodology and practice to align with the intersectional nature in the work of decolonizing media. Additionally, when we collaborate with other producers of aesthetic artifacts, particularly, those living within the communities we observe, researchers engage in a much more emic approach to our studies, wherein the voice of the subject is privileged over the voice of the imposing observer. Lastly, through this type of collaboration, both researcher-artist and community-artist bring their unique skill sets and understandings forward to compose a much more complex and thematically rich series of works.

Art can be a tool in developing not only Black consciousness but also the consciousness of all audiences—hence, artivism.[4] The conflict, though, is often the competing interests of the academic researcher and the artists—the often-pedantic and formulaic nature of both quantitative *and* qualitative research, and the free, albeit purposeful, creative process of the conscientious artist. A solution might be in finding new protocols, methodology, and theory for new creative collaborations between artists and researchers—this was another hopeful outcome of the *Vivisection* project.

Black Female Bodies as Sites of Violence

The extant literature around hidden curricula is often centered around addressing the ways in which students come to schools infected with unsanctioned curricula that may reinforce, conflict, or intersect with the goal of schooling. Jackson (1968) first observed that lurking beneath the ethos of the primary classroom were unspoken norms and rules, which he defined as "the hidden curriculum." More researchers have examined how the hidden curricula implanted into the populace reinforce desirable behaviors in members of various social-class strata and gender presentations (Bowles & Gintis, 1976; Anyon, 1980; McLaren, 1988; Apple, 1993). Hidden curricula can maintain the social order, for instance, by ensuring girls are inculcated with the belief that they are indubitably destined for motherhood, and, therefore, they may choose to forgo education, or they may go into the helping professions; or hidden curricula may reinforce, in members of the working class, a belief that their most prized skills include obedience and submission. Meanwhile, managerial or upper-class youth are taught, and concomitantly celebrated for leadership behavior, such as vociferousness—a behavior that would be viewed as deviant by poor boys and met with swift punishment (Giroux and Penna, 1983; Horn, 2003; Vallance, 1983). Of course, hidden curricula are present in formal learning environments, such as schools, but hidden curricula are present in any place where people congregate and communicate. Thus, a hidden curriculum is a set of beliefs, values, and lessons that are not formally taught but are implicitly so, and members adapt to and understand them (Anyon, 1980; Giroux and Penna, 1983; Horn, 2003). These values and lessons are often obfuscated, yet community members are expected to and do comply with them. Media, in multitudinous forms, particularly social media for purposes of this piece, are powerful conductors for these implicit and obfuscated values and lessons.

Feminists have explored the female body as a site of both resistance and subjugation, and the multiple ways that the physical body, or our conceptualization of its meaning, allows for analysis of gender, sex, beauty, disability, and death (Butler, 1993; Scarry, 1985; Grosz & Probyn, 1995). Butler's (1993) *Bodies That Matter* addresses the ways in which the gendered body is depicted. Similarly, our project concentrates on the physical form of the Black woman as depicted historically and contemporarily. Feminists conceptualize the physical body, the flesh, as a site of trauma. The colonial imagination reduces the Black female body to an object. An ironic result is an "irresistible [for the viewer, yet], destructive [for the Black woman-turned-object] sensuality" (Spillers, 1987, p. 67).

In the ontological relationships that come as result of a colonial project, an individual can take one of two different roles: an agent of the colonial authority or subject. The colonial project relation has a single property associated with it: control. The individual entity has several identifiers associated with it that inform how an individual functions under the system of domination, such as race, gender, class, and geopolitical positioning.

In *Vivisection*, we intended to disrupt those identifiers and trouble the ways those identifiers are used to categorize one within the power structure. We thought we'd decenter the colonial agent but depict the remnants of his work— the ripped flesh, the lesions. Just his implements. The subject, the Black woman, while not the agent of the colonial authority, who is conspicuously absent in our images, is the agent of our gaze—she resituates the way the eye and her narrative are prioritized. The story privileged here is not the discourse of the state but the narrative of the resituated subject. I suggest the work troubles, rather than destroys, the relationship because as long as the colonial project embedded in the media's hidden curriculum exists, these subtype relationships are interminable. The wounds are present as are the agent's implements—the handiwork is present while the agent hides his hands in the same way the brutality of the executors of these women are, too, out of sight. Officers, as colonial agents, are presented publicly as heroes, protectors, and do-gooders acting on behalf of a benevolent authority. They appear in courts in suits and ties, and in the media in their blues with badges emblazoned across their chest. Victims are either unnamed, shown in mugshots, or in blurry, unflattering images snatched from social media.

Vivisection is an effort to resist the dehumanizing colonial project that constructs Black women as disposable. However, the colonial project, specifically how it has been executed in the Western Hemisphere, is reliant on brutally dehumanizing indigenous and enslaved Africans by dismembering, disemboweling, maiming, and destroying the body of colonized peoples. Spillers argues that the agents of the western hemispheric version of the colonial system rely on the destruction of Black and Brown bodies to establish its order:

> [The colonial] order, with its human sequence written in blood, represents for its African and indigenous peoples a scene of actual mutilation, dismemberment, and exile. First of all, their New-World, diasporic plight marked a theft of the body—a willful and violent (and unimaginable from this distance) severing of the captive body from its motive will, its active desire. Under these conditions, we lose at least gender difference in the outcome, and the female body and the male body become a territory of cultural and political maneuver, not at all gender-related, gender-specific. (1987, p. 67)

While Spillers contends gender is erased through this dehumanizing effort, I argue that rather than the erasure of male bodies, males are defaulted to female, as female bodies are the least regarded yet most exploited. Further, while Spillers (1987) contends Black women and men were "ungendered," I argue Black women retained femaleness but were stripped of femininity and any benevolent protections the patriarchal order had offered to those regarded as feminine. The destruction of Black folks, not just through the taking of land and resources but also through the destruction of the spirits, minds, and bodies of the invaded, is the end game of the colonial system. Therefore, the re-membering of stories of survival by Black females (the incarnation of the *other*) is *the* mechanism to destabilize the loci of the colonial narrative; thus, "[d]ecolonizing gender is necessarily a praxical task. It is to enact a critique of racialized, colonial and capitalist heterosexualist oppression as a lived transformation of the social" (Lugones, 2010, p. 746). Thus, in *Vivisection* we contend the coloniality of power did not end with colonialism (Quijano, 2000); its ideology exists in and permeates throughout the modern capitalist system, globalism, and the English language. The ideology that has constructed otherness and is reliant on its continual propagation has continued long after the end of explicit colonial rule. Capitalism is a system that only came to exist thanks to colonization and the exploitation of the mental, emotional, and physical labor of Black and Brown bodies and their lands' natural resources, which served as the material basis of Europe's pecuniary domination. Certainly, its power structures are reliant on the psychosocial division of labor (exemplified in commodified violent misogynoir in mainstream rap, which our work "puts on blast"), where the objectified Black woman's body is an exportable resource. Coloniality affirms that modernity cannot exist without the colonized other. Decoloniality counters such colonial modernity schemes—wherein othered places and the peoples that inhabit these territories are not premodern—and, instead, insists Black and Brown folks have been included in that same modernity project but as subaltern (Spivak, 1988).

Preliminary Artwork in Context

FIGURE 1.1

The first figure, figure 1.1, in the series depicts a fully nude woman, whose buttocks protrude and whose musculature is exposed. The work was to be labeled to point out the muscles focusing on the buttocks and genitalia. The piece is an homage to Saartjie Baartman;[5] deemed the Hottentot Venus by her exploiters, Baartman was a South African Khoikhoi woman exhibited throughout nineteenth-century Europe as an oddity in freak shows for what was viewed as her oversized buttocks and labia. Baartman was later relegated to sex work and, according to several historians' accounts, died due to syphilitic infection. After her tragic death, Baartman was dissected, and her brain, skeleton, genitalia, and a cast of her body were on display in the Museum of Man in Paris. Over a century later, her remains were repatriated to South Africa, where Baartman was buried in her Khoikhoi homeland during the country's National Women's Day festival in 2002. The sketch and the poetry created to accompany the image were devised to historicize the ways in which Black women's sexualized bodies have been portrayed in whitestream discursive spaces as uncivil, savage, inhuman, odd, deformed, divergent from the norm, and defiant. According to Osha,

> The colonizing agent either unduly romanticized the colonized subject by virginizing her/him through a powerful process of de-agentialization and also by objectification/[fossilization] in the Euro-erotic imaginary) or by hypersexualizing her/him employing tropes of excess, unrestrained carnality, irrationality, and violence. (2014, p. 154)

Collins's (2000) conceptualization of the Jezebel controlling image seems to best embody the archetype we were trying to portray here.

Hidden curricula are, indeed, shaped by issues of race, class, and gender (Martin, 1994; Thorne, 1993; Weis & Fine, 1993). One understudied hidden curriculum that media consumers adapt to and understand is the one where Black women and the bodies they inhabit are objects of scorn and degradation. Scholars have examined how students' and teachers' views about Black people affected how they interacted with Black students, their views on Black folks' citizenship, and what teachers taught as it related to race (Gillborn, 1992); and how race and gender shaped how women of color negotiated their roles and promoted a culture of femininity that informed interactions on university campuses (Margolis et al., 2001). Less has been done to evaluate how media's hidden curriculum denies Black women humanity and the attributes of femininity (as defined by the dominant culture), and little has been done to assess how this curriculum shapes the ways in which learners adopt detrimental beliefs about

FIGURE 1.1. *Billa Anesthesia no. 1*, by Fabian Williams, 2015.

Black women—beliefs that affect how Black women are viewed and treated. With the awareness that hidden curricula are shaped by intersecting issues of race, class, and gender, we can interrogate how hidden curricula use Black female bodies as instruments of oppression and resistance to understand unspoken norms and rules (Gair & Mullins, 2001). A premise in direct contrast to the statistics that show Black women are no more, and in some cases less likely to be, promiscuous and that Black women experience sexual assault more than white women.

The first figure grounds our work in history and illustrates the ways in which white supremacy has successfully embedded the idea of Black women's invulnerability and unrape-ability. Black feminist scholars extend this notion of the unrape-ability of Black women and argue that their bodies take on figurative meanings in popular discursive spaces that "confirm the human body as a metonymic figure for an entire repertoire of human and social arrangements" (Spillers, 1987, p. 66). Black women and girls are often viewed by consumers of media and popular culture as oversexed (as represented early on through figures like Baartman) and, therefore, unable to be sexually assaulted; or when murdered, Black women—especially sex workers and those viewed as sexually deviant—are viewed as deserving of death. Such beliefs confirm the social hierarchy by affirming that Black women are expendable commodities.

FIGURE 1.2

The next figure, figure 1.2, depicts a Black woman whose chest has been opened, and we see disembodied male hands prodding around in her chest cavity. The head is turned with the eyes open. The speculating hands—cutting the subject's chest. The examining devices, including the speculum, represent the constant infusion of authorities into the body of women. Using the speculum and other examination devices as symbols of patriarchal intrusion into the lives of women is not a new idea: "The speculum is a male instrument for the further penetration of the woman" (Moi, 2002, p. 130). The sketch was done on brown paper with purple watercolor ink, the print in archived ink. (Usually medical sketch notes are penned by the team conducting the work. In this case the notes will be written in free verse and rhyme are the thoughts of the unnamed subject).

There is a historical record of Black women having medical procedures forced on them by the state. Because Black women have had their femininity and humanness stripped, medical and governmental personnel did not view their practices as harmful. In *Medical Apartheid: The Dark History of Medical Experimentation on Black Americans from Colonial Times to the Present* (2006), Harriet Washington contends her examples are only a small sample of the medical violence approved and facilitated by governmental authorities with the intent of, unethically, using the Black female body for experimental purposes. Washington relays the history of J. Marion Sims, a nineteenth-century physician considered the father of modern gynecology. Sims used an enslaved African woman to conduct his insidious experiments. The women were often not anesthetized, and it is reported that his unwilling subjects were examined on all fours while held down by other enslaved women. His place in medical history, due to his brutal practices, has come under

FIGURE 1.2. *Billa Anesthesia no. 2*, by Fabian Williams, 2015.

scrutiny. The American Gynecological Association issued a statement, however, arguing that Sims's contributions are innumerable and deserving of celebration, including his invention of the bivalved vaginal speculum. Sims would argue that Black females should be subject to experimentations without their consent. Even after the establishment of the Institutional Review Board, Sims' successors maintained the position. Experiments on enslaved women provide the inspiration for the sketches reproduced in this volume.[6] Notwithstanding these cases there is a historical record that demonstrates medical experimentation conducted by governmental authorities to sterilize the "undesirable" and "feeble-minded." We accessed as a point of subject the public lynchings of Black women and used these images in constructing and talking about this project and to imagine the "materialized scene of unprotected female flesh" (Spillers, 1987, p. 68).

FIGURE 1.3

Figure 1.3 depicts a woman wearing a crown, with an area of her cheeks exposed. These areas of the face depict the muscles that allow the jaw to move. The crowned woman represents the ability to express speech. The vocal cords are not damaged or exposed, yet the subject's ability to be heard is diminished due to the low opening functionality. The subject's face is opened to represent the surgically precision to ensure the silence of Black women. The scalpel, an instrument used to spread tissue, is absent as are the hands seen in figure 1.2. The absence of the instrument and its wielder suggests that the silencing occurs without prompting.

FIGURE 1.4

The sufferings of Black women were ignored during the nineteenth-century anti-vivisection movement, where activists organized against animal vivisection and the unanesthetized gynecological surgeries performed on poor European women subjected to the surgical instrument of unscrupulous physicians (Lansbury, 1985). The hieroglyphics of the Black female body position the Black woman as the primordial and permanent other (Spillers, 1987) (figure 1.4). Because Black women are defeminized and perpetually othered by the white supremacist metanarrative, the failure of anti-vivisectionists to advocate for Black women is not surprising. Bakare-Yusuf emphasizes that generally the female body is a site of "physical and psychological trauma," as our bodies are conflated with labor, desire, and scientific exploitation (1999, p. 312). Yet, Bakare-Yusuf questions how the Black female body, specifically, has also become a site for "white racist violence, diseases, perverse heterosexism, pervasive addictions and unemployment" (1999, p. 312).

The National Association for the Advancement of Colored People (NAACP) keeps a history of lynching, and the organization explicitly reported (from 1882 through 1968) the horrors heaped on each victim. The image was inspired by Mary Turner,[7] whose execution was quite brutal; figure 1.4, depicting a pregnant subject's open womb, is an homage to her. The figure also seeks to speak to the ways women and children are also subject to police violence. Between medical experimentation and the extrajudicial lynching of Black people, one must question the motivations of such brutality. White supremacy and misogynoir, embedded in

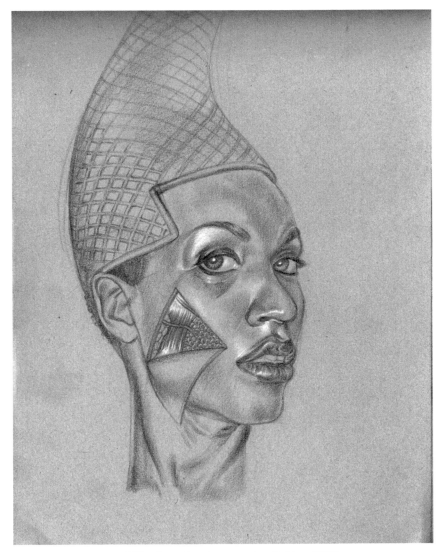

FIGURE 1.3. *Billa Anesthesia no. 3*, by Fabian Williams, 2015.

the hidden curriculum of our media outlets and enshrined in the metanarrative of Americanness, are the culprits; the imaginations of those who embrace whiteness allow such to exist with little to no thought. Tools of vivisection—rope, scalpel, bone saw, and speculum—are symbols of this ideology. The state and its agents, through these symbols, make the Black female body the metonym for death and dismemberment.

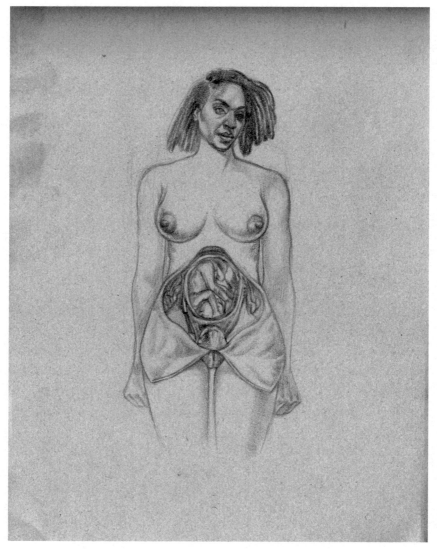

FIGURE 1.4. *Unyonyaji* (exploitation), by Fabian Williams, 2015.

Discussion and Collection Thoughts

Our principal aim here is to analogize the current hegemonic apparatus of social control, with the nineteenth- and twentieth-centuries experimentation on the bodies of Black women. Historians contend that vivisection, or dissection of human subjects with little or no anesthesia for research purposes, has its roots in antiquity. Even then, it was met with a moral quandary—wherein the major lines of inquiry involved notions of power and the morality of dissecting a sentient human being. Philosophers and practitioners alike have questioned their own ethical subjectivity as well as the subjectivity of their participants (the unwilling and willing). However, with the advent of scientific racial classifications, phrenology and other pseudoscientific theories of biological determinism designed to dehumanize non-white subjects, conceptions of what constituted humanness were all but abandoned when applied to Black bodies. Scientists argued that, indeed, Blacks were not human, did not suffer pain, and were not any more sentient than lesser primates (DeGruy, 2005). Since then, guidelines for experimentation on human subjects have been established, vivisection thoroughly denounced, and the medical innovations from these resulting experiments have left much for later scholars to ponder.

Our project, which blends poetry, hip-hop, and fine art, interrogates how, in the modern era, police act as vivisectors, uphold the power of an immoral colonial authority, and sustain the metanarrative of the hidden curriculum that renders Black women inanimate chattel and, thus, cast them as objects synonymous with death/nonlife. Rather than scalpels and speculums, the instrument to render Black women lifeless is the police service revolver. Because the womanist triad of concern (Phillips, 2006) allows for the invocation of ancestral (re)membering; accesses storytelling as resistance; and emphasizes human-human, human-spiritual, and human-nature relationships, we decided that we would use womanism and decoloniality to think about how we would decenter the whitestream hidden curriculum. As artivists, we present *Vivisection* as countercurriculum to the hidden one, and Fabian and I show how stories can be used as theoretical and methodological tools to challenge power. Although I have invoked feminism and Black feminist scholarship throughout, our exhibit is grounded in womanism and decoloniality. We acknowledge that womanism is not just feminism light. It is a distinct way to view the world. From a problem-solving perspective, womanism and feminism are complementary; but for us, womanism provides a more integrative methodology (which was important, as Fabian and I work in a way that crosses disciplines). Also, womanism readily links to decolonial thought, which ideologically grounds our work in the idea that anti-Blackness is global and pervasive and used by the powerful to reify hierarchies that place the darkest members of the colonial paradigm at the bottom. Most important, the spiritual aspect of womanism allows us to think about reanimating the inanimate, and our performance is, in a sense, a spell, ancestral hoodoo—a symbolic effort to give breath and summon spirit into women such as Mary Turner, the victims of J. Marion Sims, Sandra Bland, Rekia Boyd, and Koryyn Gaines. Inspired by Spillers's assertions, as a Black American woman of African descent, rooted in the enslaved experience in the Americas, Black female death is not just a metonym, when faced with a literal extermination. Our positionality, in terms of the work's creation allows a loose narratological reading of these images rather than just semiotic one; the images both explicitly and implicitly transmit meaning, but I also interrogate the storytelling aspect of the images. So, we ask—what counternarrative(s) do the sketches, when taken together as a collection, tell about the victims of state-sanctioned violence and the ways in which the spectacle of death is consumed? Indeed, "[i]f we think of the 'flesh' as a primary narrative, then we mean its seared, divided, ripped-apartness, riveted to the ship's hole, fallen, or 'escaped' overboard" (Spillers, 1987, p. 67).

The conceptual bifurcation inherent in the imagery of the text between the Black female subject and the disembodied, looming vivisector reflects a disruptive decolonial womanist aesthetic. We agree with Phillips's contention that

> [h]uman beings are "energy transforming machines." Womanist activism changes social and ecological realities by changing their foundations in consciousness (hearts & minds) and by creating the social and environmental structures that make new and vivifying forms of human existence sustainable. (2013)

As a methodological and analytic tool, our images destabilize the foundations of the colonial hidden curriculum in consciousness, in that these texts center the perspectives of Black women. Our artifacts depict the unnamed subject's inner life and omit the executor's notes, image, and therefore, his perspective, but his presence is known via the (re)memory of the wounds inflicted upon his subject—both seen and unseen. The pieces insist on disrupting time and space via a convergence of social media iconography, ancestral spirituality, antiquated medical sketches, and hip-hop. Without seeking majoritarian epistemic validation or rewards by fondly depicting the mammy and mule figures primarily as conduits of healing for others rather than themselves, or demonizing the alternate Sapphire or independent Black woman character as selfish and emasculating, our figures must heal for themselves while others still adventitiously benefit. Our representation and treatment of racialized female bodies decolonize the metanarrative by re-memorializing the lived realities of Black bodies in the past and present. As we explore the nature of being Black and female bodied, it is essential that we script our own herstories—even when they are terrible.

Notes

1. Sandra Bland, a twenty-eight-year-old Chicago woman traveling through Waller County, Texas, in 2015, was assailed by a local police officer over a routine traffic stop. Unable to make bail, Bland was found hanging in her cell three days later. Authorities claim she took her own life. The officer conducting the traffic stop was cleared of wrongdoing, and the Waller County officials found that the officers on duty were not involved in Bland's death.

Rekia Boyd, a twenty-two-year-old African American woman, was murdered in 2012 by an off-duty Chicago police detective after firing into a crowd of Boyd's friends. Bystanders claimed the officer was drunk. The officer was charged but later cleared of wrongdoing.

In 2016 twenty-three-year-old Koryyn Gaines was fatally shot in her home after a six-hour standoff with Baltimore County, Maryland, police armed in riot gear there to serve a warrant for a traffic violation. Her young son was also shot. Holding a shotgun, Gaines live-streamed her stand-off affirming her rights to protect her home from unlawful entry by authorities. Facebook ended her live stream, and police shot and killed the young mother of two.

Because I experience a mental health condition, when referencing the intersectional nature of my own marginalized identity, I use the term "neurodivergent"—a term coined by disability activists to challenge the notion of cognitive normality and to embrace the diverse ways in which humans process the world. The term succinctly describes the different ways in which I view what happens around me and challenges the dominant contention that those living with neurodivergence are broken, flawed, or ill. Bland had been treated for depression and Gaines for cognitive dysfunction resulting from lead poisoning—I further found myself in sisterhood with these women.

2. White (1999) describes the image of the Sapphire as an aggressive and emasculating Black woman. The Sapphire, a stereotype popularized early in the nineteenth century through minstrelsy and later through other forms of American entertainment, was used to dehumanize Black women and contrast them with an idealized genteel white femininity.

3. The project is in the genesis stage and at the time of this publication being workshopped.

4. "Artivism" is a portmanteau of art and activism.

5. Osha (2014) contends Baartman's body shaped the colonial discourse wherein all African women came to symbolize savagery, shameless nakedness, and ferocity. Such beliefs were used to justify the White Man's Burden narrative (rooted in Rudyard Kipling's poem of the same name that charges White men with the Christian duty to civilize Black and Brown folks through imperial campaigns). Symbolism works, but I argue that the Black female body is, instead, representative of another of Burke's (1969) master tropes, metonymy, wherein the Black female body is synonymous with death, not just representative of it. Burke's term "master" is also intentionally used here to impugn the ways in which master narratives are shaped through the rhetorical strategies privileged in Eurocentric media.

6. Other models and I were used in the sketch prototypes.

7. Mary Turner was a heavily pregnant, young, Black mother who was victim of a grisly lynching in 1918 by a white mob in Lowndes County, Georgia, for pushing for justice for her lynched husband, Hazel "Hayes" Turner, who, along with ten other Black citizens, had been accused of murdering a White farmer.

References

Anyon, Jean. (1980). Social class and the hidden curriculum of work. *The Journal of Education, 162*(1), 67–92. Retrieved from http://www.jstor.org/stable/42741976

Apple, Michael. (1993). *Official knowledge: Democratic education in a conservative age.* New York, NY: Routledge, 1993.

Bakare-Yusuf, Bibi. (1999)."The economy of violence: Black bodies and the Unspeakable Terror." In J. Price & M. Shildrick (Eds.), *Feminist theory and the body: A reader* (pp. 311–323). New York, NY: Routledge.

Bowles, Samuel, & Gintis, Herbert. (1976). *Schooling in capitalist America: Educational reform and the contradictions of economic life*. New York, NY: Basic Books.

Burke, Kenneth. (1969). Appendix: Four master tropes. In *A grammar of motives*, by Kenneth Burke (pp. 503–517). Berkeley: University of California Press.

Butler, Judith. (1993). Bodies that matter. In J. Price and M. Shildrick (Eds.), *Feminist theory and the body: A reader* (pp. 235–245). New York, NY: Routledge.

Collins, P. H. (2000). *Black feminist thought: Knowledge, consciousness, and the politics of empowerment*. New York, NY: Routledge.

DeGruy, Joy. (2005). *Post traumatic slave syndrome: America's legacy of enduring injury and healing*. Milwaukee, WI: Uptone.

Gair, M., & Mullins, G. (2001). Hiding in plain sight. In E. Margolis (Ed.), *The hidden curriculum in higher education* (pp. 21–42). New York, NY: Routledge.

Gillborn, D. (1992). Citizenship, "race" and the hidden curriculum. *International Studies in Sociology of Education, 2*(1), 57–73. doi:10.1080/0962021920020104

Giroux, H., & Penna, A. (1983). Social education in the classroom: The dynamics of the hidden curriculum. In H. Giroux & D. Purpel (Eds.), *The hidden curriculum and moral education* (pp. 100–121). Berkley, CA: McCutchan.

Grosz, E., & Probyn, E. (1995). *Sexy bodies: The strange carnalities of feminism*. New York, NY: Routledge.

Horn, R. (2003). Developing a critical awareness of the hidden curriculum through media literacy. *The Clearing House: A Journal of Educational Strategies, Issues and Ideas, 76*(6), 298–300. doi:10.1080/00098650309602024

Jackson, P. W. (1968). *Life in classrooms*. New York, NY: Holt, Rinehart, and Winston.

Lansbury, C. (1985). Gynaecology, pornography, and the antivivisection movement. *Victorian studies, 28*(3), 413–437. http://www.jstor.org/stable/3827303

Lewis, T. (2015). *Conversations with Toni Cade Bambara*. Oxford: University Press of Mississippi.

Lugones, M. (2010). Toward a decolonial feminism. *Hypatia, 25*(4), 742–759. Retrieved from www.jstor.org/stable/40928654

Margolis, E., Soldatenko, M., Acker, S., and Gair, M. (2001). Peekaboo: Hiding and outing the curriculum. In E. Margolis (Ed.), *The hidden curriculum in higher education* (pp. 1–20). New York, NY: Routledge.

Martin, J. R. (1994). *Changing the educational landscape: Philosophy, women, and curriculum*. New York, NY: Routledge.

McLaren, P. L. (1988). Culture and canon? Critical pedagogy and the politics of literacy. *Harvard Educational Review, 58*, 213–234.

Moi, T. (2002). Patriarchal reflections: Luce Irigaray's looking glass-speculum. In T. Moi (Ed.), *Sexual/textual politics: Feminist literary theory* (2nd ed.) (pp. 126–130). New York, NY: Routledge.

Osha, S. (2014). *African postcolonial modernity: Informal subjectivities and the democratic consensus*. New York, NY: Palgrave Macmillan. Retrieved from https://doi.org/10.1057/9781137446930

Phillips, L. (2006). Introduction. In L. Phillips (Ed.), *The womanist reader* (pp. x–xx). New York, NY: Routledge.

Phillips, L. (2013). *Womanism, feminism, & moving social/ecological change forward*. PowerPoint presentation, WCW Lunchtime Seminar. Wellesley Centers for Women. Retrieved from https://wcwonline.org/pdf/lss/WCWwomanismLSSslides4.26.13.pdf

Quijano, A. (2000). Coloniality of power and Eurocentrism in Latin America. *International sociology, 15*(2), 215–232.

Scarry, Elaine (1985). *The body in pain: The making and unmaking of the world*. Oxford: Oxford University Press.

Spillers, Hortense. (1987). Mama's baby, papa's maybe: An American grammar book. *Diacritics, 17*(2), 64–81. Retrieved from www.jstor.org/stable/464747

Spivak, G. C. (1988). Can the subaltern speak? In C. Nelson and L. Grossberg (Eds.), *Marxism and the interpretation of culture* (pp. 217–313). Urbana: University of Illinois Press.

Thorne, B. (1993). *Gender play: Girls and boys in school*. New Brunswick, NJ: Rutgers University Press.

Vallance, E. (1983). Hiding the hidden curriculum: An interpretation of the language of justification in nineteenth-century educational reform. In H. Giroux & D. Purpel (Eds.), *The hidden curriculum and moral education* (pp. 9–27). Berkeley, CA: McCutchan.

Washington, H. A. (2006). *Medical apartheid: The dark history of medical experimentation on Black Americans from colonial times to the present*. New York, NY: Harlem Moon Broadway Books.

Weis, L., & Fine, M. (Eds.). (1993). *Beyond silenced voices: Class, race, and gender in United States schools*. Albany: State University of New York Press.

White, D. (1999). *Ar'n't I a woman*. New York, NY: Norton.

2

Breath, Spirit, and Energy Transmutation

Womanist Praxes to Counter Coloniality

JILLIAN FORD

One evening a few years ago, my yoga instructor Sula demonstrated the warrior 2 pose as she reminded us, "Pull your muscles to your bones. Push your right hip forward, so it's even with your left hip. Focus intention on your core." One piece I always loved about Sula's teaching style was the way she reminded us of individual considerations for each pose; in this way she effectively taught across wide ranges of experience in each class. Hers was a pedagogy against assimilation: Sula helped create the space for and proliferation of individual bodies, breaths, movements, and styles. Amidst our individual enactments, our breathing connected us to one another. Windows slightly ajar, we interconnected with the trees in her yard: no scarcity of oxygen to inhale. We acknowledged the opportunity to reciprocate with exhaled carbon dioxide. Balance. I had been practicing with her for over a year by that time, so her reminders served mostly for me as a method by which she vocally maintained rhythm in class. The quality of our own breath served as both a mirror of our own state and as a reminder of the oceans. I was used to Sula's phrases that accompanied most poses. But that night she followed a familiar phrase with, "Force with no movement creates pressure. You see, that's the metaphysics of it all." As soon as she said that, I felt a wave of energy vibrate from my heart down my outstretched arms through the tips of my fingers, down my legs out the bottom of my heels, and up through my spine out the top of my head. I felt like I was shining: steady, strong, and new. Instead of just one vibrational wave, the energy continued to flow: I embodied the origin of the light. Feeling this level of freedom was new to me.

Before she uttered those words, it was the pebbly bass cello in Sula's voice that grounded me. The yoga studio sat at the back of her family's home, just beyond a space typically brimming with life being lived: bicycles harnessed to pulleys overhead, Sula's sons' artwork, fresh vegetables, incense: a warm and intentional Diasporically inspired energy adorned their home. Always there were folks, one or two cats in the common area, and palpable love.

Sula's idea that *force with no movement creates pressure* became a clear metaphor for my ongoing battles with depression (pressure) resulting in part from my participation in efforts to resist anti-Black state violence in schools (force) within the context of a colonial arm of the state: public education (no movement). "Force with no movement creates pressure" made me feel free: it pulled back a curtain, unlocked a door. As a former high school teacher and by then a teacher educator, moments of freedom seemed increasingly rare. Freedom felt fleeting mostly because the static curriculum in the United States continued to propagate the Eurocentric grand narrative, the evermore-standardized assessments enduringly threatened teachers' opportunities to employ engaging pedagogies, and teacher education remained saturated with Whiteness. All of this against a backdrop of cops killing Black folks with impunity. My increasing understanding of the all-encompassing nature of the state-led war on Black people enveloped me with an intensity that sank me. Black feminism, feminisms of Color, and womanism provided the maps I needed to get well, such that I could rejoin efforts of historically situated resistance.

Perhaps the experience occurred the way it did because I had been engrossed in reading Frantz Fanon's *Wretched of the Earth* (1963) for much of the day leading up to the yoga class. I was struck by his notes of the psychiatric patients with whom he worked throughout Algeria's war for independence, in particular, his findings that mental illness "loomed so large among the perpetrators of 'pacification' and the 'pacified' population" (p. 181). To illustrate his point, Fanon presented ten cases of what he called "psychotic reaction" wherein "priority [was] given to the situation that triggered the disorder" (p. 183). He asserted connections between the war and his patients' psychoses by giving detailed firsthand accounts of war-induced symptoms. *It is not my intention to imply that experiences in my life have been remotely similar to anyone who lived through war.* Instead, I wish to lift the general concept that psychiatric diagnoses can be directly related to the state-mandated rules of society and state-sanctioned violence.

This chapter is my attempt to explain some of the tools I used to propel myself out of madness, or at least out of the agony that madness can create: breath, spirit, and energy transmutation. I say "myself" to indicate that which in the end only I could do; my overall healing was anything but solitary. Those closest to me rallied hard to bring me back. Learning to harness my breath, tap into Diasporic and cosmically attuned spirit, and transmute energy, I was able to constitute myself enough to reach back to their outstretched arms of support. Until that point, I had remained untethered.

I realized I was compiling a nexus of lived experiences and theoretical understandings that until that evening in Sula's yoga studio, I regarded as disparate. Sula's declaration about metaphysics dissolved the barriers that had blocked my understanding of the ways in which my difficulty sustaining mental wellness connected to the violence of coloniality through schooling (Ford, 2017; Grande, 2015; Ladson-Billings & Tate, 1995). I recognize that my experiences with schooling account for a part of a much-broader ecology of influences, relationships, and dynamics that shaped my life; it was not solely schooling that damaged my well-being. Schooling was, however, a significant factor, and it was that which played out in public. Black feminist, feminist of Color and womanist writing and community building served as gateways to engage the coloniality I had to confront for healing.

Womanist worldviews run counter to mainstream logics of patriarchy and racial capitalism (Robinson, 2000), such as valuing private ownership and accumulation, revering competition, and normalizing the structures that ensure some peoples' excess wealth derived from other peoples' labor and abject poverty (Amoo-Adare, 2004/2006; Lemons, 1997/2006). Womanism takes seriously embodied epistemologies, spirituality, and energy's role in social change. This energy can be generated from our awareness of and connection to our breath, spirit, and light. Practicing a meditation on energy allows us to be keen observers of its quality, movement, and power (Maparyan, 2012).

Internalized Coloniality

In *Spiral to the Stars: Mvskoke Tools of Futurity*, Laura Harjo defines colonialism "as a practice and ideology that extends across time and space throughout the world and includes elements such as land regimes based on Western conceptions. Settler colonialism, then is not a historical moment but rather a hegemonic bloc of time that still persists today" (Harjo, 2019, p. 65). Coloniality refers to the contemporary manifestation of colonialism; that which was ushered in alongside the brutal beginnings of modernity (Mignolo, 2007). As part of European conquest of Africa and the Americas, the Europeans created race as a stratification tool for domination. Conquering "settlers" stole land, attempted genocides, and enforced chattel slavery as parts of the colonial project, a project which is "ongoing yet incomplete" (Patel, 2018, p. 102).

Despite my developing knowledge of the ways coloniality shaped much of contemporary US society, it was not until my early adulthood that I began to interrogate the way coloniality manifested in my family of origin, the ways it lived inside of me. As a queer Black-identified Black/White biracial (currently) able-bodied ciswoman to whom mental wellness seemed elusive, how had coloniality set the stage for an internal war among my multiple identities?

Audre Lorde reminded us that "we must move against not only those forces which dehumanize us from the outside, but also against those oppressive values which we have been forced to take into ourselves" (1984/2007, p. 135). What had I been forced to take into myself? What had I allowed in? In what ways was it festering? In the foreword to the first edition of *This Bridge Called My Back: Writings by Radical Women of Color*, Toni Cade Bambara explained that the volume recorded "particular rites of passage." In the text she identified racism, classism, homophobia, and gender-based violence as some of the brands of violence the anthology contributors had experienced. She continued:

> And coming to terms with the incorporation of disease, struggling to overthrow the internal colonial/pro-racist loyalties—color/hue/hair caste within the household, power perversities engaged in under the guise of "personal relationships," accommodation to and collaboration with self-ambush and amnesia and murder. And coming to grips with those false awakenings too that give us ease as we substitute a militant mouth for a radical politic, delaying our true coming of age as committed, competent, principled combatants. (2015, p. xxx)

Like Bambara described, I had absolutely experienced false awakenings. Her description of our tendency to weaponize words prior to developing "competent [and] principled" methods of combat eloquently described some of my prior (less than eloquent) actions. I identified with Cherríe Moraga's courageous admission in her essay "La Güera" from *This Bridge*, "I feel angry about this—the years when I refused to recognize privilege, both when it worked against me, and when I worked it, ignorantly, at the expense of others. These are not settled issues" (2015, p. 29).

Black feminisms do not seek to settle issues; dynamism is a characteristic tenet, as is an imperative for praxis. Linking with others who have experienced, theorized, articulated, and acted to change damaging effects of schooling connected me to community in life-affirming ways. I was absolutely not alone. One of the most damaging consequences of individual battles with mental illness is the way it can close folks off from the most worthwhile projects, such as contribution to collective liberation, and the self-love fortification necessary for actions that contradict capitalist hegemony (such as anything beyond reaction and consumption).

Schooling and Madness:
Pathologizing Nonassimilation

US public schools are dictated by corporate interests that coincide with the carceral logics (Kaba, 2021; Meiners, 2016) that seek to normalize Indigenous genocide (Grande, 2015) and premature Black death (Dumas, 2018; Gilmore, 2007; McKittrick, 2011). As such, the colonialist structures of contemporary schooling sponsored by the state can be soul-crushing. One of the most insidious elements of the racial violence that characterizes pre-kindergarten through twelfth grade (P–12) schooling in the United States is the neutral or even benevolent position that many schools assume in local communities.

In *Decolonizing Educational Research: From Ownership to Answerability* (2016), Leigh Patel states, "In the United States, education figures prominently within the public imaginary as deliverance from iniquities in society. . . . This widely held belief in the promise of education is echoed in policies and governmental actions" (p. 16). The problems with this are many. Education's benevolent status in the public imaginary typically rests on liberal values that champion individualism and claim schools are meritocratic spaces. Because these beliefs exist alongside deeply entrenched realities of educational inequities, "commonsense" notions of who is responsible for educational failure abound. The misguided thinking is that because success belongs to those who work hard, those who do not succeed have not worked hard. This paradigm ignores the systemic inequities that constitute the infrastructure of the United States.

Since its inception, schooling in the United States was built with the understanding that Indigenous genocide and Black enslavement were permissible elements in the establishment of a nation so defined by its allegiance to democracy. Most states' social studies curriculum standards make this clear by propagating the grand narrative of American exceptionalism that is characterized by *moves to innocence* (Mawhinney, 1998; Tuck & Yang, 2012). That is, perpetrators of conquest, genocide, and enslavement are crafted as nonviolent explorers, who should be lauded for their bravery and ingenuity. The architects of this democratic experiment embedded these narratives into the foundational level of the nation-state through schooling, its most widespread agent of coloniality. Curricular justifications of Indigenous genocide embedded within the glorification of the "Founding Fathers" and Manifest Destiny remain strong in the vast majority of official curriculum in the United States today (Shear, Knowles, Soden, & Castro, 2015). If P–12 students are to learn to critique these colonialist conceptions in school, it is due to individual teachers' pedagogical and curricular decisions to go beyond—and in some cases disobey—the official curriculum standards.

One of many examples of this is that Black and Indigenous kids are expected to swallow an education that valorizes Andrew Jackson. This is the ongoing assault: the way mainstream social studies curriculum and pedagogy function as poison. The Indian Removal Act of 1830, which Jackson signed, is a standard to be covered, with no consideration of students' affective responses to the violence of the history nor to possible harm by the teacher.

In *Red Pedagogy: Native American Social and Political Thought* (2015), Sandy Grande illustrates how the articulated ideals of liberal democracy that continue to constitute the civic mission of schools in the United States have always viewed Indigenous sovereignty and self-determination as threats to the narrow aim of enfranchisement. She also points to President Jackson's refusal to abide by the US Supreme Court's ruling that the state of Georgia did not have authority over people or affairs within the Cherokee Nation—and his subsequent federal order to remove Eastern Indians to reservations—as certain confirmation that the virtues of "democracy" were applicable only to the White people. Grande calls the period between 1871 and 1968 an era of *imposed democracy for Indigenous people*, wherein the US Congress dissolved Indians' rights to argue on their own behalf in treaties and ended their ability to represent themselves at the federal level. Simultaneously, the United States used enfranchisement to collapse all American Indian nations into a homogenous entity against which laws and policies were levied in more streamlined and totalizing ways.

The spirit-murdering realities of the curriculum, structure, and aims of colonialist schooling have wreaked havoc on Black and Indigenous communities (Love, 2019; Williams, 1987). Western psychiatry and psychology often add more harm to the damage done, as they share some of the fundamental colonialist assumptions. For example, the *Diagnostic and Statistical Manual of Mental Disorders, Fourth Edition* (DSM IV, 2000) defines mental health as "a state marked by the absence of illness." This misses worlds of meaning from traditional Indigenous and Black cosmologies. As opposed to Western medicine's formation around illness, most Indigenous healing is structured around a wellness model (Linklater, 2014). Black and Indigenous culturally-based conceptions of health encompass holistic notions of wellness by addressing the material and spiritual consequences of coloniality that often manifest in addiction, suicide, and other forms of individual and community despair.

Until the evening at Sula's yoga studio described in the opening vignette, my battles felt internal; beyond that, they felt inescapable. Decolonial theory prompted me to ponder the origin of my beliefs, which easily uncovered the insidious nature of coloniality in diagnoses of pathologies. Indeed, my previous guilt and shame were largely predicated upon the Western construct of "normalcy" and the expectation that the colonial context is healthy for a colonized people. As Fanon's writing helped me consider the social contexts and constructions of mental illness, "my" ill health started to make sense to me.

It was not coincidental that my aforementioned epiphany occurred while I was deeply immersed in a yogic pose. By engaging multiple senses, students are afforded significantly deeper and more complex understandings than they are in the solitary cognitive apparatus valued in US public education. One of the various shortcomings in contemporary Western curricula is the extent to which abstract knowledge is valued to the complete exclusion of embodied knowing. Enlightenment ideals of mind over body exist throughout the colonized world. This dichotomy values positivistic formulas to deduce Truth (Berila, 2016; Ng, 2011/2018).

Schooling as a colonial system largely ignores the centrality of physical bodies' role in comprehension and knowledge (Berila, 2016; Ford, 2016), except for the privileged few. As such, the healing education that my illnesses pushed me to find, in this case, yoga, is itself an act of resistance to colonial curricula that ignored embodied learning. Engaging embodied epistemologies was helping me (re)member my spirit (Dillard, 2012), which I thought had left completely. I recognized it immediately. It is the self-efficacy that comes from knowing that one's truth is a valid truth.

There is very little in contemporary schooling that echoes nature. That which cannot be measured is routinely disregarded in US P–12 education. Curricula have been developed to justify coloniality through the social studies and language arts, mathematics and science, physical education and the arts, and beyond. That is, instead of emulating nature, contemporary schooling attempts to rewrite what is natural and in so doing encourages maintenance of the status quo. This directional inversion results in widespread miseducation that leads individuals and groups away from wellness instead of toward it.

In *The Killing Rage: Ending Racism* (1995), bell hooks asserts that "like all mental health disorders, the wounded African-American psyche must be attended to within the framework of programs for mental health care that link psychological recovery with progressive political awareness of the way in which institutionalized systems of dominations assault, damage, and maim" (p. 138). As I have written elsewhere (Ford, 2016), access to breath and spirit are political matters due to the role they play in overall well-being.

Phillis Sheppard, a self-identified Black lesbian womanist professor of theological studies at Vanderbilt Divinity School, advises

> [F]or those of us who teach social justice, the persistence of injustice must not be an opportunity to lapse into cynicism, or despair, that will paralyze us in our vision and our teaching. It will render us hopeless, turn our activism into caricatures of the past, and our classrooms into rote recitations announcing the advent of death. No, instead in facing the hegemonic imagination, the historical ethos, and colonized minds in the cultural, caring, activist, loving pedagogical spaces where we are, we must . . . teach as if our lives depended on it. (2020)

Sheppard's guidance from cynicism to womanism illuminates the core of what I experienced in the opening vignette. She offered an accurate diagnosis for the spiritual malady that left a gaping hole for cynicism and paralysis to enter my soul. Unlike other forms of social change, womanism asserts the most essential site of healing is self. In her 2012 text *The Womanist Idea*, Layli Maparyan suggests that the domains for progress toward optimal well-being begins with individuals and expands to communities. From communities, positive vibrations can best expand to humanity, then all living kind. Devotion to ecological and humanitarian betterment widens our consciousness of care to planet Earth. The cosmos could be considered as a still-larger domain to consider.

In what follows, I describe three womanist principles that allowed me to reconnect with myself and my communities in order to reengage in the work of collective liberation. Specifically, I present attention to breath, spirit, and energy transmutation as vehicles for soul healing. The chapter ends with a womanist vision that returns to an elevated position of where I began this journey: my own and others' inner light.

Pedagogies of Invitation

Curriculum and pedagogy characterized by coloniality are nonconsensual expressions of epistemological and ontological power. These are hegemonic technologies created and sustained to hide preconquest histories, to discourage collective agency, to smother creativity. Anzadúan scholar and professor AnaLouise Keating describes "status-quo stories" as the numbing scripts that insidiously structure individual, collective, and social realities. Fundamentally, status-quo stories propagate "self-enclosed individualism" (2013, p. 171), a term Keating employs to denote hyperisolation and impermeable boundaries between self and other. She makes clear that while individual agency and integrity are vital, it is the hierarchical form of individualism that disallows collaborative work for social change. In an effort to help students become aware of status-quo stories that underpin the high value Western society places on rugged individualism, I draw on what Keating calls "pedagogies of invitation" (2013, p. 167).

Although pedagogies of invitation are multiple, context-dependent, and not prescriptive, Keating does describe three premises:

* We are interrelated with all existence: All human and nonhuman life is interconnected and interdependent.
* Transformation is optional and always—in some way or other—exceeds our conscious efforts, attempts, and expectations.
* Transformation is more likely to occur when educators remain flexible, open-minded, and willing to be changed by what and who we teach. (2013, p. 183)

All living things are both constituted by systems and constitutive of larger systems, simultaneously. As such, it was critical for me to begin with my own well-being to affect meaningful change in my classroom and the larger society. Gloria Anzaldúa's concept of conocimiento—deep consciousness paired with radical interconnectedness—is central to understanding pedagogies of invitation. Drawing on Anzaldúa's work, Maparyan (2012) suggests intra/interpersonal connectedness and cellular consciousness engage in catalytic processes that both reflect and generate peaceful energetic vibrations. These same vibrations connect with other living and nonliving entities to make change. Anzaldúa's courage sanctions augmentations of my own:

> It's not on paper that you create but in your innards, in the gut and out of living tissue—organic writing I call it. . . . The meaning and worth of my writing is measured by how much I put myself on the line and how much nakedness I achieve. (Anzaldúa, 2015, p. 170)

The coloniality of schooling wreaked psychological havoc on me, as it has on large numbers of Black, Indigenous, and People of Color for generations. By engaging the womanist ways described below, I was practicing pedagogies of invitation within myself and with myself in connection to others. I offer these, therefore, as a means of illustrating invitational pedagogies that have aided both me and—directly or indirectly—my students.

BREATH

In what ways does our breath connect us to ourselves? How does it link us with others over time and through space? In *Undrowned: Black Feminist Lessons from Marine Mammals* (2020), Alexis Pauline Gumbs reminds us,

> Breath is a practice of presence. One of the physical characteristics that unites us with marine mammals is that they process air in a way similar to us, though they spend most or all of their time in water, they do not have gills. We, too, on land are often navigating contexts that seem impossible for us to breathe in, and yet we must. (p. 21)

Breath is a practice of presence
Inhale
Breath is a practice of presence
Exhale
Breath is a practice of presence
Inhale
Breath is a practice of presence
Exhale

Breath, Spirit, and Energy Transmutation

Trusting our bodies as sights of knowledge, we learn to drop into our bodies and draw awareness to individual molecules of oxygen entering through our nostrils and trace that awareness throughout our bodies as a way to scan for areas with tensions and pain. In discussing the power of Middle Passage narratives, Ashon T. Crawley explains about breathing:

> There is something that occurs in these texts that typically goes unremarked, or if remarked, is only done insofar as there is a spectacular instance of such. What goes unremarked, though certainly produced is the occasions of recounting movement, is the necessity of the breath, of breathing itself, as a performative act, as a performative gesture. What goes unremarked is how breathing air is constitutive for flight, for movement, for performance. (2017, p. 32–33)

In the same way that breathing air is constitutive for flight, for movement, and for performance, it is necessary for discourse, for collaboration, and for learning. The colonialist curriculum in P–12 schools is removed from students' lives. It is static. It does not need breath, it is dead. This stands counter to what we know about learning theory; students learn when the pedagogies are relevant, sustaining, and engaging. Breath is central to worthwhile pedagogies.

Angela Y. Davis provides insight into her awareness of breath in the 2016 volume *The Wind Is Spirit: The Life, Love, and Legacy of Audre Lorde*, edited by Gloria Joseph. In the anthology, Davis relays an occasion of a visit she made to the Alameda County Juvenile Hall to talk with the youth. She explained, "Because this juvenile facility is located only a few minutes from my house, and because I literally breathe the same air as the children who are incarcerated there, they are especially close to my heart" (p. 250). Davis describes a feeling of deep interconnectedness with the youth, who she described as well read, attentive, and loving.

While engaging with the youth about the reality of her fears during the time she was underground and running from the Federal Bureau of Investigation, Davis drew on Audre Lorde's assertions that courage and fear were not mutually exclusive, that she had to act despite being afraid. Davis explains in the text that despite not articulating Lorde's name, she was consciously invoking her spirit. After her dialogue with the larger group, Davis relates, she went to a classroom to find a young man for whom she had a message about the bureaucratic delays on his impending release, despite his being wrongfully detained. To her surprise, she saw a poster with Jean Weisinger's photograph of Lorde with her arms stretched overhead, and words from *The Cancer Journals*: "When I dare to be powerful—to use my strength in the service of my vision, then it becomes less and less important that I am afraid." In my interpretation, the breath Davis identified sharing with the young people by way of their proximity was also shared over time by way of conjuring Lorde's spirit. Awareness of breath as a connective force manifested in both cases.

Focus on our breath allows for manipulation of our heartbeats and our emotions. It is true that physiology plays an integral role in how we engage one another in the public sphere. What is not true is that our (often *learned*) immediate physiological reactions have to be those upon which we act. Habitual awareness of the available options opens a space for connecting—with oneself, other people, the planet, and/or the cosmos—between each and every inhale and exhale.

SPIRIT

In addition to the biological necessity of breath, awareness of our breath connects us with the strength of spirituality (Hanh, 1996). It is helpful to surround ourselves with goodness to inhale that quality. This *is* inspiration. This chapter discusses the ways spirit broke open in me through yoga. Because the moment was so profound, and it provided a crack in the shell in which I was encased that was caused in large part by the coloniality of schooling. Before and since that time, I have experienced the grace of spirit in numerous other ways: the gumminess of my nephew's smile, laughter over shared meals with chosen family, sunlight's reflection off the San Francisco Bay, the purr of my cat on my chest as I heal from surgery. I have witnessed spirit in the classroom when my students share stories of their childhoods, encourage one another through vulnerable moments, and take assignments way beyond what I had envisioned as outcomes. The commonalities in these examples lie often in the synchronization of consciousness that connect us to one another and to the nonhuman world.

From M. Jacqui Alexander, in *Pedagogies of Crossing: Meditations on Feminisms, Sexual Politics, Memory, and the Sacred* (2005), I learned that, perhaps, it was a fire that ignited within me on the yoga mat to produce the light that I experienced. If so, the clarity and freedom I felt were a divine alignment that she describes between individuals' internal fires and that which burns at the center of the universe. The feeling was so different from what came before and after it that it created within me the need to pursue it. I knew I needed it and that access to it would require stretching and strength building.

Numerous scholars have named spirit as central to pedagogies and paradigms for positive change. Eschewing ontologies that separate mind from body and people from one another, these scholars also honor interconnectedness and shared aims of communal empowerment and wellness. Womanism espouses an ever-present spirit in all that exists. This is important because it allows for individual and collective understandings that there is much to behold beyond what can been seen.

Cynthia Dillard (2012) offers *endarkened feminism* as a way for African ascendant teachers and researchers to (re)member those traditions coloniality has attempted to erase. Building on the work of other Black feminist scholars, Dillard explores epistemologies as ground for expansion. In particular, she uplifts the global and spiritual dimensions of our experiences as central to our ways of knowing. Dillard's use of endarkened feminism is an anti-colonial move from the start, a challenge to colonization of African American and other marginalized groups' mental, intellectual, and spiritual lives (2000). Loving Blackness from the inside out is fundamental for Diasporic connections and strength. Dillard explains that cultural memories allow us to tap into all our senses and to form spiritual connections across Diasporic time and space. In addition, endarkened feminisms allow us to consider Black lives against a backdrop of Blackness.

So much of contemporary schooling focuses on positivistic "knowledge," valued by its ability to be hypothesized, tested, observed, and found "true." A spiritual pursuit of knowledge asks about what and how truths matter in our everyday lives and asserts that feeling is a legitimate category for certain types of knowledges. Spiritually situated teaching, learning, and research involve a strong connection of self with the aims of the research and the methodologies, as well as the communities within which one is conducting the research.

ENERGY TRANSMUTATION

Womanist theory declares that "everything is energy, and all social or environmental change is fundamentally changing energy." Applied metaphysics, the investigation of the nature, principles, and problems of ultimate reality, is a crucial component of womanism. This leads to "miracles" by transforming oppressive energy into energy used for social, political, or material change. Maparyan explains, "If existence is sacred and life is sacred and humans are sacred and self is sacred"—all of which is so in womanist thought—"then social change activity must, by association, also be sacred or capable of serving as a conduit for sacred energy or the transmutation of energy from a less to a more sacred form" (2012, p. 118–119).

Democratizing miracle manifestation can begin with studying and employing the millennia of wisdoms contained in mysticism. Recognizing that this process is achievable by a much-wider segment of humanity than the traditionally limited number of gurus, prophets, and mystics opens the door to thousands of years of meaning making that was previously considered off limits to most people (Maparyan, 2012). This reconciliation between humanity and the spiritual realm is essential for the type of planetary healing that womanism demands.

Womanists submit the centrality of energy and understand that we can learn to affect it. According to the laws of physics, strong energies act as magnetic streams toward which other energies are attracted. Drawing on David R. Hawkins's (2002) mathematical representation of energy bands, Maparyan (2012) explains that interactions that commonly register as positive (I love you, you just made my day, etc.) trump those that commonly register as negative (I hate you, you just ruined my day, etc.). What some may write off as flowery naivete, womanists understand that how we show up in the world *matters*.

Students in Westernized P–12 schools and institutions of higher education study energy through the sciences. The public school science curricula in the United States include standards that address energy in biology (e.g., the food chain and the technical aspects of the nervous system), chemistry (e.g., caloric measurement and the theories of thermodynamics), and physics (e.g., the role of movement in kinetic energy and the role of position in potential energy). Although these concepts of energy are foundational to natural science, they do not address metaphysical dimensions of energy.

Humans and plants affect energy form and direction on metabolic, behavioral, emotional, and other levels. Consider digestion or photosynthesis; cheering up a friend or petals bending stems toward the sun. While cellular-level energy transformation occurs on an automatic level and is set in motion by transmuting some forms of energy (e.g., from chemical to thermal), conscious energy transmutation is intentional and can be practiced at the individual and community levels. In what follows, I outline a method by which we can develop the strength of our consciousness, which, in turn, can help determine our ability to access it as a source of power to transmute energy.

RECOGNIZING INNER LIGHT

In *The Womanist Idea* (2012), Maparyan introduces a concept she calls *Luxocracy*, or "rule by light." The light in this case is that which every being has innately, known also as soul, inner divinity, higher self, or spirit. To build a Luxocracy, one must recognize one's own sacredness, the sacredness of all people, and the sacredness of all things in the cosmos. As part of its spiritual foundation, consideration of Luxocracy involves a dimension of energy. Tracing one's energy back to the sun allows us to understand both the divine and observable role of energy in our teaching and learning.

Maparyan distinguishes between Luxocracy and other forms of social structure:

> Like democracy, Luxocracy is egalitarian; unlike democracy, Luxocracy rests on a foundation of spirituality. Like anarchy, Luxocracy eschews formal, hierarchical structures of governance; unlike anarchy, Luxocracy is thoroughly benevolent and nonviolent. Like theocracy, Luxocracy is spiritualized and spiritually centered; unlike theocracy, Luxocracy rests on internal, personal notions of spirituality, rather than external, organized religion. (2012, p. 4)

By drawing on the life-affirming elements of existing political paradigms, Luxocracy offers a way to redirect our gaze toward pathways to liberation. In a similar manner, Luxocracy's womanist origins imbue it with an eclectic approach to various forms of spirituality. It is based in an assumption of abundance, drawing on the reality of our resources if we can harness those systems that prioritize collaborative production and shared access. Luxocracy is situated on a combination of three elements, which Maparyan describes as innate divinity, the value of commonweal, and the potential for strength born of a planetary identity. Creating a society that honors these characteristics would involve undoing the colonialist structures and pedagogies that define contemporary schooling.

In a recent issue of *Sierra* magazine, Gumbs describes the California Nebula, a red expanse in outer space. She explains that the nebula is the length of five full moons, which is equal to one hundred light-years. Its distance is ten times its spread, so she reminds us that what we see today is what the star looked like one thousand years ago. She goes on to answer a self-posed question regarding why she looks up to see something that is no longer. According to Gumbs, it is, "because I crave a longer perspective. Looking up, allowing myself to perceive or imagine light reflected to me from 1,000 light years away makes me feel both small and expansive" (2021, February 8).

Feeling both small and expansive as a teacher is a powerful way to engage with one's students in an effort to resist coloniality in schooling.

In real life, my yoga instructor Sula is a community gem. She is an ultimate light-bender. She is unabashedly dedicated to Black liberation and has incredible gifts that manifest magnificently, often in the form of community building. Sula embodies what generations of Black women teachers, community and school based, do: a warm demanding love for herself, her family, her communities, the natural environment, the cosmos. Her comment "Force with no movement creates pressure" sent me on a journey to understand new levels of embodied liberation for myself and for the communities of which I am a part. Her invitational pedagogy helped me to uncover my entrenchment within a colonialist system, and womanist principles helped guide me out. Braiding together strands of energy constitutive of and produced by breath, spirit, and energy transmutation, light emerges as another component of communal uplift. Antithetical to colonialist logics of scarcity, these forces are abundant. As teachers, we can channel these renewable resources—made stronger through love and harnessed through awareness—to create spaces for learning and transformation. Perhaps, if force with *no* movement creates pressure, force *with* movement can create freedom.

References

Alexander, M. J. (2005). *Pedagogies of crossing: Meditations on feminisms, sexual politics, memory, and the sacred.* Durham, NC: Duke University Press.

Amoo-Adare, E. A. (2004/2006). Critical special literacy: A womanist positionality and the spatio-temporal construction of Black family life. In L. Phillips (Ed.), *The womanist reader*, 347–358. New York, NY: Routledge.

Anzaldúa, G. (2015). Speaking in tongues: A letter to Third World women writers. In C. Moraga and G. Anzaldúa (Eds.), *This bridge called my back: Writings by radical women of color* (pp. 163–172). Albany: State University of New York Press.

Anzaldúa, G., & Moraga, C. (Eds.). (2015). *This bridge called my back: Writings by radical women of color* (4th ed.). Albany: State University of New York Press.

Bambara, T. C. (2015). Foreword to the first edition, 1981. In C. Moraga and G. Anzaldúa (Eds.), *This bridge called my back: Writings by radical women of color* (pp. xxix–xxxii). Albany: State University of New York Press.

Berila, B. (2016). *Integrating mindfulness into anti-oppression pedagogy: Social justice in higher education.* New York, NY: Routledge.

Crawley, A. T. (2017). *BlackPentacostal breath: The aesthetics of possibility.* New York, NY: Fordham University Press.

Davis, A. Y. (2016). Audre Lorde in the twenty-first century. In G. Joseph (Ed.), *The wind is spirit: The life, love, and legacy of Audre Lorde* (pp. 250–252). New York, NY: Villarosa Media.

Dillard, C. (2000). The substance of things hoped for, the evidence of things not seen: Examining an endarkened feminist epistemology in educational research and leadership, *International Journal of Qualitative Studies in Education, 13(6),* 661–681. doi:10.1080/09518390050211565

Dillard, C. (2012). *Learning to (re)member the things we've learned to forget: Endarkened feminisms, spirituality, & the sacred nature of research & teaching.* New York, NY: Lang.

Dumas, M. J. (2018) Beginning and ending with Black suffering: A meditation on and against racial justice in education. In E. Tuck and K. W. Yang (Eds.), *Toward what justice? Describing diverse dreams of justice in education* (pp. 29–45). New York, NY: Routledge.

Fanon, F. (1963). *The wretched of the Earth* [Les damnés de la terre]. (Richard Philcox, Trans.). Paris, France: Présence Africaine.

Ford, J. C. (2016). "'I'm feelin' it': Embodied spiritual activism as a vehicle for my queer black liberation." In B. Berila, M. Klein, & C. J. Roberts (Eds.), *Yoga, the body, and embodied social change: Intersectional feminist analysis* (pp. 29–40). Lanham, MD: Lexington.

Ford, J. C. (2017). "No really . . . Call me crazy": Reclaiming identity through vulnerability in teacher education. In B. Picower & R. Kohli (Eds.), *Confronting racism in teacher education: Counternarratives of critical practice* (pp. 67–73). New York: Routledge.

Gilmore, R. W. (2007). *Golden gulag: Prisons, surplus, crisis, and opposition in globalizing.* Berkeley: University of California Press.

Grande, S. (2015). *Red pedagogy: Native American social and political thought.* (10th anniversary ed.) London: Rowman & Littlefield.

Gumbs, A. P. (2020). *Undrowned: Black feminist lessons from marine mammals.* Chico, CA: AK Press.

Gumbs, A. P. (2021, February 8). [Twitter: "My telescope and I."] Retrieved from https://twitter.com/alexispauline/status/1358792697381871616/photo/3

Hanh, T. N. (1996). *Breathe! You are alive: Sutra on the full awareness of breathing*. Berkeley, CA: Parallax Press.

Harjo, L. (2019). *Spiral to the stars: Mvskoke tools of futurity*. Tucson: University of Arizona Press.

Hawkins, D. R. (2002). *Power vs. force: The hidden determinants of human behavior*. Carlsbad, CA: Hay House.

hooks, b. (1995). *Killing rage: Ending racism*. New York, NY: Holt.

Kaba, M. (2021). *We do this 'til we free: Abolitionist organizing and transforming justice*. Chicago, IL: Haymarket.

Keating, A. (2007). *Teaching transformation: Transcultural classroom dialogues*. New York, NY: Palgrave MacMillan.

Keating, A. (2013). *Transformation now! Toward a post-oppositional politics of change*. Urbana: University of Illinois Press.

Ladson-Billings, G., & Tate, W. F. (1995). Toward a critical race theory of education. *Teachers College Record, 97*(1), 47–68.

Lemons, G. L. (1997/2006). To be Black, male, and "feminist": Making womanist space for Black men. In L. Phillips (Ed.), *The womanist reader* (pp. 96–113). New York, NY: Routledge.

Linklater, R. (2014). *Decolonizing trauma work: Indigenous stories and strategies*. Halifax, Canada: Fernwood.

Lorde, A. (1984/2007). *Sister outsider: Essays & speeches by Audre Lorde*. Berkeley, CA: Crossing Press.

Love, B. (2019). *We want to do more than survive: Abolitionist teaching and the pursuit of educational freedom*. Boston, MA: Beacon Hill Press.

Maparyan, L. (Phillips, L.). (2006). *The womanist reader*. New York, NY: Taylor & Francis.

Maparyan, L. (2012). *The womanist idea*. New York, NY: Routledge.

Maparyan, L. (2015). "A womanist perspective on development." Lecture. Retrieved from https://www.youtube.com/watch?v=rC4yn8oyYds

Mawhinney, J. (1998). *"Giving up the ghost": Disrupting the (re)production of white privilege in anti-racist pedagogy and organizational change* (master's thesis), Ontario Institute for Studies in Education, University of Toronto. Retrieved from http://www.collectionscanada.gc.ca/obj/s4/f2/dsk2/tape15/PQDD_0008/MQ33991.pdf

McKittrick, K. (2011). On plantations, prisons, and a Black sense of place. *Social and Cultural Geography 12*(8): 947–963.

Meiners, E. R. (2016). *For the children?: Protecting innocence in the carceral state*. Minneapolis, MN: University of Minnesota Press.

Mignolo, W. D. (2007). Introduction. *Cultural Studies, 21*(2), 155–167. doi:10.1080/095023 80601162498

Moraga, C. (2015). La Güera. In C. Moraga and G. Anzaldúa (Eds.), *This bridge called my back: Writings by radical women of color* (pp. 22–29). Albany: State University of New York Press.

Ng, R. (2011/2018). Decolonizing teaching and learning through embodied learning: Toward an integrated approach. In S. Batacharya and Y. R. Wong (Eds.), *Sharing breath: Embodied learning and decolonization*. Edmonton, Canada: Athabasca University Press.

Patel, L. (2016). *Decolonizing educational research: From ownership to answerability*. New York, NY: Routledge.

Patel, L. (2018). When justice is a lackey. In E. Tuck and K. W. Yang (Eds.), *Toward what justice? Describing diverse dreams of justice in education* (pp. 101–112). New York, NY: Routledge.

Robinson, C. J. (2000). *Black Marxism: The making of the Black radical tradition*. Chapel Hill: University of North Carolina Press.

Shear, S. B., Knowles, R. T., Soden, G. J., & Castro, A. J. (2015). Manifesting Destiny: Re/presentations of Indigenous Peoples in K–12 U.S. history standards. *Theory & Research in Social Education, 43*:1, 68–101, DOI: 10.1080/00933104.2014.999849

Sheppard, P. (2020). This is woman's work: The worth and witness of womanist work in times like these. Zoom Roundtable Discussion. Retrieved from https://www.facebook.com/watch/live/?v=274215623695282&ref=watch_permalink

Tuck, E., & Yang, K. W. (2012). Decolonization is not a metaphor. *Decolonization: Indigeneity, Education & Society 1*(1), 1–40.

Williams, P. (1987). Spirit-murdering the messenger: The discourse of fingerpointing as the Law's Response to Racism. *Miami Law Review 42*, 127–157.

PART II

Transforming Interventions

I release you, my beautiful and terrible
fear. I release you. You were my beloved and hated twin, but now, I don't know you
as myself. I release you with all the pain I would know at the death of my daughters.

—Joy Harjo, "I Give You Back"

3

Discursive Colonialism of Hmong Women in Western Texts

Education, Representation, and Subjectivity

LEENA N. HER

During my first year in graduate school, I enrolled in a course on "urban youth" in US schools. In this course, "urban" was used as an indicator of race and ethnicity and not geographic location. The readings and classroom discussions focused on ethnic and racial minorities in US schools. Although we did not encounter many Hmong or Southeast Asian youth through our course readings, the topic of Hmong American youth was brought up in class one day as we discussed how cultural belief systems affect the school achievement patterns of ethnic minority youth. One of my classmates who had been a teacher for many years in San Jose, California, brought up the example of the Hmong as an example of a cultural group whose cultural practices and belief systems contributed to gender disparities in educational success. In the Hmong community, she explained, Hmong girls were not encouraged to go to school and were encouraged to marry young at the age of fourteen or fifteen. Although I am a Hmong woman, I did not raise my hand to object to this statement. I had grown weary of culturally based explanations to explain academic failure in ethnic and minority communities when structural, political, and cultural factors seemed much more important in understanding patterns of academic achievement.

I begin this chapter with this personal account as an entry point into a discussion of how Hmong gender dynamics are represented in academic discourse. This event occurred at a time when I did not have a language to understand how written texts sanctioned by institutions and scholarly practices produced, circulated, and sustained particular ideologies of Hmong women (and men) (de Certeau, 1988; Smith, 1999); I only felt the consequences of these ideas in my life and the lives of other cultural and linguistic minorities. In this paper, I invoke this event to discuss the implications of how Hmong women have been written in Western academic texts and the consequences of their subjectification (Bhabha, 1994). Although other regimes of representation have been contested in Hmong studies—media representations (Schein, Thoj, Vang, & Jalao, 2012) and narrative works of fiction, poetry, and other literary representations (Moua, 2002; Hmong American Writers' Circle, 2011), there has been little attention on the production of and implications of gendered Hmong subjectivities in academic text (Vang, Nibbs, & Vang, 2016). There exist significant works about the Hmong of academic research that have contributed to the field of Hmong studies and to practice-based fields, such as social work and education. In this chapter, my critique of two works, selected for their wide circulation in research and higher education classrooms, does not dismiss their contributions toward expanding and contributing to knowledge about the experiences of Hmong refugees in the United States. Yet, there is room within these texts to explore how Hmong women are represented and the implication and productivity of these representations in continuing to perpetuate subaltern Hmong women subjectivities.

While I am influenced by the work of Western scholars, such as Michel Foucault (1972) and Michel de Certeau (1988), who have questioned and critiqued methods, practices, and epistemologies in the production of scientific knowledge, I choose to privilege scholars from decolonial studies (Bhabha, 1994; Grosfoguel, 2011; hooks, 1992; Perez, 1999; Smith, 1999) who speak from the vantage point of the colonized. I find that there exist overlapping connections between the experiences of colonized people and the experiences of the Hmong diaspora, who have historically resided in colonial states in which they have settled or resettled. Equally important is the overlap between the emancipatory methods decolonial scholars write about and the emancipatory methods used by Hmong scholars, writers, and activists to tell their own stories.

Hmong Women Subjectivities in Western Texts

My well-meaning colleague, despite her lack of interaction and engagement with the Hmong community in the United States, obtained much of her knowledge about the Hmong community from the research archives. There has been a lot of interest in studying the assimilation and acculturation experiences of the Hmong population in the United States and other Western countries since their resettlement as refugees in the 1970s. This interest is due to the identity of the Hmong as a stateless people who have been described as a cultural group, who fiercely guard their cultural beliefs and practices (G. Y. Lee & Tapp, 2010; Quincy, 1995).

Currently, the Hmong diaspora extends across several continents in a multitude of countries, such as China, Vietnam, Laos, Thailand, the United States, Australia, and several countries in Europe. Historical records and linguistic analyses suggest that the Hmong originated in southwest China. Historical records describe the Hmong as refusing to be acculturated into the expanding Chinese empire. Therefore, they migrated to regions of Southeast Asia in the late early 1800s, settling in mountains of Laos, Thailand, and Vietnam. Many Hmong living in the United States came from Laos as refugees during the late 1970s and 1980s. During the 1960s many ethnic minority Hmong were recruited to fight alongside agents from the Central Intelligence Agency (CIA) when the United States increased its presence in Laos in an effort to fight communism by establishing a military-aid program to train a pro-American Lao army. Many Hmong and other hill-tribe groups living in the highland region of Laos were recruited to serve as US allies in the covert operations. Hmong participation in the war resulted in an estimated thirty thousand troops, fifty thousand civilians, and two hundred thousand refugees (G. Y. Lee & Tapp, 2010). When the United States lost the Vietnam War and pulled out of Saigon in 1975, it ended its covert activities in Laos. Many Hmong fled Laos as political refugees, due to fears of being prosecuted as American allies in the new communist regime.

Since the arrival of Hmong refugees to the United States in the late 1970s and early 1980s, researchers have extensively studied the experiences of the Hmong community by examining resettlement, acculturation, and assimilation in Western nations (Chan, 1994; Faderman, 1998; Hutchinson & McNall, 1994; Meredith & Rowe, 1986; Winland, 1994), mental and medical health issues (Gerdner, Cha, Yang, & Tripp-Reimer, 2007; S. Lee & Chang, 2012), and assimilation and incorporation into the American educational system (Trueba, 1990; S. J. Lee, 2001, 2002, 2005; Ngo, 2008; Ngo, Bigelow, & Wahlstrom, 2007; Ngo & Lee, 2007). Of particular interest to researchers is the gender hierarchy that exists in the Hmong community. In this discourse, Hmong women occupy the periphery of Hmong social order and are constrained by their position in all circumstances of their lives. This subjugation begins prior to birth, based on Hmong kinship structure. Jo Ann Koltyk uses the metaphor of a tree to describe Hmong kinship structure.

> The Hmong conceive of the links to their ancestors as their origins or roots; sons are considered the roots of the family, especially as families branch off into separate lineages within the patrilineal clan line. Daughters, on the other hand, do not carry the weight of the past. They will marry out and bear children for other patrilineal clans. (1997, p. 39)

Within this patriarchal society, Hmong boys and girls are socialized differently. Although boys may be tolerated for challenging their parents, girls are often not encouraged to have any voice at all (G. Y. Lee & Tapp, 2010, p. 158). Instead, young girls are taught to be "good girls" so that they may be able to attract husbands. Hmong parents want "obedient daughters-in-law and urged their sons to choose compliant girls" (Donnelly, 1994, p. 139). Once they are married, Hmong women continue to exist on the periphery of the family structure. Nancy D. Donnelly explains that "in terms of domestic power, their security coming from their sons, while men were central and commanded obedience" (1994, p. 82). Thus, in all these texts, Hmong women bear children, listen to their husbands, and choose social and ideological norms regarding women's role dutifully and silently and with little contestation (Donnelly, 1994; Koltyk, 1997; Rice, 2000; Winland, 1994).

The Productivity of Discursive Colonialism

The composite image of Hmong women in Western literature created by scholars, policy makers, journalists, photographers, and others is an act of discursive colonialism (Bhabha, 1994; Mohanty, 1988) where cultural difference and otherness figure significantly in the making of Hmong woman subjectivity. Homi K. Bhabha explains that the "predominant strategic function" of colonial discourse is:

> the creation of a space for a "subject peoples" through the production of knowledge in terms of which surveillance is exercised and a complex form of pleasure/unpleasure is incited. . . . The objective of colonial discourse is to construe the colonized as a population of degenerate types on the basis of racial origin, in order to justify conquest and to establish systems of administration and instruction. . . . [C]olonial discourse produces the colonized as a social reality which is at once an "other" and yet entirely knowable and visible. (1994, p. 101)

The possibilities of being knowable and visible rely on enunciatory practices. Bhabha argues that the enunciatory subject "is a subject in performance and process" (1994, p. 19). In the process of meaning-making, knowledge is authorized and/or deauthorized, and differences and similarities are negotiated and articulated. In this discourse, Hmong women's agency is often judged against a set of tacit Western assumptions of what it means to be liberated. In contrast to the Western liberated woman, analyses and descriptions of the agency, or lack thereof, of Hmong women subjects rely on the paradigm of patriarchal Hmong culture and the proclivity of the patriarchal social order to serve as a cultural code and constraint. Mohanty (1988) describes this act as a process where the "material and historical heterogeneities of the lives of women are rendered invisible thereby making it possible to produce and re-present a composite, singular Woman" (p. 62).

Bhabha suggests that intervention of colonialist discourse must shift from judgments of images and narratives as either positive or negative toward an understanding of the *"processes of subjectification"* where one must engage in "its effectivity" (1994, p. 95, emphasis original). He continues, "In order to understand the productivity of colonial power it is crucial to construct its regime of truth, not to subject its representations to a normalizing judgment. Only then does it become possible to understand the *productive* ambivalence of the object of colonial discourse—that 'otherness' which is at once an object of desire and derision, an articulation of difference contained within the fantasy of origin and identity" (1994, p. 96).

As the event that opens this essay indicates, discourses about the highly constrained lives of Hmong women within Hmong culture are productive in silencing alternative explanations of school-achievement patterns in the Hmong community by focusing solely on Hmong culture. A review of the educational research literature finds that this discourse is used to frame differences in educational attainment by Hmong boys and girls as an outcome of deeply rooted cultural values and practices that constrain Hmong girls' educational aspiration (Donnelly, 1994; Hutchinson & McNall, 1994; S. J. Lee, 1997; Meredith & Rowe, 1986; Walker-Moffat, 1995). Researchers have also suggested that Hmong parents have higher educational expectations for their sons than daughters (Goldstein, 1985; Ngo & Leet-Otley, 2011; Walker-Moffat, 1995). Early studies completed by researchers asserting that the high dropout rates and low achievement levels of Hmong girls were connected to "patrilineal and patriarchal norms that tend to devalue females among the Hmong" have been particularly influential (Rumbaut & Ima, 1988, p. 104). In particular, "early marriage" is determined to be a cultural practice that extremely limits the low educational achievement of Hmong women in academic and nonacademic contexts. This research cites from and is validated by institutionally sanctioned scientific discourse of the Hmong community, particularly, studies that examine gender dynamics in the Hmong community (Donnelly, 1994; Koltyk, 1997; Rice, 2000; Thao, 2003).

Critical textual analysis of texts from these studies finds that there exist limited possibilities of being a Hmong woman in Western academic texts (Her, 2016). Within this academic archive, the diverse experiences of Hmong women are limited to the experiences of three subfigures: the authentic Hmong woman of the homeland, the refugee woman of Western relocation sites, and the assimilated Hmong woman caught between two opposing cultural worlds (Her, 2016). In the following section, which traces the effectivity of the Hmong women subject in the academic archives, I argue that imperialist notions of education, as formal schooling, are used as means to substantiate and objectify Hmong women into the three subfigures of the Hmong woman subject.

Authentic Hmong Woman

The figure of the authentic Hmong woman of the homeland originates in Laos and Thailand (Donnelly, 1994; Rice, 2000; Symonds, 2004). An example can be seen in *Calling in the Soul: Gender and the Cycle of Life in a Hmong Village* by Patricia Symonds (2004). In this study, Symonds insists that in order to study the birthing practices of Hmong refugees in Rhode Island, she must return to Thailand. The homeland not only serves as the site of authenticating Hmong identity and culture but also the site constituting inequitable gender relationships. In the homeland, this woman occupied a lower social status as a marginal family member and obedient worker. Anthropologist Robert Cooper describes the relationship between a man and a woman in the homeland as a "master-servant" relationship premised on the psychological distinction where a Hmong man can control a Hmong woman (1984, p. 136).

Another rendering of the subfigure of the authentic Hmong woman is predicated on her being illiterate and uneducated. For example, the opening scene in Nancy Donnelly's (1994) ethnography of Hmong women in Seattle, Washington, provides a depiction of uneducated Hmong women of the homeland, who are not only illiterate but disinterested in becoming educated. The reader is introduced to Hmong women in the first chapter, "Discovering the Hmong." Here Donnelly adopts a common narrative trope in ethnographic narratives (Marcus & Cushman, 1982) by constructing her arrival story and the meeting of the culturally different other. Donnelly explains to the reader that she first meets the Hmong when she responds to an ad to teach English to Southeast Asian women. She begins by describing the thirty-five Hmong and Mien women as "good-natured" and "friendly" but acting out with odd behavior: "Their behavior was unexpected: they blew their noses in the drinking fountain or wandered away during lessons" (1994, p. 3). While some were "intent on learning English," others had little interest in learning the "useful skills" and "approached class like play" (1994, p. 3). In her classroom of eleven women, she discovered that they were "entirely ignorant of English," unable to understand the difference between singular and plural nouns, "did not understand money and could not add or subtract" (1994, p. 3). Donnelly connects this ignorance and inability to the country of Laos.

> Later I learned that in rural Laos most women didn't handle money. They engaged in gift exchange, and only men traded with cash. But at the time I was surprised at this hole in their information. They were fascinated by this new concept, and quick to learn it. Women who after dozens of repetitions could not turn a statement into a question could whip pennies from pile to pile with hardly any errors. (1994, p. 3)

Then, she compares the mind of the uneducated Hmong woman of the homeland to her own intelligence and way of processing information and develops a plan for how to educate them:

> I realized that my mind works through abstractions, molded by years of schooling, while theirs, I thought, were literal, shaped by the actual material world and their experiences of it. The best way to teach them would be to tie every concept to something real that could be touched, and to slip abstract ideas like plurality in sideways. (1994, p. 3)

Donnelly's decision to use this description to construct a narrative of the Hmong women refugee population is telling of the play of power present in the making of Hmong women subjectivities. Although she had numerous accounts to draw from in her experience working with Hmong women who created and sold textiles in a textile co-op in Seattle, she begins her narrative by presenting Hmong women as childlike and ignorant. The knowledge and capabilities of the Hmong women in the narrative are traveled *through* when Donnelly tells the reader that the success of the sewing co-op and the abilities of the Hmong women do not originate from their skills or knowledge but from the American women with whom they were working:

> The refugee women had no previous experiences selling needlework or anything else in the American market. They did not know ordinary business practices, and they lacked business foresight. Also, they lacked skill in English, as well as in salesmanship and in knowledge of their market. They could not have continued selling their needlework, especially through a retail outlet, without the help of the American women. (1994, pp. 90–91)

Other significant texts written about the Hmong community and used widely in US high school and university classrooms also render Hmong women as ignorant and uneducated. Anne Fadiman's *The Spirit Catches You and You Fall Down* (1997) has been used widely in university classrooms in the United States. This story centers around the real-life case of a young girl, Lia Lee, the second-eldest daughter (of fifteen children) of Foua Lee, who emigrated to the United States with her husband and their family. In the university, the volume is often included in common book lists for first-year college students to read. It is also used widely in medical schools to impart cultural competence to health care practitioners. Although the book is hailed as a significant text for teaching Western students about cultural difference and intercultural competence, it also teaches the reader about the uneducated Hmong women based on narrativizations of Foua, one of the book's main characters.

In this text, Foua is presented as uneducated and obtuse. Fadiman uses Lia's epilepsy to interpose the Hmong and US culture in a framework of difference and conflict. Although Foua has resettled in the United States, her experiences and actions are framed and understood within the context of the subject position of the Hmong woman of the homeland. As utilized by Fadiman, Foua's lack of English proficiency is not constructed as a condition of resettlement into a new country but used to explain her thought process and inability to be agentive. For example, Fadiman explains, "Foua never thought to ask [to take her placenta home], since she speaks no English, and when she delivered Lia, no one present spoke Hmong" (1997, p. 6). Foua's uneducated status as a refugee woman serves as a central barrier toward the treatment of her daughter. Fadiman tells the reader that Foua does not know her birthday or how to sign her name and is illiterate. Fadiman does little to soften the criticism or to sympathize with Foua when one of the doctors treating Lia describes Foua as "either very stupid or a loonybird" when she is unable to answer questions during medical in-take or when hospital staff judge her harshly for becoming pregnant for the fifteenth time and force her to consider tubal ligation (1997, pp. 47, 58).

The reader first meets Foua through a retelling of the birth of her daughter Lia. Fadiman begins with what Lia's birth may have looked like in Laos:

> If Lia Lee had been born in the highlands of northwest Laos . . . her mother would have squatted on the floor of the house that her father built from ax-hewn planks thatched with bamboo and grass. . . . She remains proud to this day that she delivered each of them into her own hands, reaching between her legs to ease out the head and then letting the rest of the body slip out onto her forearms. (1997, p. 3)

But since resettling into the United States, Foua gives birth to Lia in a Western hospital. Fadiman takes the reader to the sterile hospital bed where Foua is described as "laying on her back on a steel table, her body covered with sterile drapes, her genital area painted with a brown Betadine solution, with a high wattage lamp trained on her perineum" (1997, p. 6). In these contrasting images, Foua is rendered as a gendered birthing body whose role is to produce children. In Laos she is a capable vessel able to perform her role during the birth of her children. In the United States, she is stripped of this capacity and agency, depicted as a body strapped onto medical devices and first exposed and constrained by Western medicine and now, on text, available for the reader to gaze upon.

Through this birth story, Fadiman is able to tell the reader the cultural practices, beliefs, and taboos associated with pregnancy, birthing, and child-rearing. As the chapter progresses, more stories are told to set up a contrast between Hmong conceptions of health and healing and Western medicine. Hmong culture is presented as a set of beliefs centered on mysticism and irrational ideas. For example, the reader is told that "no woman of childbearing age would ever think of setting foot inside a cave, because a particularly unpleasant kind of *dab* [monster] sometimes lived there who liked to eat flesh and drink blood and could make his victim sterile by having sexual intercourse with her" (Fadiman, 1997, p. 4).

The process of objectification is achieved when Western medicine and the two doctors who struggle with and against the Lees to provide medical care for Lia are depicted as complex individuals who are torn by their desire to take care of Lia despite their disdain for her parents' stubborn unwillingness to adopt Western medication and treatment. The Lees' unwillingness to work with the doctors is framed as originating from their culture. Here, Hmong culture is presented "as a reified, essential, static thing" that not only is essential and static, it determines everything they do (Taylor, 2003, p. 160). Janelle S. Taylor provides an excellent critique of cultural determinism inherent in Fadiman's narrative:

> There is a certain circularity here: Hmong immigrants exhibit Hmong culture, which is characterized by a fierce attachment to Hmong culture, which has the effect of preserving Hmong culture (which is characterized by a fierce attachment, etc.). To read history in this way is really to rule history out of court altogether: nothing ever changes, and in fact it *cannot* change, because these people are destined to act just this way. (2003, p. 165)

In this text, Hmong culture is not dynamic, flexible, negotiable, or contested but a fixed entity that determines the behaviors and actions of the Lees. Fadiman mummifies Hmong culture to make possible the story of cultural conflict that she wants to tell. Fanon provides an analysis of the underlining assumptions of the mummification of culture and the constraints how subjects' actions are theorized:

> This culture, once living and open to the future, becomes closed, fixed in the colonial status, caught in the yolk of oppression. Both present and mummified, it testifies against its members. . . . The cultural mummification leads to a mummification of individual thinking. . . . As though it were possible for a man to evolve otherwise than within the framework of a culture that recognizes him and that he decides to assume. (1967, p. 34)

Refugee Hmong Woman

Scholars who move away from using Hmong culture as a determining factor construct a second kind of Hmong woman figure. This figure is the refugee Hmong woman who encounters Western ideas of gender equity while trying to make a new life for herself in relocation sites of Western nations. The refugee Hmong woman figure was born in the refugee camps, where she began to acquire material wealth made possible by the support of Western women who gave her the idea of selling her *paaj ntaub* (textiles) overseas. Later, when this woman resettles into Western nations, she begins to work outside of the home, which poses a threat to Hmong patriarchal society. As a consequence, her husband experiences loss of prestige, self-esteem, and authority (Bays, 1994; Chan, 1994; Donnelly, 1994; Faderman, 1998). This Hmong woman is torn between two cultures: oppressive and patriarchal Hmong culture and Western culture, where liberatory opportunities for education and advancement exist. Even though Hmong women are active agents participating in social change within their community, they continue to be under the constraints of Hmong patriarchal social order (Julian, 1998).

One example of this narrative can be seen in Wendy Walker-Moffat's study of Hmong education in the United States. In *The Other Side of the Asian American Success Story* (1995), Walker-Moffat begins her narrative with a story about a Hmong girl she names Si Chi. Si Chi is described as a young woman who values education. Walker-Moffat tells us that Chi's desire to learn and her curiosity would make her a successful student. Yet, Chi was not just a student, she was also a Hmong wife. Through Walker-Moffat's text, we learn that Chi's role as a wife made it difficult for her to juggle and manage her life as an American student.

Walker-Moffat dichotomizes Chi's identity as a Hmong wife and as a student. On the one hand, she is a young woman who desired schooling. On the other hand, she is a Hmong wife who willingly accepts her role and duties as a daughter, daughter-in-law, wife, and mother, roles that the reader learns are secondary to those of her father, her husband and his family, and later, her child. Walker-Moffat's analysis of Chi's acceptance of her Hmong self and the rejection of her potentially liberating American student identity is based on her interpretation of what Chi learns as a Hmong woman. She writes: "Si Chi's role models are women who are married and producing families. She does not know any educated Hmong women who could serve as alternate role models. . . . For her having children is the essence of being Hmong, and having an education is the essence of being American" (1995, p. 4).

The line between the analyst and the subjects is blurred here. Do Hmong women see schooling as an American enterprise and motherhood as the essence of being Hmong? Or is the incommensurability of education and motherhood Walker-Moffat's? Critical Hmong studies scholars provide distinction by offering up competing narratives of the educational aspirations of Hmong women in Thailand and Laos and troubling hegemonic images of Hmong women as uneducated and subservient (Vang, Nibbs, & Vang, 2016, Duffy, 2007). For example, John M. Duffy's book *Writing from These Roots* (2007) provides insight into the literacy practices of the Hmong community in Laos, Thailand, and the United States and challenges characterizations of the Hmong as a preliterate society. His analysis of literacy practices of the Hmong provides several accounts of women participating actively in literacy practice prior to coming to the United States. Several authors in *Claiming Place: On the Agency of Hmong Women* (Vang, Nibbs, & Vang, 2016), a collection of essays and research articles seeking to expand and challenge the research archive on Hmong women, also provide counternarratives to the assumptions made by Walker-Moffat about Hmong women and education. Furthermore, stories by writers of *Bamboo among the Oaks: Contemporary Writing by Hmong Americans* (Moua, 2002), *How Do I Begin? A Hmong American Literary Anthology* (Hmong American Writers' Circle, 2011), and *The Latehomecomer: A Hmong Family Memoir* (Yang, 2008) provide examples of Hmong women as shamans, medicinal healers, skilled silversmiths, and businesswomen. Walker-Moffat's (1995) analysis that being a mother is the essence of being Hmong is momentarily hers, but it belongs to a historical analysis that has relied on the association of Hmong womanhood as mother, nurturer, bearer of Hmong tradition, obedient, hardworking, and passive receptor of patriarchal practices and as such is circumscribed and limited by Hmong society (Donnelly, 1994; Koltyk, 1997; Rice, 2000; Winland, 1994).

Assimilated Hmong Woman

More recently, researchers have pushed against a method of analysis in which Hmong women acquiesce to Hmong culture. This becomes necessary, as Hmong women who have resettled in Western nations have been successful in business, education, politics, and a myriad of other fields. These women constitute the third subfigure, the assimilated Hmong woman. In the academic archive, they are Hmong women who have adopted Western notions of gender equity and modernity (G. Y. Lee & Tapp, 2010; S. J. Lee, 1997). Hmong women "who have assimilated mainstream values that promote equality between the sexes" (G. Y. Lee & Tapp, 2010, p. 159) are considered "trailblazers" and role models whose "initiatives will contribute to Hmong women becoming more confident and skilled in achieving better conditions for themselves" (Julian, 1998; G. Y. Lee & Tapp, 2010, p. 160). Although these Hmong women no longer acquiesce to Hmong culture, scholars continue to present this subfigure of Hmong women as individuals whose lives continued to be constrained by ideologies of Hmong culture and male patriarchy. Education, according to Western scholars, comes at a great cost to acculturated Hmong women:

> I can suggest one immediate structural change, following upon the observation that while Hmong girls attended American schools, educated girls quickly fell into disfavor as wives, since traditional parents wanted obedient daughters-in-

law and urged their sons to choose compliant girls (often fitting their own preferences).... Educated girls seems to have been marrying down the educational ladder, or sometimes marrying non-Hmong. The goals of such traditionalist families can be assumed to be maintaining traditional social relationships in the household. (Donnelly, 1994, p. 139)

Educated Hmong women are trailblazers because there are so few of them. One barrier to Hmong women's education is the cultural practice of "early marriage" (Donnelly, 1994; Hutchinson & McNall, 1994; S. J. Lee, 1997; Ngo, 2002; Rumbaut & Ima, 1988). This is exemplified in Stacey J. Lee's (1997) study of Hmong American female pursuit of higher education. In this study, she complicates the cultural difference explanation of low academic achievement of Hmong American women by directing attention to social, racial, and other structural conditions that hinder their academic success. Despite her attention to structural issues that persist in the lives of immigrant Hmong women, she maintains that early marriage and motherhood are cultural norms and, thus, a barrier inherent in the Hmong community. Hmong American women pursue higher education but face a lowered status as a consequence of holding off marriage. By framing the actions and decisions of the educated Hmong American woman against what it means to be a traditional Hmong woman, culture and patriarchy continue to serve as a significant analytic methodology to understand the pursuit of higher education.

Bic Ngo also rejects the cultural difference analysis and argues that the decision to marry is not about competing cultural values: "Hmong American women's decision to marry early may be an expression of contestation that stems from female students' struggles with structural inequalities and power.... Early marriage, as perceived and practiced by Hmong girls and young women, is a form of opposition to two central institutional experiences—family and education." Ngo wants to draw attention to "conception of early marriage in the Hmong community" to highlight the "fluid and dynamic character of Hmong American experiences" to reveal "the ways in which so called 'traditional' or 'cultural' practices are not fixed, but are being negotiated, disrupted, and transformed" (2002, p. 166).

While Ngo is concerned about how culture is used to explain and analyze the educational decisions Hmong women make, she still works within the premise that Hmong culture is a significant determining factor in the educational lives of Hmong women. A close reading of her article suggests that the literature on early marriage and its impact on the educational achievement and aspirations of Hmong women inspired her to propose a new theory to complicate the practice by suggesting that Hmong women are negotiating, disrupting, and transforming this practice. What is problematic about this position is the tacit assumption that early marriage is a Hmong practice, even if it is going through a process of cultural change. One could ask, however, What is early marriage? Doesn't it denote that there is a norm from which one has diverged? What, then, is this norm but an imposed notion of when a person should get married? Prior to being in Western context, where educational problems are often explained in cultural terms (McDermott & Varenne, 1995), was early marriage a phenomenon and then a problem to be resolved?

Furthermore, Ngo argues that Hmong women elect to marry early due to structural issues related to the institutions of family and education (2002, p. 166). Within the family, Hmong women may choose to marry due to intergenerational conflicts that occur between them and their parents on issues of dating, assimilation, and acculturation. Ngo's analysis relies on the assumption that Hmong patriarchy creates an ironic and contradictory situation where Hmong women escape the oppressive family situation only to find themselves oppressed after they marry. She substantiates her claims by citing the accounts of other scholars who use patriarchy as *the* central analytic frame to analyze the experiences of Hmong women:

> Ironically, young women who marry to escape their parents' control and social restrictions find themselves under the constraints of another authority figure— their mother-in-law (Donnelly 1994; Lee 2001). Although Hmong women may perceive marriage as an option for escaping parents' control, they actually end up replacing one set of authority with another. The consequences of marriage may thus be great. Some parents-in-law may prohibit their daughter-in-law from pursuing higher education, even if the daughter and her parents wish her to continue (Ngo 2000). Divorce is infrequently an option, because it is greatly discouraged and often results in disdain and rejection from Hmong society (Donnelly 1994; see also Smith-Hefner 1999). (2002, p. 182)

In determining how to write Hmong woman in Western texts, being educated plays a significant but tacit ideology structuring how Western scholars objectify Hmong women and construct their subjectivities. In the examples that I provide, being educated is framed exclusively in Western terms, where literacy is limited to reading and writing (in English) dichotomies of concrete and abstract concepts frame judgments of cognitive ability, and being an educated person is only gained through formal schooling. What is promising is that this framework is not only being dismissed; it is being displaced by the work of critical Hmong scholars and writers. The next section discusses the emancipatory works of scholarship and literature that take on Emma Perez's call: "We are spoken about, spoken for, and ultimately encoded as whining, hysterical, irrational, or passive women who cannot know what is good for us, who cannot know how to express or authorize our own narratives. *But we will. And we do*" (1999, p. xv, emphasis original).

Scholarship, Critical Literacy, and Decolonial Methodologies

Decolonial scholars argue that it is in critical literacy where colonized subjects can liberate themselves (Perez, 1999). Bhabha states, "Literacy is absolutely crucial for a kind of ability to be responsible to yourself, to make your own reading within a situation of political and cultural choice" (as cited in Olson & Worsham, 1998, p. 3). Over the past forty years, Hmong writers, scholars, and artists have taken on Perez's call to narrate their own stories. As Mai Neng Moua, editor of *Bamboo among the Oaks*, explains: "It is essential for the Hmong and other communities of color to express themselves—to write our stories in our own voices and to create our own images of ourselves. When we do not, others write our stories for us and we are in danger of accepting the images others have painted of us" (2002, p. 7). These works offer spaces to tell new stories and shape new enunciatory subjects.

The writers in *Bamboo among the Oaks* produce a set of narratives that challenge the hegemonic knowledge of the Hmong as "simple, preliterate, illiterate, welfare-dependent, and, most recently, violent" (Moua, 2002, p. 7). As writers who identify and are identifiable as Hmong, their narratives do not seek out to essentialize the Hmong experience for others. Moua explains that the stories and poems should not be read as social histories to convey information about the Hmong. She aptly warns the reader, "It is not an overview, 'Hmong life in America 101'" (2002, 14). Instead, the authors are trying to obtain power, a power that "consists in the ability to make others inhabit your story of their reality" (Gourevitch as cited in Moua, 2002, p. 3). Unlike the narratives constructed by Fadiman (1997) and Donnelly (1994), which set out to essentialize Hmong culture in order to tell the perpetual immigrant narrative of cultural conflict and adaptation, the writers of *Bamboo among the Oaks* seek out to tell a story that is not essentially Hmong for others or essentially Hmong for other Hmong but to tell a story that others can *inhabit*.

Nine years after the publication of the first anthology by Hmong writers and artists, another literary text, *How Do I Begin?* was published by a group of writers who identify themselves as the Hmong American Writers' Circle. The collection of stories in *How Do I Begin?* seeks to redefine and represent the experiences of Hmong men and women who negotiate and contend with cultural, national, and gendered identities. Several authors focus on gender, gender disparities, and gender ideologies within the Hmong community.

Each collection of poetry, stories, and/or photographs is preceded by an introduction of the writer, who articulates his/her social identity and geopolitical location and how these positions shape the narrative that they present. Hmong identity factors significantly into the social identities of the writers, but so, too, do identities as refugee, immigrant, and, most significantly, as writer. Founder of the Hmong American Writers' Circle, Burlee Vang explains the importance of writing in shaping collective and individual identities:

> I've come to believe that as writers of Hmong descent—by inquiring, disassembling, reclaiming, and reinventing our past and present—we will have finally shaped our collective and individual identities on that blank page where our author abandoned us long ago. (2011, p. xix)

Decolonial scholar Ramón Grosfoguel explains the importance of the "locus of enunciation," the "geo-political and body-political location of the subject that speaks" (2011, p. 4) in decolonial epistemologies. He explains that the decolonization of knowledge requires the insights and perspectives of speakers from subalternized bodies. He distinguishes between the epistemic location and the social location to explain that it is not the location of the speaker (global south) and how she/he has been racialized, ethnicized, or gendered that marks knowledge as decolonized. Grosfoguel argues that decolonial knowledge is "knowledge coming from below that produces a critical perspective of hegemonic knowledge in the power relations involved" (2011, p. 5). As texts written from the social and epistemological locations of subalternity, where the identities of the speakers are self-proclaimed as Hmong, the texts provide readers with alternative accounts to the narratives of Hmong women and men portrayed in Western academic texts. It is significant that *How Do I Begin* and *Bamboo among the Oaks* are used in college and university classrooms in ethnic studies, Asian American studies, and Hmong American studies courses across major universities in the United States.

My intent in this chapter is to contribute to the work of decolonial and transnational feminist projects to deconstruct imperialist constructions of ethnic minority women (Mohanty, 1988; Perez, 1999). As the event that opens this chapter reveals, these descriptions are consequential to schooling and education. Educators and scholars utilize these sources as relevant knowledge to make sense of the issues they encounter in their research sites and classrooms. In writing this essay, I stake my claim as an enunciatory subject against the academic canon that has been written about Hmong women. As a Hmong woman, there are particular moments when my gender has been a point of contention and struggle for me, not unlike other women in other cultural and political spaces. What remains important for me and other Hmong women scholars, activists, and writers is that we be able to displace stories that have been written about us with new stories where we can break out of the subject positions that have claimed our diverse, complex, and nuanced experiences.

In the social sciences and humanities, scholars in the field of critical Hmong studies are also speaking back to the field. It is an interdisciplinary field composed of scholars in the fields of history, ethnic studies, anthropology, education research, and sociology who not only recognize the importance of the foundational work of scholarship on the Hmong but also recognize that within these narratives there exist imperialist ideations of ethnic and racial otherness. As the field of critical Hmong scholarship advances from critical and necessary deconstruction work to constructions of new narratives and subjectivities, it is with utmost importance that scholars adopt decolonial methodologies (Smith, 1999). As Grosfoguel (2011) argues, it is not enough to adopt postcolonial or postmodernist perspectives, it is important to take up the methodologies of decolonial scholars in order to reshape and reclaim new narratives.

References

Bays, S. A. (1994). *Cultural politics and identity formation in a San Joaquin Valley Hmong community* (Unpublished doctoral dissertation). University of California, Los Angeles.

Bhabha, H. K. (1994). *The location of culture.* London: Routledge.

Chan, S. (1994). *Hmong means free: Life in Laos and America.* Philadelphia, PA: Temple University Press.

Cooper, R. (1984). *Resource scarcity and the Hmong response: Patterns of settlement and economy in transition.* Singapore: Singapore University Press.

de Certeau, M. (1988). *The writing of history* (T. Conley, Trans.). New York, NY: Columbia University Press.

Donnelly, N. (1994). *Changing lives of refugee women.* Seattle: University of Washington Press.

Duffy, J. M. (2007). *Writing from these roots: Literacy in a Hmong American community.* Honolulu: University of Hawaii Press.

Faderman, L., with Xiong, G. (1998). *I begin my life all over: The Hmong and the American immigrant experience.* Boston, MA: Beacon Press.

Fadiman, A. (1997). *The spirit catches you and you fall down.* New York, NY: Noonday.

Fanon, F. (1967). *Toward the African revolution* (H. Chevalier, Trans.). New York, NY: Grove.

Foucault, M. (1972). *The archaeology of knowledge and the discourse of language* (A. M. Smith, Trans.) New York, NY: Vintage Books.

Gerdner, L. A., Cha, D., Yang, D., & Tripp-Reimer, R. (2007). The circle of life: End-of-life care and death rituals for Hmong-American elders. *Journal of Gerontological Nursing, 33*(5), 20–29.

Goldstein, B. L. (1985). *Schooling for cultural transitions: Hmong girls and boys in American high schools* (Unpublished doctoral dissertation). University of Wisconsin–Madison.

Grosfoguel, R. (2011). Decolonizing post-colonial studies and paradigms of political economy: Transmodernity, decolonial thinking, and global coloniality. *Transmodernity, 1*(1), 1–36.

Her, L. N. (2016). Rewriting Hmong women in Western text. In C. Y. Vang, F. Nibbs, & M. Vang (Eds.), *Claiming place: On the agency of Hmong women* (pp. 3–27). Minneapolis: University of Minnesota Press.

Hmong American Writers' Circle, The. (2011). *How do I begin? A Hmong American literary anthology*. Berkeley, CA: Heyday.

hooks, b. (1992). *Black looks, race, and representation*. Boston, MA: South End Press.

Hutchinson, R., & McNall, M. (1994). Early marriage in a Hmong cohort. *Journal of Marriage and the Family, 56*, 579–590.

Julian, R. (1998). "I love driving!" Alternative constructions of Hmong femininity in the west. *Race, Gender & Class, 5*(2), 30–53.

Koltyk, J. A. (1997). *New pioneers in the heartland: Hmong life in Wisconsin*. Needham Heights, MA: Allyn & Bacon.

Lee, G. Y., & Tapp, N. (2010). *Culture and customs of the Hmong*. Santa Barbara, CA: Greenwood.

Lee, S., & Chang, J. (2012). Mental health status of the Hmong Americans in 2011: Three decades revisited. *Journal of Social Work in Disability and Rehabilitation, 11*(1), 55–70.

Lee, S. J. (1997). The road to college: Hmong American women's pursuit of higher education. *Harvard Educational Review, 67*(4), 803–827.

Lee, S. J. (2001). More than model minorities or delinquents: Hmong American high school students. *Harvard Educational Review, 67*(4), 505–528.

Lee, S. J. (2002). Learning "America": Hmong American high school students. *Education and Urban Society, 34*(2), 233–246.

Lee, S. J. (2005). *Up against Whiteness: Race, schools, and immigrant students*. New York, NY: Teachers College Press.

Marcus, G. E., & Cushman, D. (1982). Ethnographies as texts. *Annual Review of Anthropology, 11*, 25–69.

McDermott, R., & Varenne, H. (1995). Culture as disability. *Anthropology and Education Quarterly, 26*, 324–348.

Meredith, W. H., & Rowe, G. P. (1986). Changes in Lao Hmong marital attitudes after migrating to the United States. *Journal of Comparative Family Studies, 17*(1), 117–126.

Mohanty, C. T. (1988). Under Western eyes: Feminist scholarship and colonial discourses. *Feminist Review, 30*(Autumn), 61–88.

Moua, M. N. (2002). *Bamboo among the oaks: Contemporary writing by Hmong Americans*. St. Paul: Minnesota Historical Society Press.

Ngo, B. (2002). Contesting "culture": The perspective of Hmong American female students on early marriage. *Anthropology & Education Quarterly, 33*(2), 163–188.

Ngo, B. (2008). Beyond "culture clash" understandings of immigrant experiences. *Theory into Practice, 47*(1), 4–11. doi:10.1080/00405840701764656

Ngo, B., Bigelow, M., & Wahlstrom, K. L. (2007). The transition of Wat Tham Krabok Hmong children to Saint Paul public schools: Perspectives of teachers, principals, and Hmong parents. *Hmong Studies Journal, 8*, 1–36.

Ngo, B., & Lee, S. J. (2007). Complicating the image of model minority success: A review of Southeast Asian American education. *Review of Educational Research, 77*(4), 415–453.

Ngo, B., & Leet-Otley, J. (2011). Discourses about gender among Hmong American policymakers: Conflicting views about gender, culture, and Hmong youth. *Journal of Language, Identity, and Education, 10*, 99–118.

Olson, G. A., & Worsham, L. (1998). Staging the politics of difference: Homi Bhahba's critical literacy. In G. A. Olson & L. Worsham (Eds.), *Race, rhetoric, and the postcolonial* (pp. 361–391). Albany: State University of New York Press.

Perez, E. (1999). *The decolonial imaginary: Writing Chicanas into history*. Bloomington: Indiana University Press.

Quincy, K. (1995). *Hmong: History of a People*. Spokane: Eastern Washington University.

Rice, P. L. (2000). *Hmong women and reproduction*. Westport, CT: Bergin & Garvey.

Rumbaut, R., & Ima, K. (1988). *The adaptation of Southeast Asian refugee youth: A comparative study*. Washington, DC: US Office of Refugee Resettlement.

Schein, L., Thoj, V.-M., Vang, B., & Jalao, L. C. T. (2012). Beyond Gran Torino's guns: Hmong cultural warriors performing genders. *Positions, 20*(3), 763–792.

Smith, L. T. (1999). *Decolonizing methodologies*. New York, NY: Zed Books.

Symonds, P. (2004). *Calling in the soul: Gender and the cycle of life in a Hmong village*. Seattle: University of Washington Press.

Taylor, J. S. (2003). The story catches you and you fall down: Tragedy, ethnography, and "cultural competence." *Medical Anthropology Quarterly, 17*(2), 159–181.

Thao, Y. J. (2003). Empowering Mong students: Home and school factors. *The Urban Review, 35*(1), 25–42.

Trueba, H. (1990). *Cultural conflict and adaptation: The case of Hmong children in American society*. Bristol, PA: Falmer Press.

Vang, B. (2011). Introduction. In Hmong American Writers' Circle (Eds.), *How do I begin? A Hmong American literary anthology*. Berkeley, CA: Heyday.

Vang, C. Y., Nibbs, F., & Vang, M., Eds. (2016). *Claiming place: On the agency of Hmong women*. Minneapolis: University of Minnesota Press.

Walker-Moffat, W. (1995). *The other side of the Asian American success story*. San Francisco, CA: Jossey-Bass.

Winland, D. N. (1994). Christianity and community: Conversion and adaptation among Hmong refugee women. *The Canadian Journal of Sociology, 19*(1), 21–45.

Yang, K. K. (2008). *The Latehomecomer: A Hmong Family Memoir*. Minneapolis, MN: Coffee House.

4

A Spiritual Infusion

An Anti-Colonial Feminist Approach to Academic Healing and Transformative Education

ANGELA MALONE CARTWRIGHT

Given that classroom practices, such as curriculum design, material selection, and pedagogical decisions, are influenced by personal beliefs and commitments (Villegas, 2007), it is important for teacher educators, as well as classroom practitioners, to interrogate their epistemologies. Trained in university teacher-preparation programs, many preservice and practicing teachers are likely to privilege an Enlightenment-based, empirical worldview at the expense of other ways of knowing, including spirituality. However, the limitations of an empirical-only worldview are increasingly highlighted by educators working within anti-colonial and feminist frameworks.

The academy's willingness to explore the issue of spirituality and the role spirituality plays in society, particularly, education, is necessary for continued growth (Rendon, 2000). In his introduction to *Spirituality, Education, & Society: An Integrated Approach* (2011), Ali Abdi argues:

> the noticeable absence of spirituality from the educational research and from contemporary spaces of school, is to say the least lamentable, and the coming of this work and other treatises that should follow it, are essentially needed, and should awaken, one must hope, in all those whose perception of public education as a primary public good is authentic and present, an urgent sense of advancing the place of spirituality in all learning situations, relationships and outcomes. (p. xiii)

His concern is shared by many educators (Dillard, 2006; hooks, 2000; Palmer, 1993; Rendon, 2000; Shahjahan, 2004; Wane & Ritskes, 2011). Their calls for an infusion of spirituality, defined for the purposes of this paper as the act of intentionally seeking connections that make us more fully human (Lynskey, 2014), into the academy support challenges to the Enlightenment project by anti-colonial and feminist educators. Though the Enlightenment project continues to dominate the Western academy and teacher-education programs, spiritual infusion can create space for holistic, transformative educational experiences. This shift to include anti-colonial and feminist epistemologies can lead to healing for faculty, teacher candidates, and students.

A Spiritual Infusion

An infusion of spirituality may simultaneously increase the challenges confronting educators while creating space for renewed healing and growth. The role of spirituality is an integral part of the work of many educators from marginalized communities (Arvin, Tuck, & Morrill, 2013; Dillard, 2006; Grande, 2010; Shahjahan, 2005). It is unsurprising, then, that educators who advocate for a spiritual infusion reinforce calls from marginalized communities for multiple epistemologies and (re)evaluation of how academic and educational research is done (Dillard, 2006; Palmer, 1993). Educators calling for the inclusion of a spiritual epistemology and methodology also challenge the dominant structure of relationships within all educational settings. Further, they critique the purpose of academic and educational endeavors at all instructional levels.

A spiritual infusion into the academy would support a transformational approach to the epistemologies of preservice teachers and, thus, into kindergarten through twelfth grade (K–12) classrooms. At the heart of a spiritual epistemology is the relational nature of truth (Astin, 2004; Dillard, 2006; Palmer, 1993; Rendon, 2000). Many marginalized communities cannot conceive of truth being the possession of a single perspective nor success as individual advancement. Their resistance to the notion of universal truth is intrinsic and born of their lived experiences. Indeed, Vine Deloria Jr. (1999) reminds readers that only in relationship can a person even exist. Riyad Shahjahan astutely identifies that this worldview is in conflict with that of the academy. He explains that a "high level of individualism and competitiveness is encouraged within the academic ranks, especially in research universities. . . . But, according to many spiritual traditions, the primary site for spiritual development is through letting go of the ego" (2005, p. 692). A spiritual infusion may transform the ways in which educators interact with their peers, which can, in and of itself, be transformational. Scholar-poet Alice Walker asserts that "knowledge kept secret ceases to be knowledge; it becomes dogma and superstition. Knowledge actually requires sharing in order to exist" (2006, p. 162). bell hooks (2000) argues that hoarding knowledge is usually linked to a desire for power, which reinforces hierarchies and bolsters oppressive systems. A spiritual infusion that privileges cooperation and communal advancement would, thus, be not only transformational to the static and competitive nature of many teacher-education programs but could also empower future primary educators to be change agents themselves and to educate their students about tools of resistance to oppressive systems.

Shahjahan (2005) asserts that a spiritually infused epistemology and methodology would also privilege process over product, as opposed to the current product-driven quality of the academy and, thus, primary and secondary education. In a spiritually infused academic environment, educators would be focused on trying to learn, not trying to know. Knowing implies a static quality to the subject, which can be limiting, if not overtly counterproductive (Deloria, 1999). As Deloria argues, it is the Western tradition "which seeks to freeze history in an unchanging and authoritative past" (1999, p. 42; see also Said, 1978). Educators must acknowledge the flexibility of cultures in diaspora, the processes of evolving cultures. Intrinsic in their evolution is the presence of elements of the dominant culture, both informative and limiting to the traditional culture (Deloria, 1999; Hall, 1999). A type of hybrid culture can begin to emerge, evidenced in the appearance of Western-style, Native-themed works of literature in the early postcolonial era (Appiah, 1992). The process of hybridization influences and transforms dominant culture, as well, though the imbalance of power raises questions of cultural appropriation, both within the academy (Arvin, Tuck, & Morrill, 2013) and in primary and secondary settings.

A spiritual infusion would be challenging to the status quo in many ways, challenging educators to interrogate the balances of power that have, in some cases, been previously unquestioned. The interrogation process will be particularly important and difficult for educators from dominant traditions. Deloria argues that the dominant Western "assumption that the world operates in certain predetermined ways, that it operates continuously under certain natural laws, and that the nature of every species is homogenous, with few real deviations" is the source of many consequences, both intentional and unintended, which result in "trauma[s]" (1999, pp. 102–103). Spiritual epistemologies and methodologies may create space in which to acknowledge, interrogate, and make restitution for these consequences and healing for these traumas.

The healing process that could be inspired by a spiritual infusion may have far-reaching effects. Teacher-preparation programs, as they are still largely the purview of colleges and universities, remain grounded in the Enlightenment assumptions that inform the larger academy. Though teacher preparation is admittedly only one aspect of the larger academy, it is uniquely situated to act as a catalyst for societal transformation. The importance of transformation at all levels of education cannot be overstated. Instead of a tool for self-determination (Deloria, 2001b), school has been experienced as "a site of social struggle where asymmetries of power are played out" (Grande, 2003, p. 337). Compulsory education is a site of indoctrination (Deloria, 2001b) and cultural (and physical) abolition and genocide (Grande, 2010). Students who resist annihilation and invisibility, overtly or by simply retaining their cultural knowledges (Tuck & Yang, 2011), are considered deficient (Gallegos, Villenas, & Brayboy, 2003) and "not nearly as bright" as their dominant peers (Deloria, 2001b, p. 133). These traumas must be healed, and Cynthia Dillard (2006) argues that a spiritual infusion can enable educators to become healers.

Educators have already begun to envision the possibilities, many of which share the goals embraced by scholars from marginalized communities. Parker Palmer envisions transformational educational experiences that prepare "us to see beyond appearances into the hidden realities of life—beyond facts into truth, beyond self-interest into compassion, beyond our flagging energies and nagging despairs into the love required to renew the community of creation (1993, p. 13). Palmer's (1993) privileging of truth and community are in conflict with the dominant, Enlightenment-based model of education today. However, his words resonate with anti-colonial feminist calls for a conception of truth not based solely in authority but also in contextually situated communities.

Thomas Moore (2005) argues that the Enlightenment model of education emphasizes the mind at the expense of the soul. Though students may learn the "correct" answers to politically and economically expedient questions, the result is likely that they will become good consumers, even good students, but not good citizens and lifelong learners (Lynskey, 2013). Moore rejects the Enlightenment project's desire for knowledge at the expense of wisdom, arguing instead that education "cultivat[es] . . . a certain kind of ignorance," privileging not knowing in the same way it privileges knowing (2005, p. 15; see also Deloria, 2001b). He promotes a holistic spiritual education, one that provides "healing" through "the discovery of what the soul wants" (2005, p. 13). Walker concurs, asserting that "the soul wants to know the truth; what is really going on" (2006, p. 215).

Edmund O'Sullivan proposes an alternative model of emancipatory hope, one that challenges educators (indeed, all citizens) to see past the dominant market model into what he calls the "Big Picture" (2005, p. 69–71). When the focus is on only the isolated pieces of information that will be tested, we miss the opportunities to explore complexities and interconnectivity. O'Sullivan compels educators to, instead, act as "strange attractors," those creative elements in society act as catalysts for transformation, and to "situate ourselves in a 'great work'" in which we ask "great questions" (2005, pp. 73–76). Educators who desire transformational learning must ask the difficult questions of *why* and, even more significant, *how could it be otherwise* in their pursuit of great work (Lynskey, 2013). Acknowledging the inequities and epistemological violence inherent in dominant educational and institutional systems is simply not enough; we must go further, actively seeking to disrupt them in pursuit of more-just and more-equitable systems. Teaching and learning are meaningful activities when approached with the goal of transforming society and creating space for multiple epistemologies and opportunities to create truth in community encourages students to pursue alternatives not available in a hierarchical system that privileges a Western, Enlightenment approach at the expense of other ways of knowing.

The Enlightenment Project

In contrast with the relational ways of knowing privileged by Indigenous and non-Western societies, the Enlightenment ushered in a worldview that privileged the concept of a self-evident universal truth that could be discovered through reason and empirical evidence, with science as its own authority and the standard by which all things would be measured. A scientific approach to truth created a system that privileged objectified knowledge where "reality [is] basically physical, and knowledge thereof basically mental or verbal" (Deloria, 1999, p. 104). While this perspective has long been unquestioned in the Western academy, it is incongruent with many non-Western worldviews, particularly, as they relate to religion and spirituality. Deloria explains: "Truth is in the ever-changing experiences of the community. For the traditional Indian to fail to appreciate this aspect of his own heritage is the saddest of heresies" (1999, p. 42). In addition to disagreement regarding the nature of truth, some marginalized worldviews also challenge the idea that truth can be fully known, particularly, by those who lack the cultural knowledge to appreciate the context of that which they observe (Dei, 2000; Deloria, 1999, 2001a; Tuhiwai Smith, 1999).

In much the same way that truth has been objectified by science, so has spirituality been framed as an experience that can be empirically observed and quantified (Nye & Hay, 1996). While this may have been necessary in order to begin the academic discussion, it has limited the extent to which educators could investigate the impact of spirituality. An objectified, scientific approach decontextualizes and idealizes religion and spirituality in order to conform to the Enlightenment principles of objectivity and universality (Laible, 2000; Shahjahan, 2005; Tisdell, 2007; Wright, 1997). The apparent inability of spirituality and other nonempirical epistemologies to conform to Enlightenment ideals is one of the primary reasons they have been largely disregarded in the academy. However, the growing rejection of Enlightenment ideals by educators from marginalized communities has created space for an interrogation of the assumptions that inform the modern

Western academy and teacher-preparation programs (Paris, 1995). Shahjahan's (2005) assertion that science has become the new religion of the Western education succinctly frames the discussion. Indeed, if one compares the characteristics of academics in the age of Scholasticism to those that guide inquiry since the age of Enlightenment, it is clear that little has changed but the source of authority from which one may learn the truth.

Joseph Rickaby (1908) described Scholasticism as characterized by its orthodoxy, dualism, optimism, and stasis in medieval Europe. While the variety of topics investigated by Scholastic intellectuals was not limited to the Catholic Church, great pains were made to ensure that their findings were never in conflict with the doctrine of the church. This commitment to orthodoxy guaranteed funding and approval by the powerful medieval Church, but it limited the extent to which scholars could follow their findings. Scholastic dualism focused on separating the human experience from the larger world, as well as detaching God from the natural world. These dichotomies were an additional safeguard to the aforementioned orthodoxy. Scholastic optimism is described by Rickaby (1908) as faith in the ability of scholars to discover absolute truth. As scholars approached the doctrines of the Catholic Church with the similar certitude, Scholastic work was largely guided by a particular religious conception of truth. If an emerging truth was not reconcilable to the teachings of the Church, it could not be the absolute truth. A significant effect of this influence is found in Rickaby's (1908) fourth characteristic of Scholasticism, its belief in the stasis of truth. While this belief evidenced itself most often in the study of the natural world, its philosophical implications would certainly have affected scholars' interpretations in other inquiries, particularly, as they expanded their inquiries into the natural world to include Indigenous peoples. Acknowledging only a singular, timeless, and universal truth, scholars could not appreciate the increasing complexities of the expanding world.

With the advent of the Enlightenment, the relationship between religion and the academy was turned on its head. No longer did scholars have to make their scientific and philosophical findings align with Catholic doctrine; on the contrary, doctrine that opposed science was discarded or reinterpreted to match scientific evidence. However, while the hierarchy of authority was reversed, the characteristics that informed Scholastic inquiry maintained their privileged status in the modern academy. The modern Enlightened scholar's allegiance is no longer to the orthodoxy of the Church but to the orthodoxy of science. The scholar's dualistic worldview is reinforced by the dichotomous nature of the academy, with its drive to classify the world and its inhabitants while maintaining academic distance and neutrality. The academy's optimistic faith in empiricism remains intact, as is evidenced by the privileged position of quantitative research methods over qualitative. This portrait of a modern scholar in the Western academy speaks to the fourth characteristic of Scholasticism stasis. Despite significant shifts in worldview and authority within the academy, the underlying assumptions remain: orthodoxy, dualism, optimism, and stasis.

This privileging of epistemologies that favor these characteristics impacts teacher-preparation programs, as well. Trained in an era of punitive standardized assessments, preservice teachers may have insufficient preparation to counter dominant narratives (Lynskey, 2015) that continue to encourage orthodoxy to authority, the dualistic separation of students' cultural selves from their academic selves, the optimistic belief that test scores equate to learning, and the lack of political will to challenge the status quo. Douglas Sloan critiques this dominant, Enlightenment-based model of education as one that seeks to "homogenize, standardize, and regulate the human being" and rejects it in favor of models that encourage educators and students to acknowledge and privilege our full humanity (2005, p. 43). Standards-based, assessment-driven models of education ignore students' full selves, and static, culturally based conceptions of truth influence not only what is taught but also how. These educational realities are potentially harmful to students, especially in K–12 classrooms. This is particularly true for students from marginalized communities, as their epistemologies are many times among those disregarded in favor of the dominant Enlightenment model. By forcing students into fixed categories that ignore the complexities of their lived experiences, the dominant models of education are complicit in the unjust labeling of children from marginalized communities as at-risk (Gallegos, Villenas, & Brayboy, 2003) because these models disregard the parts of the students that don't fit neatly into the categories, a reflection of the Enlightenment project's drive to classify the world and everything in it.

For many students from marginalized communities, religion and spirituality are among the difficult-to-quantify parts of themselves that are disregarded by the academy (Deloria, 1999; Du Bois, 1990; Paris, 1995; Shahjahan, 2005). With the shift in authority regarding truth, there is little doubt that religion and even spirituality have lost the place of privilege they held in the pre-Enlightenment Western world (Lincoln, 2003). Not only are their places of privilege lost but spirituality and religion are also often rejected, described by Njoki N. Wane and Eric J. Ritskes as being "silenced and marginalized as a discourse or embodied knowledge in the academy" (2011, p. xv). Spirituality and religion are no longer acceptable sources in the search for truth. Educators who embrace a spiritual worldview are caught in a difficult situation, which hooks voices, saying, "Taught to believe that the mind, not the heart, is the seat of learning, many of us believe . . . we will be perceived as weak and irrational" (2000, p. xxvii). Many educators engage in a kind of covering to hide their spiritual lives so that their commitment to and competence in their disciplines will not be questioned (Yoshino, 2006).

Challenging hierarchies, such as those institutionalized by the Enlightenment project, is at the heart of Riane Eisler's (2005) alternative transformational model of holistic education. Her partnership model is based on relationships, which she privileges equally with reading, writing, and arithmetic goals in education. Eisler argues that both what we teach and how we teach it influence the ways in which our students interact with others. She challenges educators to interrogate how, where, and what we teach for the elements of hidden curriculum that undermine the importance and development of healthy relationships. Because healthy interpersonal relationships, priorities, and definitions of success are integral to transformative education, Eisler's partnership model seeks to create a template for information based on "linking rather than ranking," challenging the hierarchal structure of the dominator model (p. 51). Challenges to the dominator model, thus, include challenges to both epistemology and methodology, focusing instead on the more relational truths and inquiries of the partnership model.

Indeed, as George Dei highlights the holistic and relational nature of Indigenous knowledges, a holistic approach to education can be seen as the practical application of a spiritual infusion, as opposed to the academy's historic commitment to dualism, under both the Scholastic and Enlightenment project worldviews (2000; see also Miller, 2005; Taggart, 2001). Holistic education endeavors to "nurture the development of the whole person," including "the intellectual, emotional, physical, social, aesthetic, and spiritual" elements (Miller, 2005, p. 2). Interestingly, Shaikh Mabud identifies goals similar to these when he describes a Muslim view of religion and education, explaining that "the religious view speaks of a *total* human being in whom the senses, mind, intellect and spirit work as part of the whole person" (1992, p. 89, original emphasis). In a holistic education model, the student is not required to compartmentalize or cover; instead, full integration of the self in the learning environment is encouraged. The whole self is more than empiricism and reason; Dei's description of self includes the "spiritual, emotional, cultural, and psychological," as well as "physical and material embodiment" (2000, p. 126). Holistic models of education include space for students and educators coming from marginalized communities to incorporate their lived experiences and cultural knowledges into the learning environment.

Wane and Ritskes argue that the purpose of spiritual learning is embracing "the things that make us whole" (2011, p. xvi). For many scholars, educators, and students, embracing that which makes us whole will necessitate a (re)claiming of stolen, lost, and excluded knowledges that have long been absent from the academy. Julie Kaomea draws on Michel Foucault when she describes this possibility as "an insurrection of subjugated knowledges" (2006, p. 336). For teacher educators, this will entail (re)imagining the ways in which subjugated knowledges can be included in course readings, learning activities, grading, and field placements.

Likewise, K–12 practitioners can actively seek ways in which to make course curriculum, materials, learning activities, and assessments more inclusive.

Anti-Colonialism and Transformative Education

Anti-colonial educators are pushing back against the dominant Enlightenment model of education. Despite its long history of disregarding Indigenous knowledges (Deloria, 2001a), educators from marginalized communities continue to speak truth (Dillard, 2006) to the academy. The emergence of postcolonial discourse, born from Edward Said's (1978) concept of Orientalism, helped to create space within the academy for multiple, contested worldviews. Robert J. C. Young (2001) describes postcolonialism as being concerned with (re)viewing history with an intentional focus on the perspectives of the oppressed, as well as the long-term consequences of their subjugation. However, postcolonialism works under the assumption that imperial practices are in the past only. It "dehistoricizes and homogenizes human identities" as they are shaped by continuing colonial impulses (Dei, 2000, p. 116).

Although a postcolonial approach is gaining popularity, many educators from marginalized communities have begun to reject it in favor of anti-colonial discourse. Linda Tuhiwai Smith (1999) rejects postcolonial discourse as another imperialistic attempt by the West to maintain its control over the naming and framing of the world. Conversely, anti-colonial discourse names the processes of global capitalism as recolonizing tendencies. In addition to acknowledging current colonial impulses, anti-colonialism privileges Indigenous cultures and knowledges as sites of resistance (Dei, 2000).

One of these sites of resistance is challenging the Western conception of science as the only source of truth. Deloria rejects science as "having no moral basis" and being "entirely incapable of resolving human problems except by the device of making humans act more and more like machines" (2001a, p. 4). Many educators from marginalized communities consider science flawed, as it represents only an Anglo-European ideological perspective and a religiously inspired goal of dominating nature, which has historically portrayed nature as an intrinsically evil entity doomed to destruction, thus not requiring our responsible stewardship (Deloria, 1999; see also Abdi, 2011; Dei, 2000; Palmer, 1993). These epistemological differences have substantial impacts on what is taught in K–12 science and civics courses.

Anti-colonial educators also resist the Enlightenment project's reliance on scientific dualism, which forces educators to operate under imposed dichotomies aimed at separation (Dei, 2000; Deloria, 2001a; Narayan, 2003). While desirable in the Western model, especially in the standardized environment of K–12 education, dualism and dichotomies ignore the complexities and interconnectedness that are central to many Indigenous worldviews (Deloria, 2001b). The Enlightenment-based drive to separate and categorize is related to its inability to tolerate mystery and ambiguity (Deloria, 2001b). Indeed, at the heart of Dillard's (2006) endarkened feminist epistemology is a call to privilege the mystery. The Enlightenment project privileges the known, and many preservice teachers are trained to perceive truth as that which can be discovered or, at least, constructed. However, the inclusion of marginalized voices reveals that no single version of the truth can be complete, and some truths appear to be contradictory to others. Because truths are built in community (Palmer, 1993), educators should privilege the mystery, that which is yet to be learned, above that which we think we understand.

As Dillard (2006) illustrates with her deliberate wording when naming her theory, privileging the mystery will require educators to (re)think and (re)name our academic infrastructure. The Enlightenment is framed as the time when Western civilization left the darkness of superstition and embraced empiricism as the way to know truth. While some benefits of scientific development are clear, the correlating abandonment and subjugation of alternative epistemologies have been costly. Privileging Enlightenment however it is defined and by whom necessarily subjugates those perceived as still in the dark. However, the darkness is where the mystery is, where the dialogue can begin, and where hope for reconciliation and restitution lives. In the darkness is where we can let go of our certainty and become truly relational beings, more truly human.

The importance of relationship and recognition of our shared humanity is apparent not only in the need to change our epistemologies but also our methodologies (Deloria, 2001a, 2001b; Shahjahan, 2004, 2005; Tuhiwai Smith, 1999). The necessity of these challenges is evident in Tuhiwai Smith's description of the Indigenous perception of research: "[T]he term 'research' is inextricably linked to European imperialism and colonialism. . . . [It] is probably one of the dirtiest words in the Indigenous world's vocabulary. . . . [I]t stirs up silence, it conjures up bad memories, it raises a smile that is knowing and distrustful" (1999, p. 1). Tuhiwai Smith attributes Indigenous distrust of research to the relationship between research and conquest but also to the manner in which information is gathered, interpreted, and (re)presented by conquering researchers (1999; see also Dei, 2000). She draws upon Said's (1978) concept of Orientalism to explain that the basic function of early research on Indigenous peoples was for the purpose of understanding in order to rule (Tuhiwai Smith, 1999).

Said described Orientalism as "a style of thought based upon an ontological and epistemological distinction made between 'the Orient' and (most of the time) 'the Occident'" (1978, p. 2). At the heart of Orientalism is the dualism of "us" versus "them," with the defining characteristic of "us" being that we are not "them." As Said explains, our definition of "them" is largely our own invention. It does not accurately portray those whom we have Othered, but that does not stop our portrayal from becoming definitive and damaging. Orientalism is "a Western style for dominating, restructuring, and having authority over the Orient" (Said, 1978, p. 3). European and, later, American scholars approached non-Western cultures as sites for experimentation, exploitation, and domination in the successive names of religion, empire, science, and progress. It is these experiences that make Indigenous peoples wary of the scholar-researcher. As the work of the scholar-researcher becomes the K–12 curriculum, the objectification and caricature of nations and peoples becomes codified and reified into truth, taught in classrooms and influencing the work to come.

Anti-Colonial Feminism and Transformative Education

Educators from marginalized communities apply anti-colonial critiques to the Enlightenment-based, Eurocentric assumptions that underlie critical theory, much of the scholarship considered progressive and inclusive (Tuck & Yang, 2011). A particularly productive example of anti-colonial theory utilized to challenge the dominant notion of inclusivity is "whitestream" feminism (Grande, 2003). Sandy Grande asserts that mainstream feminism, which overwhelmingly reflects White culture, has silenced women from marginalized communities with its focus on the grand narrative of the Enlightenment-based patriarchy, with its artificial binary of masculine rationality versus feminine emotionalism (2003; see also Arvin, Tuck, & Morrill, 2013; Dillard, 2006). Focusing on and rejecting this specific binary distinction enable White women to abdicate responsibility for the role women play(ed) in colonial activities and ignore the continued colonial tendencies that support globalization (Grande, 2003; Kaomea, 2006).

In addition, the whitestream feminism's framing of feminism as a primarily academic endeavor illustrates the gulf between whitestream feminism and the feminism of women of color (Grande, 2003). Grande advocates instead for a feminism transformed by acknowledging the real-life experiences of women of color, one that acknowledges power dynamics between and among women as it seeks to dismantle colonial structures (2003; see also Dillard, 2006). These tensions manifest in teacher-education programs, where preservice teachers are taught research-based best practices to enhance student achievement but are provided with insufficient guidance on how to enhance student growth. As we continue to deprofessionalize and standardize teacher education, preservice teachers can enjoy academic achievement in the form of high marks though they fail to develop the necessary skills of critical thinking, problem solving, and relationship building. The art of the profession is being lost in the efforts to quantify it into a science. Including the epistemologies, methodologies, and pedagogies of feminists of color creates space for preservice teachers to engage the complexities of both their content and pedagogical decisions while also encouraging them to seek connections and guidance from many cultural contextual sources.

Arvin, Tuck, and Morrill (2013) take up Grande's (2003) call for a contextualized feminism, indicting disciplines based both in feminism and multiculturalism for their failure to address the unique experiences of Indigenous women and their communities. As opposed to inclusion and equality within Enlightenment-based, Western structures, assumed to be the desirable end-goal for all marginalized communities, Arvin, Tuck, and Morrill (2013) argue that Indigenous communities are more concerned with sovereignty and self-determination (see also Grande, 2010). Indigenous scholars also problematize the assumption that Enlightenment-based ideas of "rights and justice" and progress are universally desired (Grande, 2003; Tuck & Yang, 2011). Though these educators challenge the academy as a whole, their indictment is of significant import for colleges of education: the entities responsible for preparing the nation's teachers. Though multiculturalism remains an educational buzzword, despite its lack of required, let alone effective coursework (Butin, 2007), the work of these scholars indicates that multiculturalism that remains comfortably within the dominant, Enlightenment-based models of education falls short of being truly multicultural. Therefore, it is likely that our underprepared preservice teachers' limited exposure may be doing even less than we think in preparing them to bridge the distance between the dominant, Enlightenment-based model of education and the embodied experiences of their students.

As is demonstrated the problematization of the concept of progress by Indigenous educators, naming and framing, the acts of defining the world in which we live, learn, and work, are significant (Grande, 2010). Indeed, Deloria advocates for a rejection of the entire Western framework, asserting that true liberation requires more than an "intellectual reorientation alone" (1999, p. 101). He argues that "if we are to talk seriously about the necessity of liberation, we are talking about the destruction of the whole complex of Western theories of knowledge and the construction of a new and more comprehensive synthesis of human knowledge and experience" (1999, p. 106).

Asad (1993), like Deloria (1999), suggests that in order to be truly emancipatory, discourses must consider Indigenous and non-Western epistemologies. He provides a relevant critique of the Western-conception religion, arguing that it cannot be applied to non-Western experiences. In the Western framework, religion is an individual experience based on beliefs (orthodoxy), while in the non-Western framework, largely rejected in Western institutions, it is considered communal experience based on action (orthopraxy). He argues that only in the West is religion relegated to the margins as an individual, belief-centered enterprise. Asad elaborates, explaining that this perspective on religion developed in the West as the Enlightenment reversed the distribution of power that existed in premodern Europe (1993; see also Lincoln, 2003; Tweed, 2008). As religious and spiritual truths were subjugated to science, they had to be relegated to the realm of the personal. Asad's (1993) rejection of Western conceptions of religion has little to do with the content of the religions themselves. The locus of his anti-colonial discourse is that he challenges academic definitions of religion because of the post-Enlightenment, Western ideological underpinnings of the definitions (see also Deloria, 2001b). It is only with the acceptance of non-Western worldviews and traditions, of those marginalized and rejected, can the modern academy hope to seriously challenge its exclusionary philosophical groundings.

As opposed to the current either/or approach to Indigenous and Enlightenment models of ontology, educators can begin to adopt a both/and approach. Instead of simply reifying the basic assumptions of the past while shifting the center of authority, anti-colonial discourse challenges the academy's ideologies, epistemologies, and methodologies, creating space for new knowledges and new ways of knowing. In order to move into a deeper understanding of the world, we must embrace the painful yet necessary challenges of embracing discourses that present significant and structural challenges.

Implications of a Spiritual Infusion

Embracing the challenges that anti-colonialism and spirituality bring to the academy may lead not only to wholeness and inclusiveness but also to healing from the traumas of colonialized educational systems, including objectification and erasure. hooks draws attention to the relational nature of healing, saying, "Rarely, if ever, are any of us healed in isolation. Healing is an act of communion" (2000, p. 215). Receptivity to new epistemologies in the academy may be healing for educators and students from marginalized communities, as they have long been resisting the subjugation of their worldviews and knowledges. The pursuit of transformative education begins with such acts of healing, because, as Palmer asserts, "If teaching is to be reformed in our time, it will not be the result of snappier teaching techniques. It will happen because we are in the midst of a far-reaching intellectual and spiritual revisioning of reality and how we know it" (1993, p. xvii).

References

Abdi, A. A. (2011). Foreword. In N. N. Wane, E. L. Manyimo, & E. J. Ritskes (Eds.), *Spirituality, education, & society: An integrated approach* (pp. xi–xiii). Rotterdam, Netherlands: Sense.

Appiah, K. A. (1992). Introduction. In *Things fall apart*, by Chinua Achebe (pp. ix–xvii). Book 1. New York, NY: Random House.

Arvin, M., Tuck, E., & Morrill, A. (2013). Decolonizing feminism: Challenging connections between settler colonialism and heteropatriarchy. *Feminist Formations, 25*(1), 8–34.

Asad, T. (1993). *Genealogies of religion: Discipline and reasons of power in Christianity and Islam.* Baltimore, MD: Johns Hopkins University Press.

Astin, A. W. (2004). Why spirituality deserves a central place in liberal education. *Liberal Education, 90*(2), 32–41.

Butin, D. W. (2007). Dark times indeed: NCATE, social justice, and the marginalization of multicultural foundations. *Journal of Educational Controversy, 2*(2), article 14.

Dei, G. (2000). Rethinking the role of Indigenous knowledges in the academy. *International Journal of Inclusive Education, 4*(2), 111–132.

Deloria, V., Jr. (1999). *For this land.* New York, NY: Routledge.

Deloria, V., Jr. (2001a). American Indian metaphysics. In V. Deloria Jr. & D. Wildcat, *Power and place: Indian education in America* (pp. 1–6). Golden, CO: Fulcrum.

Deloria, V., Jr. (2001b). Higher education and self-determination. In V. Deloria Jr. & D. Wildcat, *Power and place: Indian education in America* (pp. 123–134). Golden, CO: Fulcrum.

Dillard, C. B. (2006). *On spiritual strivings: Transforming an African American woman's academic life.* Albany: State University of New York Press.

Du Bois, W. E. B. (1990). *The souls of Black folks.* New York, NY: Vintage.

Eisler, R. (2005). Tomorrow's children: Education for a partnership world. In J. P. Miller, S. Karsten, D. Denton, D. Orr, & I. C. Kates (Eds.), *Holistic learning and spirituality in education* (pp. 47–68). Albany: State University of New York Press.

Gallegos, B., Villenas, S., & Brayboy, B. (2003). Introduction. Special issue, Indigenous education in the Americas: Diasporic identities, epistemologies, and postcolonial spaces. *Educational Studies, 34*(2).

Grande, S. (2003). Whitestream feminism and the colonialist project: A review of contemporary feminist pedagogy and praxis. *Educational Theory, 53*(3), 329–346.

Grande, S. (2010). American Indian identity and intellectualism: The quest for a new red pedagogy. *International Journal of Qualitative Studies in Education, 13*(4), 343–359.

Hall, S. (1999). Thinking the diaspora: Home-thoughts from abroad. *Small Axe, 6,* 1–18.

hooks, b. (2000). *All about love: New visions.* New York, NY: William Morrow.

Kaomea, J. (2006). *Na wahine mana*: A postcolonial reading of classroom discourse on the imperial rescue of oppressed Hawaiian women. *Pedagogy, Culture and Society, 14*(3), 329–348.

Laible, J. C. (2000). A loving epistemology: What I hold critical in my life, faith and profession. *International Journal of Qualitative Studies in Education, 13*(6), 683–692.

Lincoln, B. (2003). *Holy terrors: Thinking about religion after September 11.* Chicago, IL: University of Chicago Press.

Lynskey, A. C. (2013). Occupy classrooms: Teaching from a spiritual paradigm. In C. Dillard and C. Okpalaoka (Eds.), *Engaging culture, race, and spirituality in education: New visions* (pp. 115–137). New York, NY: Peter Lang.

Lynskey, A. C. (2014). *Proceedings from AERA Annual Meeting Reflections on Engaging Culture, Race, and Spirituality.* Philadelphia, PA: Unpublished.

Lynskey, A. C. (2015). Countering the dominant narrative: In defense of critical coursework. Special issue: The Importance of Standards, Professionalization, and the Preservation of

Social Foundations of Education in PK–12 Teacher Preparation and Higher Education. *Journal of Educational Foundations 28*(1–4), 73–86.

Mabud, S. A. (1992). A Muslim response to the Education Reform Act 1988. *British Journal of Religious Education, 14*(2), 74–98.

Miller, J. P. (2005). Introduction: Holistic learning. In J. P. Miller, S. Karsten, D. Denton, D. Orr, & I. C. Kates (Eds.), *Holistic learning and spirituality in education* (pp. 1–8). Albany: State University of New York Press.

Moore, T. (2005). Educating for the soul. In J. P. Miller, S. Karsten, D. Denton, D. Orr, & I. C. Kates (Eds.), *Holistic learning and spirituality in education* (pp. 9–16). Albany: State University of New York Press.

Narayan, U. (2003). The project of feminist epistemology: Perspectives from a nonwestern feminist. In C. R. McCann & S-K. Kim (Eds.), *Feminist theory reader: Local and global perspectives* (pp. 213–224). New York, NY: Routledge.

Nye, R., & Hay, D. (1996). Identifying children's spirituality: How do you start without a starting point? *British Journal of Religious Education, 18*(3), 144–154.

O'Sullivan, E. (2005). Emancipatory hope: Transformative learning and the "strange attractors." In J. P. Miller, S. Karsten, D. Denton, D. Orr, & I. C. Kates (Eds.), *Holistic learning and spirituality in education* (pp. 69–78). Albany: State University of New York Press.

Palmer, P. (1993). *To know as we are known: Education as a spiritual journey.* New York, NY: HarperCollins.

Paris, P. J. (1995). *The spirituality of African peoples: The search for a common moral discourse.* Minneapolis, MN: Augsberg Fortress.

Rendon, L. I. (2000). Academics of the heart: Reconnecting the scientific mind with the spirit's artistry. *The Review of Higher Education, 24*(1), 1–13.

Rickaby, J. (1908). *Scholasticism.* New York, NY: Dodge. Retrieved from http://www2 .nd.edu/Departments/Maritain/etext/scholas1.htm

Said, E. W. (1978). *Orientalism.* New York, NY: Random.

Shahjahan, R. (2004). Reclaiming and reconnecting to our spirituality in the academy. *International Journal of Children's Spirituality, 9*(1), 81–95.

Shahjahan, R. A. (2005). Spirituality in the academy: Reclaiming from the margins and evoking a transformative way of knowing the world. *International Journal of Qualitative Studies in Education, 18*(6), 685–711.

Sloan, D. (2005). Education and the modern assault on being human: Nurturing body, soul, and spirit. In J. P. Miller, S. Karsten, D. Denton, D. Orr, & I. C. Kates (Eds.), *Holistic learning and spirituality in education* (pp. 27–46). Albany: State University of New York Press.

Taggart, G. (2001). Nurturing spirituality: A rationale for holistic education. *International Journal of Children's Spirituality, 16*(3), 325–339.

Tisdell, E. J. (2007). In the new millennium: The role of spirituality and the cultural imagination in dealing with diversity and equity in the higher education classroom. *Teachers College Record, 109*(3), 531–560.

Tuck, E., & Yang, K. W. (2011). Youth resistance revisited: New theories of youth negotiations of educational injustices. *International Journal of Qualitative Studies in Education, 24*(5), 521–530.

Tuhiwai Smith, L. (1999). *Decolonizing methodologies.* New York, NY: St. Martin's.

Tweed, T. A. (2008). Two: Boundaries: Constitutive terms, orienting tropes, and exegetical fussiness. In T. A. Tweed (Ed.), *Crossing and dwelling: A theory of religion* (pp. 29–53). Boston, MA: Harvard University Press.

Villegas, A. M. (2007). Dispositions in teacher education: A look at social justice. *Journal of Teacher Education, 58*(5), 370–380.

Walker, A. (2006). *We are the ones we have been waiting for: Inner light in a time of darkness.* New York, NY: World Press.

Wane, N. N., & Ritskes, E. J. (2011). Introduction. In N. N. Wane, E. L. Manyimo, and E. J. Ritskes (Eds.), *Spirituality, education, and society: An integrated approach* (pp. xv–xxiii). Rotterdam, Netherlands: Sense.

Wright, A. (1997). Embodied spirituality: The place of culture and tradition in contemporary education discourse on spirituality. *International Journal of Children's Spirituality, 1*(2), 8–20.

Yoshino, K. (2006). *Covering: The hidden assault on our civil rights.* New York, NY: Random.

Young, R. J. C. (2001). *Postcolonialism: An historical introduction.* Malden, MA: John Wiley & Sons.

5

Healing the Soul—Curando el Alma—Na' Sanna'e Ini'e Collective

A Feminist BIPOC Migrant Mixtec Serving Leadership and Research Initiative

LORRI J. SANTAMARÍA, ADRIANA DIEGO, GENEVIEVE FLORES-HARO, SILVIA GARCÍA AGUILÁR, LUISA LEÓN SALAZÁR, CLAUDIA LOZÁNO, LILIANA MANRIQUEZ, AND ALBERTA SALAZÁR

I, Lorri J. Santamaría, am the elected representative and scribe for a multifaceted, divinely complex, culturally, racially, and linguistically diverse collective of women called Healing the Soul—Curando el Alma in Spanish, and Na' Sanna'e Ini'e in the San Martín Peras variant of the Indigenous Mixtec language, which three of our members speak. Our work is a mental health–innovations project designed to serve the Mixteco/Indígena community along the South-Central Coast of California.

We respectfully position ourselves here as the collective, standing on the shoulders of the Black Indigenous and women of color (BIP[W]OC) who for more than fifty years prior have spoken, studied, researched, marched, and written their stories before us, paving the way for our work. We aim to link generations of Black and Brown *feministas* (feminists) and expand previous contributions while offering new ideas to our *comadres* (sisterhood) by way of an *ofrenda* (sacred offering) to those who will continue this work in the future. The collective brings light to the high-incidence mental-health-care practices of the Tu'un Savi peoples from Oaxaca, Mexico,[1] forty thousand in number in the South-Central

Coast of California, who have created new lives for themselves and their families in the United States.

Kimberlé Williams Crenshaw's (1989) intersectionality theoretical framework and antidiscrimination doctrine on feminist and antiracist politics "become" the collective, physically and in our worldview. Our research reflects the perspectives of cisgender, queer, Mixteca, Brown, Black, Afro Indigenous–descent, and Indigenous-descent women. With regard to our particular identities and the feminista politics they may bring to mind, we consider ourselves to be accepting of people who do not match our ethnically diverse phenotypes and unique cultural and linguistic worldviews. All but one of us uses the pronouns she/her/hers/*ella* ("ella" is "she" in Spanish). Three members of the collective are Mixtec, migrants to the United States from three different regions of the state of Oaxaca, Mexico. Mixtec members speak distinct variants of the Mixteco language: that of the *pueblos* (villages, townships) of San Martín Peras, San Francisco Higos, and Guadalupe de Morelos. One member of the group is Black African American, more specifically, she is a Spanish (Sevilla)-born Louisiana Creole of Choctaw descent. Another member is Brown with Mexican ancestry of Afro-Indigenous descent. Two consider themselves to be Xicana/x, another describes herself/themselves as Brown, all three of Mexican Indigenous descent. Every member of the group is bilingual (e.g., Spanish/English or Spanish/Mixteco), and one member is trilingual with the ability to speak English, Spanish, and Mixteco.

As Black and Brown women Indigenous scholar practitioners and authors, we acknowledge and are fully aware of the juxtaposing landmines inherent to navigating Western/modern, paternalistic, and Eurocentric colonizing academic ways and means of communicating knowledge (Mohanty, 1988; Tuck, 2009). We also understand how participation in academic discourse in these ways may be to the possible detriment of honoring languages, culture, and Indigenous ways of being for the sake of academic knowledge contribution. As one member of the collective noted early on, "[At the beginning] I often asked myself if [we were] imposing, colonizing [our] own community with this type of work. To a certain extent I [thought we were] passing on this type of Western perspective of mental health to them." She was not alone in her questioning of the work at hand. Every member struggled in similar ways with related questions. Holding this juxtaposition in mind, we also fully recognized this edited collection on disrupting colonial pedagogies as opportunities to lay these shackles of confusion aside and to enjoy our freedom and relish in the act of exercising our divine feminine power to express ourselves and our truths in the presence of other women, even for this shared and very exquisite moment of sacred literary liberation.

Centering, Grounding, and Placing Our Research

Linda Tuhiwai Smith, Indigenous New Zealand Māori scholar, writer, and activist, captures the essence of this forward-moving work taken up and transformed by migrant Mixtec Indigenous thought leadership. As a united complexly diverse multigenerational group of BIP[W]OC, we appreciate Tuhiwai Smith, in particular, when she comments: "When Indigenous peoples become the researchers and not merely the researched, the activity of research is transformed. Questions are framed differently, priorities are ranked differently, problems are defined differently; people participate on different terms" (1999, p. 193). This chapter captures the meaning of the "different terms" alluded to by Tuhiwai Smith and adds a feminist lens to engaging in feminista and decolonizing work in our communities. Tuhiwai Smith, like Django Paris and Samuel Alim (2017); Lorri J. Santamaría, Cristina Santamaría Graff, Adriana Diego, Liliana Manríquez, Doña Alberta Salazár, Claudia Lozáno, Luisa León Salazár, Silvia García Aguilár, and Genevieve Flores-Haro (2020); and Leigh Patel (2016), explore what it means to actively co-decolonize/decolonize research regarding the ways in which oppression, racism, and White supremacy are structurally and systemically reinforced in society. With these authors, we describe ways in which social institutions and conditions reinforce the perpetuity of inequity. Together we explore ways in which research can be learned and applied as a tool to unseat, interrupt, and redress continual cycles of oppression impacting BIP[W]OC.

The collective works for the Mixteco/Indígena Community Organizing Project (MICOP), an Indigenous-led and Indigenous-serving nonprofit organization. We support and uphold the migrant Mixteco/Indígena community who now live and work in Oxnard, California, are considered essential and comprise most of the agricultural workforce in the state. Research activity undertaken by the collective was funded by the State of California's Mental Health Services Act (MHSA) and administratively overseen by Ventura County Behavior Health (VCBH).[2] This semi-autonomy contributes to the *co-decolonizing* framing of our work with the "co" designation to honor the resources and funding provided to engage our inquiry and practice. This designation also speaks to the fact that all members of the collective are not from the Mixtec/Indigenous community. Our project contrasts with previous research addressing women's health within the same nonprofit community (Maxwell, Young, Vega, Cayetano, Crespi, & Bastani, 2015; Maxwell, Young, Moe, Bastani, & Wentzell, 2018). In past research endeavors, multilingual women *promotoras* (community peer health-care providers) provided researchers from outside the community with access to the people, collected multilingual data, and provided interpretation needed for data analysis. While research findings, such as those presented by Annette Maxwell and colleagues (2015, 2018) are informative and shed light on important women's health issues in the community, their findings unintentionally feed into negative stereotypes about migrant Indigenous people, reinforcing the notion that the migrant Indigenous community and in these cases the women therein need saving by way of Western medical-health interventions.

In stark purposeful contrast, the collective's efforts fall along with what can be conceived as a continuum of decolonizing research (Tuck, 2009; Tuhiwai Smith, 1999). In the words of a Xicana team member, "[In the collective] I began to sit in as an observer, an outsider, an eager student once more. Learning from peers and elder Mixtec women about the impact of Indigenous knowledge and their plan to provide it to the community." From the beginning, the collective took ownership of the research project. This included adapted culturally grounded and sourced design, training, data collection, implementation, data analysis, and dissemination to the community (see Santamaría, Manríquez, Diego, Salazár, Lozano, & García Aguilar, 2022). Our efforts were, therefore, developed organically and semi-autonomously over three and a half years, quarterly project reports notwithstanding. The work of the collective was culturally orchestrated because of multicultural, multilingual relationships, socially just and deeply respectful interactions with funders, a sense of belonging for each member, inclusion as integral to group practice, and divine femineity that guided and continues to guide the holistically healing work of every woman.

Our Praxis DNA

We purposely and philosophically locate our theory and practice alongside that of Keeanga-Yamahtta Taylor's ((2020) refreshing portrayal of the mid-1970s Black feminists' Combahee River Collective (CRC). Linked to the liberating legacy of Harriet Tubman's Underground Railroad, the CRC stated repeatedly: when Black lives matter, all lives will and, in particular, the lives of Black women. Taylor reminds us that the CRC was a visionary tour de force with its membership, including some of the greatest pillars of the Black feminist movement of the era like Barbara Smith and Beverly Smith, Audre Lorde, Demita Frazier, Cheryl L. Clarke, and Margo Okazawa-Rey, among others. The CRC engaged the kinds of actions, contributions, and women's ways of sociopolitical pushback that inspired thought leadership as captured later by Cherríe Moraga and Gloria Anzaldúa (2015) with contributing women authors.

Like the sociopolitical-racial goals of the CRC, the collective's work runs counter to patriarchal capitalism (e.g., racism, sexism, poverty), including the exclusionary brand of feminism White women engage to benefit White women. We are progressive and inclusionary, exhibiting concern for global affairs and a sense of universal social justice and equity. We are profoundly inspired by the CRC's openness to all women interested in dismantling injustice, particularly those of color, gay, straight, two-spirit, or queer contributions; ways of "showing up" in society; and culturally sustaining (vs. responsive) thought leadership. We are realists and not convinced that our work from Indigenous feminist and antiracist perspectives will result in our emancipation, not right away, anyway.

Relatedly, Eve Tuck and K. Wang Yang (2012) assert that decolonization encompasses real, concrete actions and words and that it is not a metaphor for the masses to use toward progress. This aligns with the collective's intention in framing research and community contributions as decolonizing/co-decolonizing practices (Santamaría, Santamaría Graff, et al., 2020). Our challenge as transnational women who are no longer physically nor geographically connected to our ancestral land is to recuperate and recenter our knowledge forms to *curar*/heal our wounds from social injustices and racial inequalities. There is some challenge here regarding the transnational aspect in that the repatriation of Indigenous land cannot be realized by the Mixteco/Indígena community, as people who are no longer physically nor geographically connected to their ancestral land. This third-dimensional disconnect, coupled with frequent travel, when possible, between Oaxaca and the United States for births, deaths, and spiritual observances contributes to disproportionately higher rates of stress, anxiety, depression, and other mental-health challenges. Upon reflection of the realities of migration an Afro-Indigenous descent collective member shares:

> From my experience, I believe that when families migrate here to the United States, there's a sense of self lost, not because one wants to lose it, but is forced to lose it. People are forced to lose who they are without even knowing sometimes. With that only memories are left, and there's no more knowledge being passed down of [our] ancestral ways.

However, as the collective found in our research and practice, the community can begin to return to the ways and the wisdom of its people: a repatriation of the Mixtec and Indigenous ways of being and life through traditional medicine as created through thought leadership and healing practices documented and shared. The co-decolonizing quality of our work brings us into closer alignment to the Sangtin grassroots women's collective in Uttar Pradesh, India. In the Sangtin Writers Collective's *Playing with Fire* (Anupamlata et al., 2006), the authors transcend racial, class, and linguistic borders, from multiple perspectives to discuss community responsibility, institutional-level struggles associated with feminism, freedom, and capitalism as an act of writing against the establishment. The collective was inspired by these women as they served to enact, embody, and theorize women of color's collective experiences as knowledge production to serve our local communities in meaningful ways.

Fourth/Fifth Wave BIP[W]OC Feminism

Over the entire three-and-a-half-year body of our work, as suggested by our mentors and wayshowers, we looked at and worked with one another "across culture, across language, class, and difference" toward our shared "call" of service to the community, healing our people, celebrating Indigenous knowledge, our ways of knowing, and our divinely feminine ways of being (Moraga & Anzaldúa, 2015, p. xxiii). We see our work as a continuation of third- and fourth-wave feminisms echoing the footsteps of the CRC toward transcending the barriers of colonialism, patriarchy, and the bureaucratic red tape separating the people in our community from enjoying real mental health (Taylor, 2020). The interconnected nature of our intersectionalities provided us safe passage to go together where we would not likely be able to go alone. To this end, we are stronger together than we are apart, a metaphor for the evolved bridging process that has taken place over the years and will continue long after we have crossed this threshold. Further, bell hooks describes our stance eloquently:

> Dominator culture has tried to keep us all afraid, to make us choose safety instead of risk, sameness instead of diversity. Moving through that fear, finding out what connects us, reveling in our differences; this is the process that brings us closer, that gives us a world of shared values, of meaningful community. (2004, p. 197)

We are a unified team of culturally and linguistically diverse women boldly working together to learn from the Mixteco/Indígena community to meet the mental-health needs of those seeking culturally recognizable relief. From the very beginning we perceived strength in our differences and value in what each member of the collective was able to contribute. In our efforts we honored our unique strengths and contributions that moved us ever closer to disrupting mental-health disparities impacting the Mixtec/Indigenous community.

Feminist methodology pushing the boundaries of third- and fourth-wave feminism explored by Crenshaw (1989), introduced by Moraga and Anzaldúa with other women (2015), and later developed by Rebecca Walker (1995, 2001), served as a literary mentoring for the collective (Santamaría & Jaramillo, 2014). These authors' contributions provided a sound infrastructure that matched the postmodern DNA of the women. As our group integrated new members, continually worked with women in the community, and learned about emotional, psychological, and physical healing in various Mixteco traditions; we developed ever-evolving shades and textures of matriarchal strength. We became a dynamic example of the feminism brand portrayed by BIP[W]OC scholars as their ways of being, knowing, and doing intertwined with our own emerging epistemology and that of the Mixteca women (Estés, 2008).

These elements served to drive our project and assisted us in our own exploration of the critique of what emancipation meant in our community of practice, as well as the institutional-level funding and nonprofit organizational barriers existing within the context of our realities. Though our work took place nearly fifty years after that of the CRC and we are not geographically located in the Third-World South, the collective felt (and presently feels) authentic kinship with the CRC. We are, likewise, deeply inspired by the stories of activism, feminism, and wisdom shared by the contributions of the Sangtin Writers Collective (Anupamlata et al., 2006). Centering and grounding our work on these strong foundations provide validity and reliability to our service to the community and contribution here. With feminist sojourners who are also BIP[W]OC, we sense acute urgency, virtual sisterhood, kinship, and shared struggle in our work. With them, we individually and collectively grapple with similar organizational constraints, nonprofit, for-profit, all equally challenging.

The collective adds to these rich bodies of knowledge by extending an understanding of Mixteco Indigenous migrant women's leadership practices by advancing a new Mixteca feminist theoretical research praxis. In doing so, we identify critical leadership tendencies as uniquely Indigenous ways of being (see Pihama, Reynolds, Smith, Reid, Smith, & Nana, 2014). We add a unique, emergent, and growing body of literature, suggesting culturally relevant and sustaining Indigenous leadership exist on a dynamic continuum (Santamaría, Santamaría Graff, et al., 2020; Santamaría, Manríquez, et al., 2022; Santamaría Graff & Sherman, 2020). This continuum, we argue, shifts when power differentials and ways of executing organizational leadership functions are shared or led by Indigenous women of color, opening the door to innovative and previously underexplored avenues for research (Anupamlata et al., 2006; Santamaría, Santamaría, et al., 2014; Tuhiwai Smith, 1999). And so, steeped in the traditions and ways of being and building on the thought leadership and knowledge of our BIP[W]OC sisters near and far along a shared time-space continuum, the collective story of healing the soul proceeds in four acts. Our counterstory follows the planting and harvesting cycle of the *hierbas* (medicinal plants), which the *curanderas* (Mixtec-community women healers) shared with us as part of collective healing experience (Solórzano & Yosso, 2002). Through our voices and words, we prepare the soil, plant the seed, water the plants, nurture the growth, and share the harvest of healing the soul.

Healing the Soul in Four Acts

ACT 1: PREPARING THE SOIL

From the very start there was a moral and ethical imperative to the project. Sourcing mental-health remedies from Tu'un Savi and from the wisdom of the collective immediately transformed us beyond the notion of culturally responsivity. Furthermore, each member brought her own divinely feminine personal story and lens to the project as is shared by an Afro-Indigenous descent member:

> I believed in the way my mother cured me of an illness, when I was feeling sad, when I was feeling low. I do believe in talk therapy, but I believe that it takes much more than that to heal, it will always be an ongoing process. I believe that if we trust the process and all the wisdom our ancestors left behind, it will get us closer to healing ourselves and our communities.

Members of the collective each brought a healing journey to the process and entered the project with different healing experiences and with unique points of understanding.

Objectively speaking, the collective was tasked with studying the ways in which the Mixtec community used traditional mental-health practices to remedy stress, anxiety, and depression. As a result of the research and training required, over the course of three and a half years, the collective formed a successful Mixtec-based healing cooperative that was body, mind, and spirit centered. From our mental-grounded research inquiry, a hybridity comprising our racial and ethnic backgrounds, experiences, languages, Indigeneity, femineity, and cultures brought a measure of mental-health justice to our migrant Indigenous community that was unrivaled in terms of representation of psychologists, therapists, and clients served. For example, we had focused conversations with 21 women, conducted initial survey interviews during outreach in the community with 150 community members, attended traditional Mixtec-healing modality training led by 4 Indigenous women healers over three months, and served 280 people using the healing modalities learned.

From the community advisory council, to outreach efforts, to discussions in people's homes, to healing modality training with Mixteca curanderas, including the growing from seed to harvest of healing plants from Oaxaca, our process was one of providing mental health-care access to the community from our perspectives in ways that were meaningful to them. These activities resulted in multifaceted healing opportunities marked by individual and group empowerment. As a result, we as providers of these services are fundamentally different. Those in the Mixtec/Indigenous community who participated are different, and all participants have acquired knowledge that we will never lose. In her description of this quality, an Afro-Indigenous descent member of the group recounts:

> Our collective remembering and reclaiming the essential healings of the Mixteco/Indígena community [brought] us closer to deeper healing of our essential selves, further away from clinical iciness, pharmaceuticals, and Western ways of knowing that [sat] just on the other side of the grant-funding process.

As providers and receivers, all who were involved benefited from sharing Mixtec/Indigenous knowledge with our families and our communities in ways that permeated the boundaries of the project.

The essentiality of project's tasks, such as interviewing people in five different languages in the privacy and comfort of their homes, learning how to grow medicinal plants to make healing teas, and performing breath work for proper *limpia* (spiritual cleansing) processes, shifted us into lived realizations of what it means to perform acts that were culturally sustaining (Paris & Alim, 2014). In this new "space," knowledge *for* the people came *from* the deepest ways and knowing *of* the people. This profoundly nuanced knowledge is reminiscent of the inherent, deeply moral and highly ethical wisdom exhibited through the literary traditions when Black women such as Zora Neale Hurston (1928) expressed themselves and shared their thought leadership through autoethnography, archetypes, myths, and stories (Griffin, 2012; Estés, 2008). This phenomenon, as also captured by Katie G. Cannon (2006) and conceptualized as Black women ethics, was extraordinary. The collective operated on a profound, unspoken, deeply shared ethic of care, respect, and anonymity. Early in the project we negotiated these ethics with the Mixteca elders who taught us their own healing methods so that we could test them using resources from California and Ventura County.

The traditional Indigenous-healing modality training sourced from four highly regarded elder women from the Mixtec community included unique and specific ways of curating remedies to treat symptoms associated with stress, anxiety, and depression. Members of the collective were challenged with negotiating the variations inherent to the healing modalities offered. When it came to the limpia practices, for example, team members needed to determine how to share these highly regarded spiritual practices without praying and blatantly petitioning to God, saints, or the Virgen de Guadalupe (the Mexican/Latin Mother Mary archetype) associated with Christianity. The clearing or cleansing aspect of learning treatments to remedy stress, anxiety, and depression proved to be the heart of providing relief to those struggling mentally. We had to determine a way of honoring the spiritual aspect of the healing process, which was central, without being religious. We understood our funders could not support religious-based practices; religiosity did not resonate with every member of the team. We agreed to remain inclusive in our practices, attracting all members of the Mixteco/Indígena community.

To resolve this issue, the collective looked to identify similar aspects of the limpias so that we could capture the essence of the practice in ways that would be welcoming and nonoffensive. Drawing from race, gender, and language as well as our multifaceted moral and ethical stance (Cannon, 2006; Tuck & Guishard, 2013), we agreed to keep religion, a potentially alienating force, out of the practice. Though there was a strong pull toward including aspects of Catholicism, in particular (e.g., candles, saints, prayer) as spirituality, we felt we needed to retain Indigenous equanimity through connection to nature and to retain universal life-force energy as part of this important aspect of our work. In the end the moral and ethical imperatives were spiritual inclusion, no harm, equity of access, acceptance, and unconditional love. The group found the universality and nonreligious yet spiritual and meditative aspects of Reiki to be useful. A literature review revealed the practice as a hybridized Indigenous healing modality with recent roots in Japan used to shift energy through grounding and breathwork sometimes used in Mexico as a unifying modality (Morgan-Consoli & Unzueta, 2018; Yeh, Hunter, Madan-Bahel, Chiang, & Arora, 2004). When the team presented the practice to the curanderas as an option we could all learn to conduct the highly recommended limpias, they unanimously approved. This modality agreement underscored our group ethics and exemplified the hybrid nature of the Indigenous sourced, grounded, and serving healing practice offered (Bhabha, 1994).

The limpia training, decision, and consensus process reflected ways in which the collective embodied being "on the ground, with the people," like the CRC in the 1970s (Taylor, 2020). In our interpretation of the way in which the research would be carried out, we personified pushing back, talking back, and unleashing the kind of wild, lived feminism so eloquently captured through prose and shared with the world by Moraga and Anzaldúa (2015) and other like-hearted women. While our original work was to explore healing toward addressing mental health in the Mixteco/Indígena community, it yielded much more including our individual self-concept, self-efficacy, professionalism, practical knowledge, Indigenous knowledge, and personal development. We knew we were on hallowed ground, as one Xicana member of the collective shared: "My journey was to be in the presence of ancestral energy, powerful medicine, and practicing a gift that was passed on from generations before me." And like Anzaldúa (2015), we each benefited from our engagement with the community and with each other as tangible and authentic acts of dynamic healing.

A prior example of this was our prior work with the curanderas when the collective needed to initially convince members to speak openly about aspects of healing and mental health in focus groups. We learned very quickly that these were extremely abstract topics for which the community had little expressive language in Mixteco, Spanish, or English. The entire exercise felt forced. According to the Mixteca members of the collective, focus-group interviews from methodology to associated protocols would put Indigenous community members on the defense. At the onset of the project, it was clear the concept of mental health and symptoms and remedies associated with stress, anxiety, and depression were uncomfortable triggers when the topics were discussed. The mere mention of mental health seemed to elicit shame and promote stigma within certain members of the community. The collective saw this more with the women in the community and sensed the women's need to protect for themselves, their children, and their families. Maybe, we thought, on some level our community was weary of responding to surveys in language they didn't speak, feeling like they were being studied, and experiencing information being extracted from the community as more research (see Maxwell, Young, Vega, et al., 2015; Maxwell, Young, Moe, et al., 2018). Our more seasoned Mixtec collective member suggested:

> Why don't we share our own stories of healing from our lives to get the members of the community to share theirs? They will never answer research questions or share family secrets. Would you? We need to let them know their experiences are sacred and that their participation is protected. We need to respect this wisdom at all costs.

We proceeded as was suggested by our Mixteca members, to the point that non–Mixtec-speaking members were not present during focus-group proceedings and for other Mixtec-language data-collection activities. Much of the research activity as a result occurred in Indigenous decolonizing spaces governed by Mixtec thought leadership and ways of being.

However, for the Indigenous leadership aspect, the project was not without tension among the collective, and we strove with great intentionality to mitigate unintended harm to our community.

We pressed into our work with care, caution, culturally and linguistically appropriate community methods, and transparency. As a result, over the course of the multiyear project, the collective witnessed and experienced positive and welcoming reactions and interactions from community members. This was likely because when we approached individuals, we did so as learners. During the first year of the project, a Mixteca promotora member candidly shared: "If we were to knock on someone's door wearing a tie and asking questions about mental health through an interpreter, we would never find out about traditional Mixtec medicine. We feign misunderstanding before we would tell a stranger." In the early days of the project, we let people know right away that our aim was to help the community to remember, revisit, and share ways in which we help ourselves with our remedies and Indigenous knowledge to heal mental distress and our souls along the way. This nuance, where we became learners, seekers of knowledge, to give back to the community, and where we regarded the elder women in the community as our teachers, was the first act of healing experienced in our collective resistance and knowledge reclamation.

ACT 2: PLANTING THE SEEDS

The co-decolonizing work funded by the state of California undertaken and produced by the collective occurred more than thirty years after Chandra Mohanty's (1988) assertion that research labeled as feminist does not constitute women's liberation. This is true, and our group negotiated the precarious nature of this reality on a regular basis, as did the Sangtin Writers Collective in their grassroots efforts (Anupamlata et al., 2006). We understood our active participation in a unique brand of feminist thought leadership. Thus, in our work toward identifying a Mixteca feminist theoretical framework, we in the collective asked ourselves the same questions we pose to BIP[W]OC readers and thought leaders and innovators: Which language or culture or perspective is being privileged in the work? In what ways does the work free, empower, liberate, or uplift those involved? What are the power dynamics in play? How is power being negotiated? Whose knowledge is privileged in the space? Whose voices are being featured or heard? Whose stories are being validated? Are there any conditions? Is there any psychological, emotion, or physical harm being done? If so, to whom? What is the plan for reconciliation and redress? How is the information being shared? Whom will the information benefit?

As Patricia Collins (1999) shared in her seminal work on Black feminist thought, the women in the collective faced our own challenges regarding gender, race, and linguistic discrimination. These challenges were often compounded by the realities of what it meant for some of the collective to live the life of migrant undocumented Indigeneity. Our work introduces, privileges, and celebrates our Mixteca sisters first; our Black, Indigenous, Indigenous-descent, and Afro-Indigenous–descent members afterwards; and then the divine feminine in the global sense with regard to inclusivity, thought leadership, and feminism. Our collective efforts comprise intellectual, cultural, spiritual, and traditional knowledge construction. Our work includes recounting, remembering, and extracting to invest into the community and share the ways of knowing of the Mixteco community. Empowerment was an unintended benefit that emerged because of the project (Santamaría, Manríquez, et al., 2022). Every woman in the project transcended at least one professional, educational, psychological, emotional, or physical barrier by way of being a part of the team.

Ramón Grosfoguel (2011) asks whether humanity can produce knowledges beyond Third World and Eurocentric fundamentalisms. The research process and results rediscovered in the work of the collective featured suggest a possibility of being able to create new knowledge to bridge the space between so-called Third World and Eurocentric thought forms. The notion of hybridity becomes more and more salient the closer we look at the research activity, particularly, when we consider the multifaceted adaptation process perceived through feminist, Indigenous, generational, and educational filters (Bhabha, 1984). These different perspectives fashion unique links between different kinds of knowledge and form the basis of what can be considered decolonizing behaviors and means of navigating the act of research, rendering the work more emancipatory than otherwise. If the collective didn't exist, we are sure the epistemology we share here would not have been documented nor shared in the way it is being shared here.

The introduction of a feminist, Indigenous, Mixteco, migrant research epistemology (FIMME) follows in the research influence of emergent academic Mixtec scholars, such as Pancho Antonio-Damian (2019), who studied and produced knowledge at the University of California Berkeley; Timothy M. Herrera (2015) from Texas State University, San Marcos; and Iliana Yunuen Rhi (2011), who received her master of arts from San Diego State University, as well as previous work by members of the collective (Santamaría, Salazár, Lozáno, León, & García, 2018; Santamaría, Manríquez, et al., 2022). Whereas epistemology reflects ways in which a people learn to know, the one utilized here can be described by referencing native "Hawaiian epistemology," in which Indigenous scholar Manulani Aluli-Meyer suggests Indigenous peoples naturally "develop new theories from ancient agency" in accurate response to our environments (2013, p. 148). In this way FIMME questions the complexity inherent to Tu'un Savi women's knowledge through womanist thought forms. FIMME takes into consideration the philosophical underpinnings of perceived origins of Mixteco understandings about what is or is not, ways in which Mixtec knowledge relates to perceived intelligence, and general Mixtec conceptual understandings in relation to their lives and experiences as central. In these ways, the epistemology refers to the past to look into the future. There is some evidence of these ways of creating and sharing knowledge for the Mixteco. Through examination of pre-Columbian Mesoamerican concepts reflecting the oldest held and considered by the Mixteco most sacred marks of intelligence created by Tu'un Savi themselves for themselves and for no one else, we see proof of more abstract information storing (documentation) and sharing (reporting or dissemination). This knowledge of society depicting images of religion, architecture, and agriculture can be found in world-famous Mixtec-authored codices (Miller, 1975; Nuttall, 1975).

It is absurd to think these advanced knowledge forms collected and now kept in museums on showcase to the public are the only written survivors of pre-Columbian epistemology. Information like that inscribed in the codices has also been shared and passed down orally through language by men and women alike. Indigenous researchers, authors of this work, and the Mixteco/Indígena people themselves know and believe FIMME is coded into the DNA of every Indigenous Mexican person, passed down from *abuela* (grandmother) to *mamá* to child through generation upon generation of knowledge production and transmission. This ancient epistemology has survived the patriarchally led Spanish conquest in Mexico, historical genocide, chronic racism, discrimination, and social isolation exacerbated by national and transnational migration. This is the background knowledge base for the collective's current inquiry. Today, we build on these valuable sacred stores of knowledge, including the wisdom of the community through curanderas, who are elders leading and guiding Mixteco/Indígena research produced primarily in English, informed by Spanish and several Mixteco variants, in this land 2,160 miles north of Oaxaca.

In our work, FIMME takes on the perspective that Mixtec systems of consciousness spring from nebulous lines of connection running back and forth, in and around what can be understood to be physical, spiritual, natural, linguistic, cultural, geographical, spiritual, and distinctly feminine realities. As one Xicana collective member reflected:

> [This work] offers a deep change in yourself at a cellular level. It is a deep change in your spiritual, physical, and mental self. This journey of transformation I am experiencing has helped me to connect with Mother Earth, with the Divine, with the Sacred cosmic forces, and with our ancestors.

This dynamic system of knowing is governed by the idea that though Mixteca women are here present on this time-and-space continuum, so also are ancestral lineages and those who will come after these women and their families in the future. There is a shared knowing that the Mixtec connect heaven and earth through Indigenous bodies as conduits of all that is. Like many other "surviving" Indigenous groups, Tu'un Savi and, in particular, the women, are resourceful, highly adaptable, and clannishly community-oriented. Mixteca women work for the greatest good of the group, whether it be family, community, or pueblo, sacrificing much along the way. When optimally adjusted, Tu'un Savi women describe themselves as connected, whole, and fully integrated (e.g., body, mind, soul). As such, Tu'un Savi women's ways of understanding, sharing, learning, and disseminating knowledge are highly complex and dynamic, dependent on experiential awareness.

Reflected in figure 5.1, FIMME provides an interconnected framework for organizing Tu'un Savi women's thought leadership, which may provide a basis or inspiration for similar feminist Indigenous research inquiries.

* Knowledge is firmly rooted through geographically located Oaxacan culture and language passed on from mother to child, regardless of migration.
* It is anchored by a divinely feminine communal ancient and sacred ancestral lineage.

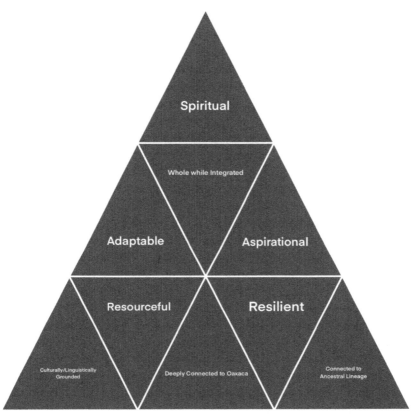

FIGURE 5.1. The basis of Tu'un Savi feminist Indigenous Mixteco migrant epistemology. Santamaría, Manríquez, et al., 2022.

* Knowing can be expressed by individual or group organization earmarked by resourcefulness (creative) and resilience (enduring).
* Intelligence is signaled by women's aspirational ability to survive by courageous adaptation as necessary.
* Intact and unchanged language and culture are evidence of spiritual quality of knowledge and women's ways of knowing.

The most concrete examples of FIMME linked to ancient, sacred ways of knowing to date are writings and drawings located in the codices reflecting pre-Columbian life, rituals, and interactions with others, which clearly take place in Oaxaca. There is no reason to believe the languages of Mixtec people today are different than those spoken at the time these communications were created. Clearly present in the codices are women and plants, presumably used in sacred healing ceremonies. From the imagery it is clear the ancient lineage is divinely feminine, sacred, and direct. As well, modern-day Mixtec artists, scholars, healers, doctors, and others who have sought training frequently take pride in serving their communities, often returning to work for their pueblos in Oaxaca as evidenced by Tu'un Savi transnational migratory patterns, many undertaken regularly by curanderas and members of the collective (González-Vázquez et al., 2016). The ability for an entire people to keep languages and culture intact over historically trying times and circumstances through countless miles of transnational migration within the Americas and the entire world can be attributed to deep Indigenous spirituality carried by the women as grandmothers and mothers. In the words of one Xicana collective member, "We do this by connecting, by having gratitude and asking for guidance, asking for protection, asking the Divine, Mother Earth, and our ancestors to show us the way to heal the Earth and all our relations."

Aluli-Meyer and the collective member's reflection above suggest it is the life-force energy "connected to all other life forces" that brings Mixtec people back to serve their community with the gifts of culturally generated, informed, and sourced knowledge, again passed down through the women (2013, p. 218). In FIMME, these elements are woven together and as such are interconnected like the fascia connecting muscle to bone in the human body. One aspect does not operate without impacting another, regardless of distance. Another facet may seemingly overlay one simultaneously. A particular aspect of the paradigm may lay dormant for centuries, while another dominates the worldview. This is the intricate body, mind, heart, head, and spirit of FIMME that provides the most appropriate foundation for the collective to understand and explore our critical work. By sharing this epistemology, it is our hope that other women who are BIP[W]OC can look within their cultures' ways of being to develop, understand, and communicate their own epistemology and unique giftings to their communities and the world at large for advocacy and service.

ACT 3: WATERING THE PLANTS

Though our work takes place within the FIMME frame, for the traditionally educated members of the collective of Indigenous descent, thoughts of colonization, subjugation, race relations, and cultural appropriation were never far from our minds (see de Rios, 1982; Skloot, 2011). We each considered working with, among, alongside, and on behalf of the Mixteco/Indígena community a privilege. Although some of us were Black or of African Indigenous descent, and all of us were Brown, we still wrestled with what hooks (1992) confronted as race relations between Black people and Indigenous people. These realities required the team to exercise sensitivity with regard to the sentiment of anti-Blackness in the migrant Mixteco/Indígena community. This was illuminated during the

Black Lives Matter movement marked by the unlawful deaths of Breonna Taylor, George Floyd, and other Black African American people during the summer of 2020, while Black, Latinx, and Indigenous people were also disproportionately impacted by the shared traumas of COVID-19 morbidity, suffering, and death. Although Mixteco/Indigenous community members share rich brown skin, dark eyes, and nearly black hair with Black and other structurally, systemically, and historically underserved folks in their region, the community did not publicly exhibit evidence of the kind of outrage exhibited by other BIP[W]OC people who showed up for protests despite the raging pandemic. There could have been fear of undocumented status or more likely nonidentification with the Black, Mexican, or Native American experience. This may also be an outgrowth of the outright ostracization and discrimination Indigenous people in Mexico experience.

Throughout the project, community accessibility to the process as well as the languages and culture of the participants was at the forefront, authentically sourced, aligned with, represented, and central to all core activities. Every aspect was led by the Mixteco/Indígena promotora team and supported by the advisory board comprising women in the community, including Mixtec and Mexican Indigenous elders. Project personnel and research leadership were representative of Mixteco/Indígena families and of the greater Indigenous community being served. Free from the male gaze, the leadership and research team explicitly integrated philosophical, spiritual, linguistic, and culturally specific aspects of the participants' community into the investigation as reflected in the trilingual name and the multilingual data collection, analysis, and dissemination.

There was an underlying decolonizing/co-decolonizing, critical-thought leadership, and social justice and equity stance taken in the research that was integrated and woven through every aspect carried out (see Santamaría & Santamaría, 2013, 2015; Santamaría, Manríquez, et al., 2022). We knew from our individual and collective, Indigenous, and Indigenous descent, Mixtec and non-Mixtec experiences working within the migrant Indigenous community that we needed to adjust the ways we approached the community throughout the inquiry. This idea was distilled by an Afro-Indigenous descent collective member when she shared: "What was missing was our culture and ancestral wisdom. Don't get me wrong we had our *pan dulce* [sweet traditional Mexican breakfast bread] and *cafecito* [coffee] when we sat down to listen and share, but it definitely takes more than that." The collective attempted to offer more depth to old ways of reaching the community and were willing to apply a more active stance and leadership that was more culturally sustaining in nature. Some of the characteristics of the approach included: engagement in critical conversations—most often with other women in the community regarding race, language, culture, difference, access, and/or equity; choosing or assuming Indigenous and social-justice lenses when making decisions about the project; the use of consensus with all constituents; trust building for optimal research activity and data collection; and accessibility. As well, inclusivity was a core characteristic of the work with the desire to add authentic counternarratives to existing information about the Mixteco/Indígena people. Leadership in the project was shared and practiced by example, helping to build greater leadership capacity for each member of the community while providing leadership as a service to the Indigenous community. These applied critical leadership (ACL) activities were evidence of thought leadership practiced by the women involved prior to the project with further development and building of these capacities because of this work with promise of sustainability moving forward (see Santamaría, Manríquez, et al., 2022).

ACT 4: NURTURING THE GROWTH

We recognize this project takes place within a beautiful unfolding of womanist and decolonizing contributions in an awakening new world of promise. The project is also unique in the ways it adds to an emergent and growing body of literature suggesting that culturally relevant and sustaining Indigenous leadership exists on an important and evolving continuum of co-decolonization (Santamaría, Santamaría Graff, et al., 2020; Santamaría Graff & Sherman, 2020). Illustrating this point, Django Paris and Samuel Alim's (2014) edited contribution of exemplars for culturally sustaining educational practice provides a unifying framework highlighting a clear shift from cultural responsivity to culturally grounded, sourced, and driven initiatives for BIP[W]OC and the communities they serve. We maintain that being culturally responsive is not enough, cultural competence is insufficient, and being culturally appropriate means the greater context or the mainstream is not aligned with the measures of diversity, equity, and inclusion needed to serve and support communities like the Mixteco/Indígena. We are not naïve, we understand that for cultural sustainability to be successful, the culture in question needs to have the leadership, infrastructure, human, and material resources to carry out and maintain the initiative being considered (e.g., wellness, health, education). In our decolonizing/co-decolonizing work, the community we served was fortunate to have attained resources to meet the community need presented. Like the Sangtin Writers Collective in India, there was underlying apprehension associated with support coming from the outside. This manifested as potential loss of authenticity regarding learning and application of the traditional healing modalities and complicated by a non-Mixtec Black director. When agreements were made among Sangtin-funding partners the research would be undertaken from within the migrant Indigenous space by and with mostly Mixteco/Indígena personnel with little oversight from state and community funding partners, the collective relied heavily on the community-based advisory board to ensure the project was authentic in terms of content and process to reflect community needs. It was determined from the start if the work would be culturally sustaining, the project needed to be grounded in community language, culture, and practices—and that the non-Mixtec director or principal investigator would largely serve as co-decolonizing facilitator or supervisor, rather than explicit driver of the endeavor.

Following the research training that led to the Mixtec retrofit, adaptation, and redesign to align with the migrant-community needs regarding questions asked, languages used, cultural approach, data collection, and analysis, it was clear the project had essentially become, as Tuhiwai Smith (1999) asserted in her description of decolonizing research: different. Along these lines, in year 4 a Mixteca promotora reflects on cultural sustainability from her perspective:

> I have more value and respect now for what I am doing. I am very grateful to God for giving me this opportunity to be able to connect with my community more. For hearing from them thanking me, in helping them to interrupt these unspoken silent diseases [stress, anxiety, and depression]. They are open with us which demonstrates they have confidence and faith in what we are doing.

Our research project became even more culturally sustaining and decolonizing/co-decolonizing when the collective took ownership of the data measures and analysis, which was a necessary function of working through sometimes up to five languages. It became additionally more so when members became students learning from the curanderas about healing modalities and herbal remedies to combat stress, anxiety, and depression. These elders who relied on oral transmission of knowledge brought fragrant herb bundles and teas for us to sip during our lessons, frowned upon our fervent note taking and diagram drawing to remember which herbs did what for whom and why, and asked us to orally recount plant names, symptoms served, contraindicators, and dosages needed. The entire experience and cumulative learning from the Mixtec elder women were life changing as a Mixtec collective member recounts:

> In my personal life I have changed in the way I process life's challenges. I take them more positively. In the spiritual sense [this work] has changed me completely. I respected plants before, but now I respect them more. I talk to them and my faith is stronger.

The learning and relationships with the elder Mixteca women continue. For example, following our training season, the team was honored to bring one of these esteemed elders with us to a county training on plant-based food as medicine. During the course through Mixtec, Spanish, and English translations, our guest was highly interactive with the presenter and added her own wisdom to the community learning forum. All participants gained much knowledge that day, and the instructor was eager to have us return with the Mixteca elder. There are many examples over the course of the project wherein the Mixtec migrant epistemology (FIMME) and Indigenous feminist ways of knowing were revealed and appreciated by the migrant Indigenous community, our funding partners, and similar organizations in the region, as well as the wider mainstream national and international audiences.

Enjoying the Harvest of Good Medicine

June Jordan reminds us that "to tell the truth is to become beautiful, to begin to love yourself, value yourself. And that's political, in its most profound way" (2002, 150). Whether we are sharing our experience with the Mixtec community to their direct benefit or sharing these contributions with "others" outside of the Mixtec/Indígena footprint, the collective members each take a staunch truth-telling stance. We envisage every aspect of our work as an opportunity to stand with Indigenous and non-Indigenous Black and Brown sisters in the spirit of womanist decolonizing truth telling. In our own way, we are disrupting and recalibrating the canon while unapologetically setting the record straight.

In this regard, research dissemination for the Mixtec/Indigenous community occurred near the end of the project by way of YouTube, Zoom presentation, flyers or pamphlets, and delivery of live *hierbas* (healing plants) directly to folks in need. We were limited by COVID-19 stay-at-home orders, and, unfortunately, community education around complementary and alternative medicine clashed with Medi-Cal (California's Medicaid system) enrollments and free flu vaccines. Project research findings indicated nearly 100 percent of the community participants who took pre- and posttests as part of the weeklong project healing regimen greatly reduced symptoms associated with stress, anxiety, and depression. Still, there were and are members of the Mixteco/Indígena community who perceive traditional ways of knowing as backward and antiquated. Can the widespread use of Western medical approaches reliant on Big Pharma and the enrollment of the migrant Indigenous community be seen as colonization? Or is access to these programs a form of liberation? Further, are the research and results of collectives like Healing the Soul Collective and Sangtin Writers Collective actual decolonizing pursuits, or are the projects merely illusions of emancipation as suggested by Mohanty (1988) so many years ago?

When for the dissemination process we stepped back, we saw ourselves as well as the 450 Mixteco/Indígena lives we impacted positively over the course of four years. Advocacy and increasing cultural and linguistic agency for our community were at the epicenter of our efforts designed to bring mental-health-care services to the people we served. The nature of the training, learning, research, implementation, analysis, and dissemination work resulted in a multifaced and complex BIP[W]OC blur of sociopolitical, historical, race, class, and gender lines. Throughout each phase of the project there was an overarching ethic of care and ambiguity that emerged because of what we understood as our shared Indigeneity (Cannon, 2006; Tuck & Guishard, 2013). The multilingual Afro/Blackness, Xicananess, Mixtecness, womanist, and even our queerness all began to merge as did seemingly our identities in the name of collective unified justice for the underserved. In a very real moment of what might be described as postcolonial decolonization, we got deliberately lost in each other's oppressions. We, as Bhabha (1994) wrote about, became fluid in the location of our individual cultures while trading our individualism for a moment to dabble in cultural hybridity. Might we have experienced a bit of what the Combahee River Collective did back in the day?

While Healing the Soul collective members felt (and feel) the learning that occurred was (and is) liberating and emancipatory in nature, we agree with Leigh Patel's perspective in her essay on learning as *marronage* (darkening) the narrative by the cumulative and repetitive practice of freedom acquisition through learning. On this theme she offers, "Learning is transformational, becom[ing] distinctly fugitive when attempted to be squelched" (2016b, p. 401). To this end, there was (is) not a lot of energy around our distinctly BIP[W]OC findings, though we know they are groundbreaking, and there aren't many folx in our own communities seeking access to the valuable information on stress, anxiety, and depression the collective has nurtured and cultivated. It is as if though our state and county partners are intrigued, and yet they are not asking too many questions about the project, they are not veering too close. The silence and lack of energy around the work feel oppressive to the group, at times, which, in turn, fuels our fire to do even more.

In the collective, stratification based on education was structurally aligned in terms of level of responsibility associated with project tasks (e.g., director or principal investigator, PhD; project coordinator or research assistant, bachelor's or master's degree; promotora, community health liaison, no professional degree needed). This could be considered an outgrowth of the mainstream governmentally bounded state and county institutional boundaries inherent to our work or a reflection of the ever-looming ubiquitous patriarchal system. We sullied those boundaries easily and often in the collective, as described by Patel, and lived the reality that "[l]earning demands a transformation of oneself for impacts and consequences that are fundamentally unpredictable" (2016b, p. 399). For example, the positionality shifts that occurred when the director or program investigator deferred to Mixteco/Indígena community members as the cultural/linguistic brokers for the project, as well as when the team learned and then transformed qualitative and quantitative research methods at the graduate level to satisfy the research needs of the grant and, more important, the community. Also, importantly, honoring all members of the collective with author and publication rights as the moral and ethical action to take moving forward.

What we learned from our experience is that women and BIP[W]OC who wish to continue this line of work can engage in two powerful actions right now to usher greater equity, inclusion, and change. These are disrupting commonly held narratives and existing canons of literature about "us" by way of truth telling and healing through formal and informal critical research activity. The collective can attest to the healing that has come out of work that is culturally sustaining. We are a living fabric of reparations and redress in our community regarding the role and value of traditional healing practices in the Mixteco/Indígena community, while we boldly add to the canon of literature and narrative about the Mixteca experience (see Maxwell, Young, et al., 2015) with our stories (Santamaría, Santamaría Graff, et al., 2020; Santamaría, Manríquez, et al., 2022). Research is a powerful tool and course of action that we can take to find at least one captured audience, one stream of discourse, or academic. On this platform we can present our perspectives and cases, telling our stories, as we are now, in our languages and voices. Moraga and Anzaldúa (2015) have shown us the way; Griffin (2012), Huber (2009), Hurston (1928), Lykes and Schieb (2015), and Solórzano and Yosso (2002) have equipped us with powerful tools (e.g., counterstories, testimonio, photovoice, autoethnography). We argue here, that like the appropriate adaptations hewn in our research, these reliable methods of inquiry are not the "master's tools" Lorde warned us to avoid (1984, p. 11). These methods are our own. Though they may have been constructed in the "master's house" right beneath his watchful eyes and sometimes by way of his "gold," these tools are most definitely ours. Now we must tell our versions of our narratives and switch our own "codes" of sophisticated and complex communication. These are the new codices—from a girls' night out to the *lavendería* (laundromat); from the bestseller list to the garden, to the classroom; and from the boardroom, dancefloor, yoga mat, and living room to our bedrooms; and beyond to the far reaches of the places we inhabit. Our delivery in every tongue, genre, and cultural space is our way of knowing, our way of sharing, and our way of showing. Our inclusionary nature and inborn accessibility promote and nurture our ultimate sustainability.

It is our intention that this essay complements other pieces like Eve Tuck's (2009) letter to communities, a counter to trauma and poverty porn (Schmidt, 2011), the baseless one-dimensional narratives concerning Indigenous folx and in our case people from Mexico who have migrated or immigrated from Oaxaca to the United States. Our multivoiced essay adds texture, dimension, warmth, truth, and multidimensional reality to the experiences of Indigenous people who live and work along California's South-Central Coast. Beyond suspending damage, we aim to reverse harm by replacing inappropriate descriptions of our lives and experiences through the lenses of well-trained, well-meaning outsiders, with descriptions of our work and lives in relation to the work, ourselves. Our contribution is part autoethnography, whole truth, and, ultimately, healing as one Xicana member shared:

> Healing the Soul changed my life and provided a path to help me heal. [It] provided a way to help our community in our journey to heal our spirits by decolonizing our ways of healing. These ways of healing, which survived are ours to decolonize, use, and protect. Healing the Soul helped me reclaim my spirituality, and I am full of gratitude for this blessing.

This work is soul-baring beyond rhetoric and a mundane reporting of quantifiable facts. The existing canon of empirical objective half-truths is being unraveled and replaced thread-by-thread as we write, and you read our words. We are happy to be a part of the divine healing enterprise that accompanies this new process and act of deeply feminist migrant Indigenous thought leadership from Mixtec, Black, Brown, Xicana, Indigenous-descent, and Afro-Indigenous–descent women as we in service to the Mixteco/Indígena community continue to do the work in addressing stress, anxiety, and depression. Let it be known that the healing we mention here may be conceptualized as consciously embodying and enacting decolonizing and co-decolonizing methodologies, leading to practices that are committed to freedom and emancipation for all. Programs and projects emanating from these methodologies "are not veiled by false rhetoric claiming to be emancipatory and then collapsing into the reproduction of Western hegemony and neoliberalism" (Santamaría Graff & Sherman, 2020, p. 21). We celebrate a concerted effort in decolonizing methodologies, particularly on the part of BIP[W]OC scholars to recognize liberation is not only freedom from systemic oppression but also is an intentional act of redressing the damage inflicted by colonization (King, 2017).

What makes women's production or contribution of knowledge radical? Is it pushback against the patriarchal reality that has dominated our discourse since time immemorial? As the perpetually oppressed, why wouldn't the women who make up the collective align with inclusive, equitable advocacy through complete sociopolitical change representing our specific yet broad, and growing, worldview. We believe that once the sleeping giant otherwise known as BIP[W]OC has arisen from our forced slumber of oppression, what was once perceived as extreme, progressive, or radical will be the new accepted and celebrated norm. Today, we witness and rejoice in this formidable awakening with Black African American women voting in blocks, participating in democracy, filling elected seats, and providing the backbone of change in the United States, even to the point of having the daughter of Jamaican and Asian Indian parents holding the second office in the land. Yes, we are happy to humbly stand on the shoulders of such giants as Hurston, Lorde, Moraga and Anzaldúa, Crenshaw, hooks, and Collins. We connect the generations hand in hand with Taylor and doing the soul-searching hard yards described by Tuhiwai Smith. We see them all, the womanist writers of *This Bridge Called My Back* and Breonna Taylor as our sisters, our radical sisters, all of us witnesses in life and in spirit of this beautiful if challenging change in our lives, the lives of our loved ones, and in the world. There is a divine feminine transcendence in this moment, and though we have not arrived, projects like Healing the Soul—Curando el Alma—Na' Sanna'e Ini'e Collective remind us that we are clearly on our way.

Notes

1. *"Tu'un Savi"* is translated as "people of the rain" and is the name Mixtec or Mixteco people call themselves. To honor language, philosophy, and Indigenous knowledge, these terms are used interchangeably in reference to Mixtec people originating from geographic zones within the present-day states of Oaxaca, Puebla, and Guerrero, Mexico.

2. Semi-autonomy is a characteristic the collective shared with BIP[W]OC in similar relationships with public funders such as the Sangtin grassroots women's collective in Uttar Pradesh, India. (Anupamlata et al., 2006).

References

Aluli-Meyer, M. (2013). Indigenous and authentic: Hawaiian epistemology and the triangulation of meaning. In M. K. Asante, Y. Miike, & J. Yin (Eds.), *The global intercultural communication reader* (pp. 148–164). New York, NY: Routledge.

Antonio-Damian, P. (2019). Mixtec parents navigating the K–12 education system in Ventura County, California. *The Berkeley McNair Research Journal, 26*, 150–172.

Anupamlata, Ramsheela, Ansari, R., Singh, R., Vaish, S., Shashibala, . . . Mohanty, C. (2006). *Playing with fire: Feminist thought and activism through seven lives in India.* Minneapolis: University of Minnesota Press. Retrieved from http://www.jstor.org/stable/10.5749/j.ctttt2nn

Anzaldúa, G. (2015). Acts of healing. In C. Moraga & G. Anzaldúa (Eds.), *This bridge called my back: Writings by radical women of color* (pp. xxvii–xxviii). Albany: State University of New York Press.

Bhabha, H. K. (1994). *The location of culture.* London, England: Routledge.

Cannon, K. G. (2006). *Black womanist ethics.* Eugene, OR: Wipf and Stock.

Collins, P. H. (1999). *Black feminist thought: Knowledge, consciousness, and the politics of empowerment.* New York, NY: Routledge.

Crenshaw, K. (1989). Demarginalizing the intersection of race and sex: A Black feminist critique of antidiscrimination doctrine, feminist theory and antiracist politics. *University of Chicago Legal Forum, 1*, 139–167.

de Rios, M. D. (1982). María Sabina: Her life and chants. *Journal of Psychoactive Drugs, 14*(3), 259–260. doi:10.1080/02791072.1982.10471940

Estés, C. P. (2008). *Women who run with the wolves: Contacting the power of the wild woman.* London, England: Random.

González-Vázquez, T., Pelcastre-Villafuerte, B. E., & Taboada, A. (2016). Surviving the distance: The transnational utilization of traditional medicine among Oaxacan migrants in the US. *Journal of Immigrant and Minority Health, 18*(5), 1190–1198.

Griffin, R. A. (2012). I AM an angry Black woman: Black feminist autoethnography, voice, and resistance. *Women's Studies in Communication, 35*(2), 138–157.

Grosfoguel, R. (2011). Decolonizing post-colonial studies and paradigms of political economy: Transmodernity, decolonial thinking, and global coloniality. *Transmodernity, 1*(1), 1–36.

Herrera, T. M. (2015, December). *Iconography of the flora depicted in the Mixtec Codex Zouche-Nuttall.* (Master's thesis). Texas State University, San Marcos.

hooks, b. (1992). *Black looks, race, and representation.* Boston, MA: South End Press.

hooks, b. (2004). *Teaching community: A pedagogy of hope.* New York, NY: Routledge.

Huber, L. P. (2009). Disrupting apartheid of knowledge: Testimonio as methodology in Latina/o critical race research in education. *International Journal of Qualitative Studies in Education, 22*(6), 639–654.

Hurston, Z. N. (1928, May). How it feels to be colored me. *The World Tomorrow, 11*, 215–216.

Jordan, J. (2002). *Some of us did not die: New and selected essays of June Jordan.* New York, NY: Basic Books.

King, J. E. (2017). A reparatory justice curriculum for human freedom: Rewriting the story of African American dispossession and the debt owed. *The Journal of African American History, 102*(2), 213–231. Retrieved from https://doi.org/10.5323/jafriamerhist.102.2.0213

Lorde, A. (1984). The master's tools will never dismantle the master's house. *Sister Outsider: Essays and speeches, 1*, 10–14.

Lyke, M. B., Scheib, H. (2015) The artistry of emancipatory practice: photovoice, creative techniques, and feminist anti-racist participatory action research. In H. Bradbury (Ed.), *The SAGE handbook of action research,* (pp. 131–42). London: SAGE Publications.

Maxwell, A. E., Young, S., Moe, E., Bastani, R., & Wentzell, E. (2018). Understanding factors that influence health care utilization among Mixtec and Zapotec women in a farmworker community in California. *Journal of Community Health, 43*(2), 356–365.

Maxwell, A. E., Young, S., Vega, R. R., Cayetano, R. T., Crespi, C. M., & Bastani, R. (2015). Building capacity to address women's health issues in the Mixtec and Zapotec community. *Women's Health Issues, 25*(4), 403–409.

Miller, A. G. (1975). Introduction. In Z. Nuttall (Ed.), *The Codex Nuttall: A picture manuscript from ancient Mexico* (pp. vii–xviii). New York, NY: Dover.

Mohanty, C. (1988). Under Western eyes: Feminist scholarship and colonial discourses. *Feminist Review, 30*(Autumn), 61–88.

Moraga, C., & Anzaldúa, A. (2015). *This bridge called my back: Writings by radical women of color.* Albany: State University of New York Press. [Originally published in 1981 by Persephone, Watertown, MA.]

Morgan-Consoli, M. L., & Unzueta, E. (2018). Female Mexican immigrants in the United States: Cultural knowledge and healing. *Women & Therapy, 41*(1–2), 165–179.

Nuttall, Z. (Ed.). (1975). *The Codex Nuttall: A picture manuscript from ancient Mexico.* New York, NY: Dover.

Paris, D., & Alim, H. S. (2014). What are we seeking to sustain through culturally sustaining pedagogy? A loving critique forward. *Harvard Educational Review, 84*(1), 85–100.

Paris, D., & Alim, H. S. (2017). *Culturally sustaining pedagogies: Teaching and learning for justice in a changing world.* New York, NY: Teachers College Press.

Patel, L. (2016a). Decolonizing educational research: From ownership to answerability. New York, NY: Routledge.

Patel, L. (2016b). Pedagogies of resistance and survivance: Learning as marronage. *Equity & Excellence in Education, 49*(4), 397–401.

Pihama, L., Reynolds, P., Smith, C., Reid, J., Smith, L. T., & Nana, R. T. (2014). Positioning historical trauma theory within Aotearoa New Zealand. *AlterNative: An International Journal of Indigenous Peoples, 10*(3), 248–262.

Rhi, I. Y. (2011). *Ñuu Savi Sini u'un Tiatyi: A renewal of Mixteco epistemology of Mother Earth.* (Doctoral dissertation). Arts and Letters, San Diego State University, San Diego.

Santamaría, L. J., & Jaramillo, N. E. (2014). Comadres among us: The power of artists as informal mentors for women of color in academe. *Mentoring & Tutoring: Partnership in Learning, 22*(4), 316–337.

Santamaría, L. J., & Jaramillo, N. (2014). Comadres among us: The power of artists as mentors for women of colour in academe. Mentoring and tutoring special issue Advancing women of color in the academy. *Research Perspectives on Mentoring and Strategies for Success, 22*(4), 316–337. doi:10.1080/13611267.2014.946281

Santamaría, L. J., Manríquez, L., Diego, A., Salazár, D. A., Lozano, C., & García Aguilar, S. (2022). Black, African American, and migrant Indigenous women in leadership: Voices and practices informing critical HRD. *Advances in Developing Human Resources, 24*(3), 173–192. https://doi.org/10.1177/15234223221100847

Santamaría, L. J., & Santamaría, A. P. (2013). *Applied critical leadership in education: Choosing change.* New York, NY: Routledge.

Santamaría, L. J., & Santamaría, A. P. (Eds.). (2015). *Culturally responsive leadership in higher education: Promoting access, equity, and improvement.* New York, NY: Routledge.

Santamaría, L. J., Santamaría, A. P., Webber, M., & Pearson, H. (2014). Indigenous urban school leadership: A critical cross-cultural comparative analysis of educational leaders in New Zealand and the United States. *Comparative and International Education/Éducation Comparée et Internationale, 43*(1), 1–21.

Santamaría, L. M. J., Salazár, A., Lozáno, S., León, L., & García, S. (2018, April 20). *Creating a Lienzo for Ñuu Savi people of the rain Mixteco/Indígena research methodology: Na Sánaeé Inié Healing the Soul Curando el Alma.* Paper presented at the Indigenous Knowledge Conference, Oxnard, California.

Santamaría, L. M. J., Santamaría Graff, C. C., Diego, A., Manríquez, L., Salazár, A., Lozáno, C., León Salazár, L., García Aguilár, S., Flores-Haro, G. (2020, September). *Co-decolonizing research methods: Toward research sustaining Indigenous and "other" community engaged ways of knowing.* American Educational Research Association (AERA) Virtual Research Learning Series.

Santamaría Graff, C., & Sherman, B. (2020). Models of school-family relations. In Oxford Research Encyclopedia of Education. *Oxford University Press.* https://doi.org/10.1093/acrefore/9780190264093.013.1247

Schmidt, R. (2011). "Children of the plains" was little more than "poverty porn." Indian Country Today Media Network.com. Retrieved from http://indiancountrytodaymedia network.com/ict_sbc/children-of-the-plains-was-little-more-than-poverty-porn

Skloot, R. (2011). *The immortal life of Henrietta Lacks.* New York, NY: Broadway Books.

Solórzano, D. G., & Yosso, T. J. (2002). Critical race methodology: Counter-storytelling as an analytical framework for education research. *Qualitative Inquiry, 8*(1), 23–44.

Taylor, K.-Y. (2020). The banality of segregation: Why Hirsch still helps us understand our racial geography. *Journal of Urban History, 46*(3), 490–493. https://doi.org/10.1177/0096144219896575

Tuck, E. (2009). Suspending damage: A letter to communities. *Harvard Educational Review, 79*(3), 409–428.

Tuck, E., & Guishard, M. (2013). Uncollapsing ethics: Racialized sciencism, settler coloniality, and an ethical framework of decolonial participatory action research. In T. Kress, Curry S. Malott, & Brad J. Portfilio (Eds.), *Challenging status quo retrenchment: New directions in critical qualitative research* (pp. 3–27). Charlotte, NC: Information Age.

Tuck, E., & Yang, K. W. (2012). Decolonization is not a metaphor. *Decolonization, Indigeneity, Education, & Society 1*(1). Retrieved from https://jps.library.utoronto.ca/index.php/des/article/view/18630

Tuhiwai Smith, L. (1999). *Decolonizing methodologies.* New York: Zed Books.

Walker, R. (Ed.). (1995). *To be real: Telling the truth and changing the face of feminism.* New York, NY: Anchor.

Walker, R. (2001). Becoming the third wave. *Identity politics in the women's movement, 3*(13), 78–80.

Yeh, C. J., Hunter, C. D., Madan-Bahel, A., Chiang, L., & Arora, A. K. (2004). Indigenous and interdependent perspectives of healing: Implications for counseling and research. *Journal of Counseling & Development, 82*(4), 410–419.

PART III

Undoing Command

Aire, with each breath may we
remember our interrelatedness
see fibers of spirit extend out from
our bodies
creating us, creating sky, seaweed,
serpent, y toda la gente.
"El alma prende fuego," burns holes in
the walls
separating us
renders them porous and passable,
pierces through
posturing and pretenses,
may we seek and attain wisdom.

—Gloria Anzaldúa, *Light in the
Dark / Luz en lo Escuro*

6

#CrunkPublicHealth

Decolonial Feminist Praxes of Cultivating Liberatory and Transdisciplinary Learning, Research, and Action Spaces

LECONTÉ J. DILL

If all you think of me is ill-fated—
shooting baskets, rolling caskets, dropping
schoolbooks, then who waits for me, breath bated?
Hold hope, with its limbs out, daydreams swopping.
Drive me to the page's edge, no footprints
There's no mail delivered, there's no address
I run up and down the block, get shin splints
Looking for a place to rest, break, recess
Tattoo my name on the corner of my wrist
Stake claim, mark territory as my own
On my forearm, the ones who've gone I list
Tennis shoes on power lines tossed and
thrown I am the gum underneath your shoe sole
Forgotten, but still stuck, no peace, no whole.
(Dill, "At Risk")

I wrote this poem as I was completing my dissertation. I was a public health doctoral student, and I was tired of hearing statistics about Black people, my people, only reported in terms of our risks—undereducated, underemployed, violent, sick, dying, dead. I knew that this is not the full story or even the real story; we are not only risks or only risky. I also knew that only reporting about risks but not offering solutions, especially community-informed solutions, was traumatic, patronizing, and futile. I was a public health doctoral student, and I was thinking, asking, listening, and writing about how urban African American and Latinx youth activate *resilience*. I was a public health doctoral student while also actively studying and writing poetry. I was in the in-betweenness of dissertation data collection and data analysis. I was reflecting of my own in-betweenness of being a student in the classroom, researcher in the field, witness in multiple spaces, and writer across genres. This poem is a sonnet, which is a form of fourteen tightly packed lines, but this form also can allow us to break apart the nuances that are underneath, in-between, and after these fourteen lines. During this time in my dissertation research and through the sonnet, I was reflecting on my research participants who were in the in-betweenness of identities as research participants and coresearchers through our participatory ethnographic approaches, and emerging poets and authors through our arts-based research methods. I was also thinking of "the hood"—be it South Central, or East Oakland, the SWATS, or Bed-Stuy— and how the places, spaces, and the African American, West Indian, and Latinx people (t)here are too-often stigmatized, (mis)labeled, and constrained.[1]

Refusing the "At-Risk" Narrative of the Public's Health

The word "risk" is not a neutral term (Douglas & Wildavsky, 1982); it has come to mean *danger*. In the field of public health, "risk" is constantly used as a synonym for "danger" (Lupton, 1993). Using "risk" to mean "danger" in public health is a colonial practice in that it always positions who is *at risk*—of disease or premature death—as people who are not of the dominant race, class, gender, or sexual orientation. Historically and globally, white male scientists and physicians have asserted that they are most suited to promote health, hygiene, and sanitation to *colonial subjects* and that this medical research and health promotion would advance imperialism (American Association for the Advancement of Science, 1900). It then follows that public health's discourse of risk is often dichotomized into "environmental hazards" in which individuals are thought to have no control or agency and into consequences of "lifestyle choices" that are deemed to be modifiable solely based on individual actions (Leahy, 2014; Lupton, 1993). Lifestyle risk is typically assessed through close-ended quantitative surveys that fail to take into account cultural, environmental, political, and structural factors of such "risk behaviors" (Lupton, 1993). Individual behaviors become moralized, and the discourse of risk becomes pervasive because it allows health problems to be quantified (Leahy, 2014). Health statistics then are viewed as the "expert knowledges" of risk (Leahy, 2014). Lupton, however, asserts that "risk therefore may have less to do with the nature of danger than the ideological purposes to which concerns about risk may be put" (1993, p. 428). Our ideologies about "sex, drugs, and rock-n-roll" shape our own shame and fears of people and their behaviors—namely, people of color, poor folks, people living in urban environments, queer folks, and young people—and lead to our (mis)labeling and stigmatization of danger and of *risk*.

Public health's focus is on the health of "the public." In contrast to the field of (Western) medicine, in public health, a broader and sometimes abstract public becomes the patient, instead of the sole treatment of individuals. Also, in public health, there is a tendency to identify an Other—as research participants, patients, clients, or community members—in contrast to the Self—as researcher, principal investigator, health care provider, or facilitator. Public health practitioners then tend to apportion blame unto marginalized, historically oppressed, dispossessed, and stigmatized "Others" (Lupton, 1993; Tuck, 2009). In public health, this othering erases the humanity from our research participants, patients, clients, and community members. We tend to see people in terms of the number of people having a certain disease. We tend to talk about health outcomes in terms of variables that may or may not be statistically significant. Research participants, patients, clients, and community members become "those people" lacking knowledge, literacy, and agency about their own bodies and lives. I call BS to this othering!

Indigenous scholar Eve Tuck reminds us that there is a trend of "damage-centered research" that renders us into thinking of ourselves as only broken and depleted (2009). In terms of public health, statistics are typically reported in terms of disability, disaster, disease, and death but not in terms of safety, peace of mind, opportunity, or wellness. This is based on an overriding ideology grounded in colonial practices in which humanity is stripped from traditional public health training and practice. For example, traditional public health training, typically administered through a program or school of public health,[2] does not regularly or rigorously include the discussion of the practices of eugenics, forced sterilization of Indigenous, African American, and Latinx women, stigmatization of people with mental illnesses, or stigmatization of queer identity that have been perpetuated by scientists, physicians, and public health practitioners and that are historical legacies of colonial practices within our field (Washington, 2006). This is not meant to be just a laundry list of marginalization but to show that science writer and medical ethicist Harriet A. Washington has *already* done the heavy lifting of unpacking these topics and more in her critical tome *Medical Apartheid: The Dark History of Medical Experimentation on Black Americans from Colonial Times to the Present* (2006). What if schools of public health across the country taught this work as a foundation text? The alternative, the norm, is an erasure and is a form of epistemic violence within the field of public health. Traditional public health training and practice do not explicitly name racism, sexism, and heteropatriarchy as contributing to the behaviors and conditions that we research and *treat*. Public health documents and documentation typically list *race, gender, age,* and sometimes *sexual orientation* as (often binary) demographic variables. What results is a tendency to focus public health curricula, research, and funding priorities on disease and not on wellness; on problems and not on assets; on combatting health disparities and not on achieving health equity. On college and university campuses, the science, technology, engineering, and mathematics (STEM) departments and classrooms are spatially and ideologically isolated away from the humanities. In clinics and hospitals, the physical health practitioners are spatially and ideologically isolated away from the mental and behavioral health ones. In governmental health agencies, analysts, scientists, and administrators are siloed into separate sections, departments, divisions, and centers. I assert that these divisions create unnecessary divisiveness, confusion, and silences, for practitioners and community members alike, and these divisions lead to the pervasive health inequities that continue to haunt us . . . to eradicate us. This unnecessary divisiveness is also the legacy of colonial practices, and it is in contradiction to the relational approaches inherent in many communities. Black feminist foremother Audre Lorde reminds us that "we do not live single-issue lives" (1984, p. 138). So, our study and pursuit of public health *cannot* be a "single-issue struggle" (Lorde, 1984, p. 138). Following Tuck, I commit to "suspending damage" and, instead, to engaging in "desired-based" research (2009), action, and teaching, through a refusal of the risk discourse and a refocus on intersectional theories and praxes within public health, which I detail throughout the rest of this chapter.

The Rememory of Black Feminisms as a Decolonizing Praxis

The work described in this chapter is committed to a decolonizing praxis, rooted in Black feminisms as epistemological foundations. Black feminisms bring the distinct and nuanced voices of Black women into the forefront (Bambara, 1970). US Black feminisms act as decolonizing praxes because they are conceptualized, articulated, embodied, and activated by descendants of the survivors of the transatlantic slave trade and the institution of chattel slavery (Dotson, 2015). US Black feminisms are enacted every day on and in lands marked by political disenfranchisement, migration, segregation, desegregation and resegregation, gentrification, and surveillance and violence enacted by the state and by vigilantes (Tuck, Smith, Guess, Benjamin, & Jones, 2014). As decolonizing praxes, US Black feminisms work to name, remember, reclaim, and imagine self-determination, resistance, and recovery in this same land and across the Black diaspora (Dillard, 2012; James, 2013; McKittrick, 2011; Tuck, Smith, et al., 2014; Tuck, Guess, & Sultan, 2014).

This chapter is informed by my understandings and embodiment of US Black feminisms (Collins, 1990; Combahee River Collective, 1977; Guy-Sheftall, 1995; Stewart, 1987), womanism (Maparyan, 2012; Phillips, 2006; Walker, 1983), endarkened feminisms (Dillard, 2006, 2008, 2012), and transnational Black feminisms (Alexander, 2005; Gqola, 2018). I resonate with Harwell (2016) in her assertion that her, and my, understanding of these frameworks is that they are not in conflict with one another. My understanding of Black feminist frameworks is informed by my mama's bookshelf, the aisles of Black-owned bookstores, my undergraduate experience at a Black women's college—Spelman—and rigorous self-study to fill in the absences of a whitestream public health canon. Collectively, Black feminisms place Black women and their/our experiences at the center of analysis. Also, Black feminisms center Black women as knowledge producers. Black feminisms acknowledge a legacy of struggle by Black women; attention to the interlocking nature of race, gender, and class oppression; sensitivity to sexual politics; the replacement of stereotypical "controlling images" with self-defined images created for and by Black women; and a belief in Black women's activism as mothers, teachers, and community leaders (Collins, 1990; Combahee River Collective, 1977; Crenshaw, 1991; Stephens & Phillips, 2003; Stewart, 1987). These core themes offer an expanded frame for decolonizing praxes.

Although Black feminisms are not new concepts or practices, I assert that many scholars and practitioners within the field of public health have either not even considered or have forgotten or distanced themselves from intersectional and holistic understandings of individual and collective wellness (Dillard, 2012), particularly enacted by and pertaining to historically marginalized communities. The "at-risk," "damaged," "diseased," overresearched yet invisible "Other" still can be discursively and epistemologically colonized by our intellectual investigations (hooks, 1990; McKittrick, 2011; Mohanty, 1991). Beckoning Toni Morrison (1987) and rooted in Black feminisms, I assert that we need to conjure up a rememory of decolonizing practices for the health and well-being of the public.[3] Rememories are moments that are not quite familiar because they have been tucked away for so long. These moments may be repressed or forgotten because of complexities that we are not yet willing to unpack (Dillard, 2012). Yet, according to Dillard (2012), who was inspired by Morrison, remembering is a Black feminist praxis and a counter to epistemic erasure. A rememory and remembering of Black feminisms for the field of public health is *not* ahistorical; it is committed to a critical and radical analysis of the social and structural determinants of health, and it works to combat the health inequities that persist. In consideration of such a rememory, Anarcha, Betsey, and Lucy,[4] Harriet Tubman, Sojourner Truth, Frances E. W. Harper, Anna Julia Cooper, Mary Church Terrell, Ida B. Wells-Barnett, Mary McLeod Bethune, and countless named and unnamed Black women midwives and nurses serve as some of our earliest nineteenth- and early twentieth-centuries Black feminist public health scholars and practitioners. These early Black feminist public health scholars and practitioners enacted pedagogies and practices related to health and wellness in plantations, swamps, churches, Black settlement houses, Black women's clubs and sororities, Black hospitals and clinics, newspapers, and schools.

A rememory of Black feminist theories and praxes can actually serve as acts of resistance to the aforementioned hegemony and risk-laden focus of the field of public health (Dillard, 2012). Such a rememory corrects us when we inaccurately assume that certain populations simply lack knowledge about healthy behaviors and health issues. Such a rememory gives us pause when we inauthentically declare that certain populations are just needing "saving."[5] Such a rememory asks us to complicate one-dimensional health behavior theories. Such a rememory demands that we defund ineffective and exploitive health interventions. Such a rememory decenters physicians and academic researchers as the primary experts. Such a rememory implores us to move from simply documenting statistics and disparities, toward radical action to achieve health equity. Such a rememory dismisses the notion of the so-called Strong Black Woman, the Angry Black Woman, and the Promiscuous Black Woman, who are too often denied adequate, accessible, and affordable health care. Such a rememory recognizes Black women's strategies of agentic coping. Such a rememory reconnects our social, physical, sexual, psychological, emotional, *and* spiritual health and well-being. Such a rememory recenters Black girls and women as knowers and doers when it comes to their/ our own health and the health of our communities (Myles, 2013). I assert that a rememory of Black feminisms for the field of public health bolsters the health of the broader population as a whole.

Framing the Pedagogical Praxis of #CrunkPublicHealth

Decolonizing praxes are visions, "not mere dreams" (James, 2013; Tuck, Guess, & Sultan, 2014), which mobilize anti-colonial knowledge systems to foster and enact critical pedagogies. I resonate with what Beverly Smith, one of the members of the Combahee River Collective and one of the authors of their 1997 statement, shared: "My involvement in both feminism and health care came at about the same time" (Lewis, 1990, p. 174). The same is true for me. #CrunkPublicHealth is my own epistemology, pedagogy, and praxis of a commitment to decolonizing and critical feminist ethics and praxes within the field of public health.

Within the academy, I first was introduced to and trained in the field of public health in the urban south, specifically in Atlanta, Georgia. Atlanta has been known as the "Black Mecca of the South" since the 1970s because of the city's civil rights heritage (Garland, 1971; Hobson, 2017), the presence of the nation's largest consortium of historically Black colleges and universities (HBCUs)—the Atlanta University Center (AUC)—the high rates of Black business and home ownership, high proportion of middle-income African Americans, and Black ascendancy to political power in the city. Atlanta is also known as the Public Health Mecca due to the clustering of public agencies, nonprofit organizations, think tanks, and institutions of higher learning focused on public health headquartered there. I was a college student in the late 1990s and early 2000s in Atlanta when and where crunk as a musical genre, a colloquial term, and a state of being was emerging. Crunk is sonic, as well as kinetic; it is emotional, as well as spatial. As a musical genre, crunk is urban, bass-heavy party music, with call-and-response patterns (Grem, 2006). Colloquially, the term "crunk" was initially named as a contraction of "crazy" or "chronic" (marijuana) and "drunk" and was used to describe a state of being under the influence (Crunk Feminist Collective, 2010; Lothian and Phillips, 2013). Colloquially, crunk also is understood as the past tense and the past participle of crank, meaning to turn on or to turn up (Crunk Feminist Collective, 2010). As a state of being, "getting crunk" is an expression of exuberance.

While soaking up the crunkness embedded in Atlanta's red clay dirt, its radio hits, and its party scene, I was also growing as a scholar at Spelman College and in the Atlanta University Center. My Introduction to Public Health class was taught by William "Bill" Jenkins, an alumnus of Morehouse College (a "Morehouse man"), one of the first Black epidemiologists at the Centers for Disease Control and Prevention (CDC) and founder of many organizations and institutions, such as the Public Health Sciences Institute (PHSI) at Morehouse College, and cofounder of the Society for the Analysis of African American Public Health Issues (SAAPHI), among others. Notably, Jenkins's research and sociopolitical standpoint and activism helped to put an end to the Tuskegee Syphilis Study. Like a true "shoe-leather epidemiologist,"[6] when his colleagues at the US Public Health Service in the late 1960s would not print more-thorough, critical analyses of the Tuskegee study, Jenkins and a comrade chose to publish in more radical and social justice–oriented news sources. Jenkins brought this history, this radicalism, and this rigorous public health training into our classroom in the late 1990s. He taught the history of the Gullah and Geechee Peoples right alongside teaching us how to perform T-Tests—giving both knowledges equal weight. Jenkins is now an ancestor (may he rest in peace), but his crunk praxis informed and inspired countless public health scholars and practitioners.

"Who You Wit?" is a question asked by crunk artists, such as Lil Jon, classic hip-hop artists, such as Jay-Z, and Christian hip-hop artists, such as Lecrae. It is literally asking, "Who are you with?" meaning who is in your crew? I take crew to not only mean friends but also those with whom we are in dialogue—in classrooms, on the page, on the bookshelf, and in the community. While an undergraduate student in the AUC, in addition to Jenkins, I continued to be trained by other scholars and practitioners, both inside and outside of the classroom in Atlanta, most of whom were also trained in the AUC or at other HBCUs. I am grateful to the teachings of Barbara Bell, Bruce Wade (rest in peace), Mona Taylor Phillips, Cynthia Trawick, Adewale Troutman (rest in peace), David Satcher, Harry Lefever (rest in peace), Cynthia Neale Spence, Brenda Dalton, Fleda Mask Jackson, Dazon Dixon Diallo, Opal Moore, Beverly Guy-Sheftall, and Billye Y. Avery. This is who I was wit! as an undergraduate student beginning to study and practice public health. Collectively, this crew of scholars and practitioners encouraged me and my peers to bring our full selves to our scholarship and to disrupt hegemonic canons and perceived boundaries of public health, the social sciences, and the humanities.

The Crunk Feminist Collective—a community of self-identified hip-hop feminist scholar-activists—also have intellectual roots in Atlanta and the urban and rural south. They define their crunk feminist standpoint as a resistance to "hegemonic ways of being" in favor of cotheorizing amongst their collective, with herstoric feminists of color, and with contemporary crunk feminists in digital, academic, and community spaces (2010). As a radical public health scholar-activist, and in the vein of Black feminisms, southern hip-hop, and the Crunk Feminist Collective, #CrunkPublicHealth is my declaration of the ways in which I resist the hegemony of the public health field and how I "get crunk" in my teaching and research praxes. I use a hashtag in the naming as a way to make my processes and work more visible through internet and social-media platforms, as well as in my lectures and presentations. Yarimar Bonilla and Jonathan Rosa refer to this as "hashtag ethnography" (2015), denoting it as a form of online fieldwork rooted in community building and activism while also noting that this work also flows between, outside of, and beyond digital spaces. I began to engage with/on Twitter more frequently in 2014 and began using "#CrunkPublicHealth" on both Twitter and Facebook then. Since then, I have encouraged my current and former students, attendees at my presentations, and anyone embodying an unapologetically decolonial feminist praxis within public health to use the term and hashtag.

Through #CrunkPublicHealth, I am also a #HealthCrit,[7] or a practitioner of public health critical race praxis (PHCRP) (Ford & Airhihenbuwa, 2010a, 2010b).

Unlike traditional health-behavior theories, as an iterative methodology, PHCRP better equips us with a culturally relevant lens in which to analyze structural oppressions that contribute to persistent health inequities. PHCRP draws from critical race theory (CRT) to move "beyond documenting health inequities toward understanding and challenging the power hierarchies that undergird them" (Ford & Airhihenbuwa, 2010b). #HealthCrits are informed by an intersectional framework to radically shift conceptualization and measurement within public health research (Ford & Airhihenbuwa, 2010a, 2010b). The health clinics and free breakfast programs established and implemented by the Black Panther Party; former surgeon general M. Jocelyn Elders's brave promotion of sexual pleasure; the Mother House as the original homeplace in the West End neighborhood of Atlanta, Georgia, of the National Black Women's Health Project (NBWHP); the Healthy Love Parties implemented by SisterLove; the narrative-oriented research and policy making of Camara P. Jones; former surgeon general Regina Benjamin starting the "hair fitness" competition at the Bronner Brothers 2011 International Hair Show; and Antronette "Toni" Yancey (rest in peace) actively reminding us to incorporate "instant recess" into our day are all examples of engaging in a public health critical race praxis.

In addition to the experiences highlighted above, I was further trained explicitly as a "transdisciplinary" public health scholar, situated along with sociology, psychology, urban planning, education, black studies, and women and gender studies, specifically. Transdisciplinary scholarship integrates and extends discipline-based concepts, theories, and methods (Neuhauser, Richardson, Mackenzie, & Minkler, 2007). Transdisciplinarity bridges academic and applied sectors, focuses on collaboration, and is seen as an evolving methodology (Neuhauser et al., 2007). This standpoint is thought to "transcend" any individual discipline's boundaries (Neuhauser et al., 2007). It is through this transcendence in which I proceed and continue to "get crunk."

A Peek into My #CrunkPublicHealth Classroom

> her work always sustenance for someone
> and an offering may her soul also be fed.
> —Ruth Forman[8]

#CrunkPublicHealth describes how I show up as a Black feminist public health educator, scholar, and practitioner in multiple spaces, including classrooms, community settings, professional organizations, and publications. I work to decolonize my syllabi by assigning scholars, practitioners, and everyday folk of color, particularly Black women. This encourages my students to disrupt the public health canon by expanding it and to read and #CiteBlackWomen.[9] Therefore, my classroom becomes one of my activist spaces. Additionally, I encourage an expansive thinking of learning spaces outside of the classroom, so I invite students on field trips to museums, theaters, art galleries, poetry slams, and radio shows, all as part of my classes in order to engage with content beyond readings and lectures.

In line with a "pedagogy of collegiality" (Chávez, Turalba, & Malik, 2006), I reframe my engagement with students and research participants as that of "colearners" and "coresearchers." My colearners have kept me accountable in teaching, conducting, and creating desire-based scholarship. Harkening back to Tuck, desire-based scholarship is "concerned with understanding complexity, contradiction, and the self-determination of lived lives" (2009, 416). For public health, such desire-based scholarship accounts for health inequities but also accounts for hope among individuals and communities. Therefore, my classroom and community-research partnerships are committed to being generative and engaging.

I see art as a decolonizing feminist praxis through its embodiment of desire (Tuck, 2009) and its mobilization of self-determination, resistance, and recovery. #CrunkPublicHealth is rooted in arts-based teaching and research methods. I center art in my lectures, presentations at professional meetings, and in my research inquiry and analyses. I am a creative writer, primarily a poet, and also and emerging playwright, so I bring my learnings, practices, and products of poetry and performance into my pedagogy. Back in 2012, I shared Langston Hughes's poem "Lament for Dark Peoples" with my students in my environmental-health class during a discussion about environmental justice (1926, p. 100). The poem reads:

> I was a red man one time,
> But the white men came.
> I was a black man, too,
> But the white men came.
>
> They drove me out of the forest.
> They took me away from the jungles.
> I lost my trees.
> I lost my silver moons.
>
> Now they've caged me
> In the circus of civilization.
> Now I herd with the many—
> Caged in the circus of civilization.

I was excited yet shocked that engaging with poetry in the public health classroom went over so well with my colearners. Now, I fully recognize that this is my pedagogy and part of my #CrunkPublicHealth praxis. I agree with esteemed poet and one of my inspirations Lucille Clifton when she spoke of both her ontology and of poetry as "a way of walking in the world, a way of seeing the world, a way of understanding the world in one's life" (Rowell & Clifton, 1999, p. 64).

At the beginning of each semester, my students and I write an "I Come From" poem, an exercise gleaned from WritersCorps San Francisco (Tannenbaum & Bush, 2005, p. 20). Also, informed by June Jordan's wisdoms, the main rule of the "I Come From" poem is to tell our truth(s) (Quiroz-Martinez, 1998). Then, the students are guided to write a ten-line statement, femifesto,[10] or list poem about from where, whom, and how we come to the classroom and to the field of public health. The students and I share our poems on the first day of class as an introduction to ourselves and our standpoints. I invite the students not to start with the caveat that they "are not a poet," though every semester there are several students that begin their introduction this way. I remind them that if they told their truth(s) and wrote ten "I Come From" lines, then they are, indeed, a poet, if even they choose to be one only for the first day of class. For public health students, many of whom were or are on the premed track, writing and sharing poetry, especially so early in the semester, seems outside of the disciplinary norms. It is with this early introduction that they learn and I am reminded about how we are going to activate #CrunkPublicHealth throughout our time together (and beyond). This illustrates my commitment to creating "brave spaces" (Atiya et al., 2013) in the classroom where students and I engage in "mutual vulnerability" (Guishard, 2009), reveal ourselves, stretch our comfort zones, and pursue lifelong learning. An excerpt from one of my "I Come From" poems is:

> I come from asthma attacks cause nightmares
>> Causes dreams of Pediatrics
>> Organic Chemistry causes nightmares
>> Causes dreams of the Health of the population
>> is Public
> I come from office hours of tissues, hugs, signatures, Track Changes
>> Pull up a chair
> I come from downloading articles, PowerPoints, subway maps, selfies,
>> poems

In their "I Come From" poems, my colearners have also shared: "I come from feminists"; "I come from artists"; "I come from Hip Hop"; "I come from translating for my mom at parent-teacher conferences"; "I come from a teen mother"; "I come from chosen family"; "I come from spirituality, but not religion"; "I come from faith"; "I come from comelibros." These working-class, migrant, immigrant, queer, Black, Brown, and urban narratives are #CrunkPublicHealth.

I bring similar poetry prompts and exercises elsewhere into my other teaching and my research partnerships and engagements, using a methodology that I frame as "participatory narrative analysis" (Dill, 2015; Dill, Vearey, Oliveira,

& Castillo, 2016; Dill, Rivera, & Sutton, 2018). Colearners, coresearchers, and I have written love notes to places and spaces that we have lost due to migrations, gentrification, forced evictions, war, disasters, or other displacements or erasures; we have written love letters to our younger selves; we have written poems to our future communities. We have bravely read these poems aloud, printed them for wider audiences, snapped our fingers, clapped, and cried. We have told our truths.

In addition to poetry, I begin and end most class sessions with playing a song, displaying a piece of visual art, or showing a performance-art piece. I strive to do this every class period, because early on in my teaching, a former student remarked, "Dr. Dill, I feel stressed," after hearing a full lecture about chronic and infectious diseases and health inequities, and then leaving class and having to ruminate on such risk factors with no sense of hopefulness and action steps. Now, I frame discussions of illness but also of healing and wellness, with artists who unpack and evoke related themes. I center artists of color, particularly Black women, in the classroom. For example, to critically analyze the complex practices and policies of residential segregation and gentrification as social and structural determinants of health, my colearners and I:

* look at the visual art of Jacob Lawrence or Varnette P. Honeywood depicting African Americans' migration to/in urban centers in the Northeast, Midwest, and West Coast;
* reflect on the photography of sheila turner and Charles Teenie Harris as social documentaries of African American life and culture;
* look at the murals of Brandan "BMike" Odums in public housing complexes in New Orleans that have been disinvested in by the city and state before, during, and after Hurricane Katrina;
* read the poetry and plays of Mary Weems exploring the foreclosure crisis;
* listen to the spoken word of jessica Care moore talking about her beloved Detroit or Roya Marsh talking broadly about the impacts of gentrification; and
* analyze the lyrics of Goodie M.O.B. detailing daily life in the "Dirty South" or Jamila Woods's love letter to Chicago.

The Embodiment of Decolonizing Feminisms through #CrunkPublicHealth

As an "othermother" (Collins, 1990) in the classroom, across campus, and in local communities, I have a loving commitment to an ethic of care, to justice, and to supporting my students' and colearners' agency. As students have vulnerably disclosed the real risks and traumas with which they are contending while they balance pursuing a public health degree and working part- or full-time in the public health field, I have realized that our personal lived experiences cannot be left out of our commitment to improving the public's health. My rememory is that:

15-, 16-, 17-year-old giggles got
lost
You listenin real good You
real good cause
you listenin so their giggles got found
So
Where you goin
now that you find yourself
in the middle

At times, academic spaces, relationships, and expectations do not recognize these lost giggles among students, nor do they prioritize finding students' giggles. #CrunkPublicHealth acknowledges that public health students and practitioners, indeed, experience multilevel stressors and traumas, and in the pursuit of achieving broader health equity for populations, we must prioritize our individual selfcare, our "#squadcare" (Harris-Perry, 2017) and allow our rage (Lorde, 1981). #CrunkPublicHealth commits to "centering wellness" by incorporating creative approaches in order to better understand and unlearn how we traditionally study and treat illness, stress, and trauma (Dill, 2019). As detailed throughout this chapter, such creative approaches, specifically poetry, have been central to my own public health practice and pedagogy and also to my daily life. I have written and studied poetry from a young age. Later, I began to identify as a poet and to teach poetry. I have personally experienced poetry as an important, healthy coping strategy in my own life and in the lives of my colearners and coresearchers. Other researchers have also illuminated the positive health effects that the arts have when coping with physical and mental-health concerns (Burch, 2021; Petteway, 2021; Stuckey & Nobel, 2010). A commitment toward cultivating individual and collective healing through incorporating the arts is a decolonial feminist approach to public health. Incorporating the arts into our public health practices invites us to center our wellness in traditionally colonial spaces, such as academic institutions, doctors' offices, and government buildings. Centering wellness is a needed disruption and is crunk!

#CrunkPublicHealth offers a paradigm toward a decolonial Black feminist alternative to traditional public health curricula, training, research, and practice. I am excited when I get to nurture or witness others activating #CrunkPublicHealth in classrooms, at presentations, in academic articles, in community settings, and on social media. Dear reader, you, yes, you, can begin to decolonize public health curriculum, pedagogy, research, and practice, as well. Critically read and teach public health critical-race theorists and public health Black feminist and transnational feminist scholars. Create brave spaces in your classrooms and offices for colearners. Add public health scholars and practitioners who get crunk to your mentoring teams, writing collectives, research labs, and citational practices. Incorporate arts-based approaches to your teaching and research. Listen to and learn from your public health students. I am so hopeful for our field knowing that students and alumni at schools such as the University of California Berkeley, the University of Michigan, and Harvard University have websites, symposia, syllabi, courses, and resources dedicated to "decolonizing public health." Anecdotally, I also know that students at HBCUs, Hispanic-serving institutions, and tribal colleges and universities are also committing to decolonial public health praxes. Our public health students are engaging in action in and out of classroom spaces. I look forward to continuing to colearn with them. Overall, let us remember that #CrunkPublicHealth is a roadmap to wellness, and may we enact it as an ongoing liberatory praxis.

Notes

I acknowledge my colearners—past, present, and future! Thank you for your openness, your expertise, and your radical witnessing. Portions of this chapter were presented at the American Public Health Association 2017 annual meeting.

1. I am referring to neighborhoods where I have grown up, lived, and/or been deeply immersed and committed to community-engaged and ethnographic research partnerships. The South Central neighborhood of Los Angeles, California, the East Oakland neighborhood of Oakland, California, the southwest area of Atlanta, Georgia, and the Bedford-Stuyvesant neighborhood of Brooklyn, New York, are all neighborhoods that had a majority population of Black residents and other residents of color since the 1940s when local and national racial restrictive covenants were being legally challenged. These same neighborhoods became redlined during this same time period and began to experience rapid White flight, residential segregation, deindustrialization, and economic disinvestment. The Black Power movement flourished in these neighborhoods in the 1960s and 1970s but then was thwarted by government surveillance and state-sanctioned violence. The crack-cocaine epidemic, deinstitutionalization of mental health facilities, and mass incarceration led to the stigmatizing of these neighborhoods and the people living in them, particularly, since the 1980s. Since at least 2008, these neighborhoods have been experiencing rapid gentrification, the foreclosure crisis, and residential and emotional displacement. These neighborhoods have been systematically disinvested. It is in these same neighborhoods that I have learned the most about resilience and resistance from the Black people and other people of color living there. For more references, see Dill, Morrison, & Dunn, 2016; Ginwright, 2010; Grady-Willis, 2006; Self, 2005; Sides, 2006; Wilder, 2000.

2. For more information about the list of accredited schools and programs of public health in the United States, see "Member Directory," Association of Schools and Programs of Public Health (2022), https://aspph.org/membership/member-directory

3. In Morrison's *Beloved*, Sethe says to Denver,

Some things you forget. Other things you never do. But it's not. Places, places are still there. If a house burns down, it's gone, but the place—the picture of it—stays, and not just in my *rememory*, but out there, in the world. What I remember is a picture floating around out there outside my head. I mean, even if I don't think it, even if I die, the picture of what I did, or knew, or saw is still out there. Right in the place where it happened. (1987, pp. 35–56)

4. Anarcha, Betsey, and Lucy are just three of the countless enslaved Black women upon whom J. Marion Sims performed gynecological experiments and surgeries without their consent and without anesthesia, in the nineteenth century. Harriet A. Washington (2006), Bettina Judd (2014), Deirdre Cooper Owens (2018), and Dominique Christina (2018) have all done important work related to the memories and legacies of these women.

5. Ruth Nicole Brown asserts that the notions of saving someone mislabeled as less than are "white-supremacist sentimentalities" (2013, p. 4), in which Black girlhoods and Black feminisms actively resist.

6. A "shoe-leather epidemiologist" refers to a public health professional who investigates disease causes and patterns by collecting rigorous mixed-methods research in the community, not solely in an isolated office or laboratory. As examples, John Snow and W. E. B. Du Bois have been described as historic shoe-leather epidemiologists.

7. Through a peer-reviewed and competitive selection, I was chosen as one of the twenty-two scholars in the inaugural Public Health Critical Race Praxis (PHCRP) Institute in 2014 at the Maryland Center for Health Equity, University of Maryland, College Park, https://sph.umd.edu/center/che/public-health-critical-race-praxis-institute. This institute was funded by the National Institute on Minority Health and Health Disparities (NIMHD) (P20MD006737). I received advanced training in PHCRP directly from Ford and Airhihenbuwa and collectively with my coscholars.

8. Ruth Forman has been an influential poetry teacher for me. I first met her on the page but first engaged with her personally during the 2003 Voices of Our Nation Arts Foundation (VONA) Voices creative writing workshop. VONA is one of my homeplaces. For more information, see https://www.vonavoices.org

9. #CiteBlackWomen is pedagogical and empirical intervention started by Christen Smith that encourages us to read the work of Black women, integrate the work of Black women into the core of syllabi, and acknowledge Black women's intellectual production. For more information, see https://www.citeblackwomencollective.org

10. "Femifesto" is a term used my Sistren Brittany Brathwaite and Mickey Ferrara at Homegirl HQ, formerly The Homegirl Box. For more information see https://thehomegirl box.com/our-story0020

References

Alexander, M. J. (2005). *Pedagogies of crossing: Meditations on feminism, sexual politics, memory, and the sacred*. Durham, NC: Duke University Press.

American Association for the Advancement of Science. (1900). The malaria expedition to West Africa. *Science, 11*(262), 36–37.

Atiya, S., Davis, S. W., Green, K., Howley, E., Pollack, S., Roswell, B. S., Turenne, E., Werts, T., & Wilson, L. (2013). From safe space to brave space: Strategies for the anti-oppression classroom. In S. Davis & B. Roswell (Eds.), *Turning teaching inside out: A pedagogy of transformation for community-based education* (pp. 105–112). New York, NY: Palgrave MacMillan.

Bambara, T. C. (Ed.). (1970). *The Black woman: An anthology*. New York, NY: Washington Square Press.

Bonilla, Y., & Rosa, J. (2015). #Ferguson: Digital protest, hashtag ethnography, and the racial politics of social media in the United States. *American Ethnologist, 42*(1), 4–17.

Brown, R. N. (2013). *Hear our truths: The creative potential of Black girlhood*. Urbana: University of Illinois Press.

Burch, S. R. (2021). Perspectives on racism: Reflections on our collective moral responsibility when leveraging arts and culture for health promotion. *Health Promotion Practice, 22*(1_suppl), 12S–16S.

Chávez, V., Turalba, R. A. N., & Malik, S. (2006). Teaching public health through a pedagogy of collegiality. *American Journal of Public Health, 96*(7), 1175–1180.

Christina, D. (2018). *Anarcha speaks: A history in poems*. Boston, MA: Beacon Press.

Collins, P. H. (1990). *Black feminist thought: Knowledge, consciousness, and the politics of empowerment*. New York, NY: Routledge.

Combahee River Collective, The. (1977). "A Black feminist statement."

Cooper Owens, D. (2018). *Medical bondage: Race, gender, and the origins of American gynecology*. Athens: University of Georgia Press.

Crenshaw, K. W. (1991). Mapping the margins: Intersectionality, identity politics, and violence against women of color. *Stanford Law Review, 43*(6), 1241–1299.

Crunk Feminist Collective, The. (2010). "Mission statement." The Crunk Feminist Collective [blog]. Retrieved from http://www.crunkfeministcollective.com/about/

Dill, L. J. (2011a). *Routes to resilience: Mechanisms of healthy development in minority adolescents from high-risk urban neighborhoods*. (Doctoral dissertation). University of California Berkeley School of Public Health. Retrieved from http://escholarship.org/uc/item/85165522

Dill, L. J. (2011b). "At-risk." In My Identity Is Community (Eds.), *Y U gotta call it ghetto?* (p. 84). Oakland, CA: Urban Diligence Press.

Dill, L. J. (2015). Poetic justice: Engaging in participatory narrative analysis to find solace in the "Killer Corridor." *American Journal of Community Psychology, 55*(1–2), 128–135.

Dill, L. J. (2019). Centering wellness: Using Black feminist literature as a public health pedagogical tool for personal healing, community health, and social justice. In A. Santella (Ed.), *Master of public health competencies: A case study approach* (pp. 45–52). Burlington, MA: Jones and Bartlett.

Dill, L. J., Morrison, O., & Dunn, M. (2016). The enduring Atlanta compromise: Black youth contending with home foreclosures and school closures in the "New South." *Du Bois Review: Social Science Research on Race, 13*(2), 365–377.

Dill, L. J., Rivera, B., & Sutton, S. (2018). "Don't let nobody bring you down": How urban Black girls write and learn from ethnographically-based poetry to understand and heal from relationship violence. *The Ethnographic Edge, 2*(1), 57–65.

Dill, L. J., Vearey, J., Oliveira, E., & Castillo, G. M. (2016). "Son of the soil . . . daughters of the land": Poetry writing as a strategy of citizen-making for lesbian, gay, and bisexual migrants and asylum seekers in Johannesburg. *Agenda, 30*(1), 85–95.

Dillard, C. B. (2006). *On spiritual strivings: Transforming an African American woman's academic life.* Albany: State University of New York Press.

Dillard, C. B. (2008). When the ground is black, the ground is fertile: Exploring endarkened feminist epistemology and healing methodologies in the spirit. In N. Denzin, Y. S. Lincoln, & L. Tuhiwai Smith (Eds.), *Handbook of critical and indigenous methodologies* (pp. 277–292). Thousand Oaks, CA: Sage.

Dillard, C. B. (2012). *Learning to (re)member the things we've learned to forget: Endarkened feminisms, spirituality, and the sacred nature of research and teaching.* New York, NY: Peter Lang.

Dotson, K. (2015, March 27). *Here be dragons: Thinking decoloniality as a Black feminist.* Paper presented at the City University of New York Graduate Center, New York, New York.

Douglas, M., & Wildavsky, A. (1982). *Risk and culture.* Oxford, England: Basil Blackwell.

Ford, C. L., & Airhihenbuwa, C. O. (2010a). Critical race theory, race equity, and public health: Toward antiracism praxis. *American Journal of Public Health, 100*(S1), S30–S35.

Ford, C. L., & Airhihenbuwa, C. O. (2010b). The public health critical race methodology: Praxis for antiracism research. *Social Science & Medicine, 71*(8), 1390–1398.

Forman, R. (2013). *Her work as worship.* Retrieved from http://www.sparkandecho.org/her-work-as-worship_ruth-forman

Garland, P. (1971, August). Atlanta, Black mecca of the south. *Ebony, 26*(10), 152–157.

Ginwright, S. A. (2010). *Black youth rising: Activism and radical healing in urban America.* New York, NY: Teachers College Press.

Gqola, P. D. (2018). *Reflecting rogue: Inside the mind of a feminist.* Johannesburg, South Africa: Jacana Media.

Grady-Willis, W. A. (2006). *Challenging US apartheid: Atlanta and Black struggles for human rights, 1960–1977.* Durham, NC: Duke University Press.

Grem, D. E. (2006). "The south got something to say": Atlanta's dirty south and the southernization of hip-hop America. *Southern Cultures, 12*(4), 55–73.

Guishard, M. (2009). The false paths, the endless labors, the turns now this way and now that: Participatory action research, mutual vulnerability, and the politics of inquiry. *The Urban Review, 41*(1), 85–105.

Guy-Sheftall, B. (1995). *Words of fire: An anthology of African-American feminist thought.* New York, NY: New Press.

Harris-Perry, M. (2017, July 24). How #SquadCare saved my life. *Elle Magazine.* Retrieved from https://www.elle.com/culture/career-politics/news/a46797/squad-care-melissa-harris-perry

Harwell, O. R. J. (2016). *This woman's work: The writing and activism of Bebe Moore Campbell.* Oxford: University Press of Mississippi.

Hobson, M. J. (2017). *The legend of Black mecca: Politics and class in the making of modern Atlanta.* Raleigh: University of North Carolina Press.

hooks, b. (1990). *Yearning.* Boston, MA: South End Press.

Hughes, L. (1926). Lament for dark peoples. In *The weary blues,* by L. Hughes (p. 100). New York, NY: Knopf.

James, J. (2013). "Concerning violence": Frantz Fanon's rebel intellectual in search of a Black cyborg. *South Atlantic Quarterly, 112*(1), 57–70.

Judd, B. (2014). *Patient*. New York, NY: Black Lawrence Press.

Leahy, D. (2014). Assembling a health[y] subject: Risky and shameful pedagogies in health education. *Critical Public Health, 24*(2), 171–181.

Lewis, A. (1990). Looking at the total picture: A conversation with health activist Beverly Smith. In E. C. White (Ed.), *The Black women's health book: Speaking for ourselves* (pp. 172–181). New York, NY: Seal Press.

Lorde, A. (1981). The uses of anger. *Women's Studies Quarterly, 9*(3), 7–10.

Lorde, A. (1984). Learning from the 60s. In *Sister Outsider* (pp. 134–144). Berkeley, CA: Crossing Press.

Lothian, A., & Phillips, A. (2013). Can digital humanities mean transformative critique? *Journal of E-Media Studies, 3*(1), 1–25.

Lupton, D. (1993). Risk as moral danger: The social and political functions of risk discourse in public health. *International Journal of Health Services, 23*(3), 425–435.

Maparyan, L. (2012). *The womanist idea*. New York, NY: Routledge.

McKittrick, K. (2011). On plantations, prisons, and a black sense of place. *Social & Cultural Geography, 12*(8), 947–963.

Mohanty, C. T. (1991). Under Western eyes: Feminist scholarship and colonial discourses. In C. T. Mohanty, A. Russo, & L. Torres (Eds.), *Third World women and the politics of feminism* (pp. 51–80). Bloomington: Indiana University Press.

Morrison, T. (1987). *Beloved*. New York, NY: Knopf.

Myles, R. L. (2013). *Unbearable fruit: Black Women's experiences with uterine fibroids.* (Doctoral dissertation). Georgia State University, Atlanta. Retrieved from https://scholarworks.gsu.edu/sociology_diss/72/

Neuhauser, L., Richardson, D., Mackenzie, S., & Minkler, M. (2007). Advancing transdisciplinary and translational research practice: Issues and models of doctoral education in public health. *Journal of Research Practice, 3*(2), 1–25.

Petteway, R. J. (2021). Poetry as praxis + "illumination": Toward an epistemically just health promotion for resistance, healing, and (re) imagination. *Health Promotion Practice, 22*(1_suppl), 20S–26S.

Phillips, L. (Ed.). (2006). *The womanist reader*. New York, NY: Taylor and Francis.

Quiroz-Martinez, J. (1998). Poetry is a political act: An interview with June Jordan. *Colorlines*. Retrieved from https://www.colorlines. com/articles/poetry-political-act

Rowell, C. H., & Clifton, L. (1999). An interview with Lucille Clifton. *Callaloo, 22*(1), 56–72.

Self, R. O. (2005). *American Babylon: Race and the struggle for postwar Oakland*. Princeton, NJ: Princeton University Press.

Sides, J. (2006). *LA city limits: African American Los Angeles from the Great Depression to the present*. Berkeley: University of California Press.

Stephens, D. P., & Phillips, L. D. (2003). Freaks, gold diggers, divas, and dykes: The sociohistorical development of adolescent African American women's sexual scripts. *Sexuality and Culture, 7*(1), 3–49.

Stewart, M. W. (1987). *Maria W. Stewart, America's first Black woman political writer: Essays and speeches*. Bloomington: Indiana University Press.

Stuckey, H. L., & Nobel, J. (2010). The connection between art, healing, and public health: A review of current literature. *American Journal of Public Health, 100*(2): 254–263.

Tannenbaum, J., & Bush, V. C. (2005). *Jump write in! Creative writing exercises for diverse communities, grades 6–12*. San Francisco, CA: Jossey-Bass.

Tuck, E. (2009). Suspending damage: A letter to communities. *Harvard Educational Review, 79*(3), 409–428.

Tuck, E., Guess, A., & Sultan, H. (2014). Not nowhere: Collaborating on selfsame land. *Decolonization: Indigeneity, Education & Society*, 1–11.

Tuck, E., Smith, M., Guess, A. M., Benjamin, T., & Jones, B. K. (2014). Geotheorizing Black/land. *Departures in Critical Qualitative Research, 3*(1), 52–74.

Walker, A. (1983). *In search of our mothers' gardens*. New York, NY: Harcourt.

Washington, H. A. (2006). *Medical apartheid: The dark history of medical experimentation on Black Americans from colonial times to the present*. New York, NY: Doubleday.

Wilder, C. S. (2000). *A covenant with color: Race and social power in Brooklyn 1636–1990*. New York, NY: Columbia University Press.

7

Activating Space and Spirit

Meditations on Spiritually Sustaining Pedagogies

SAMEENA EIDOO

> To be guided by love is to live in community with all life. However, a culture of domination, like ours, does not strive to teach us how to live in community. As a consequence, learning to live in community must be a core practice for all of us who desire spirituality in education.
>
> —bell hooks

Spirituality in secularized institutions of higher education remains a contentious subject inside and outside the classroom. The silencing and marginalization of spirituality in higher education threaten "to diminish the knowledge foundations as well as the epistemological revival of Indigenous and communal ways of knowing and social wellbeing" (Abdi, 2011, p. xii). I explore possibilities for weaving spirituality into learning and knowledge creation discourses in a secularized public university in Canada.

The University of Toronto operates on land that has been home to Indigenous peoples for millennia. Founded by royal charter in 1827, the University of Toronto "has historically been an instrument for the oppression of Indigenous peoples" (University of Toronto Truth and Reconciliation Commission Steering Committee, 2017, p. 1). It advanced the settler state by educating "generations of political leaders, policy makers, teachers, civil servants, and many others who were part of the system that created and ran residential schools" (University of Toronto,

2017, p. 1). It also perpetuated anti-Blackness through discriminatory admissions policies (Henry, 2019). The University of Toronto denied admission to Black applicants to its medical school in the 1920s (Henry, 2019). These are among the historical truths and colonial pedagogies of this institution of higher education.

I am the daughter of Muslim immigrants from India, born and raised in the Greater Toronto Area (GTA). As an educator and education scholar at the University of Toronto, I strive to disrupt colonial pedagogies by cultivating sacred life-affirming spaces on campus, particularly, for multiply marginalized Black, Indigenous, and racialized people for whom the university was not imagined in its inception. This chapter reflects on my work beyond the classroom at the University of Toronto's Multi-Faith Centre for Spiritual Study and Practice, where I conceptualized and curated programs that engaged questions of religious faith and spiritual life. I present three activations that I believe exemplify *spiritually sustaining pedagogies*.

Spiritually Sustaining Pedagogies

One of my first encounters with writing on spirituality in higher education was in *Teaching Community: A Pedagogy of Hope* (hooks, 2003). bell hooks reflected on her own spirituality, how it sustained her as a Black girl child growing up in a segregated southern United States:

> As a girl, touched by the mystical dimensions of Christian faith, I felt the presence of the Beloved in my heart: the oneness of our life. At that time, when I had not yet learned of the right language, I knew only that despite the troubles of my world, the suffering I witnessed around and within me, there was always available a spiritual force that could lift me higher, that could give me moments of transcendent bliss wherein I could surrender all thought of the world and know profound peace. (2003, p. 160)

For hooks, mystical Christianity was a protective salve and a portal through which she could freely imagine a way of being Christian that did not require her "acceptance of oppressive hierarchies" (2003, p. 161). hooks's desire to cultivate her inner world pulled her toward the study of Buddhism. She named Thich Nhat Hanh as one of the most influential spiritual teachers in her life and shared the following response to one of his teachings:

> Thich Nhat Hanh speaks of the efforts to go back [home] in terms of the recovery of one's self, of one's integrity. I began to use this vision of spiritual self-recovery in relationship to the self-recovery of colonized and oppressed peoples. I did this to see the points of convergence between the effort to live

in the spirit and the effort of oppressed peoples to renew their spirits—to find themselves again in suffering and in resistance.

Here is my concern: What is the place of love in this recovery? What is the place of love in the experience of intimate otherness? (2003, pp. 161–162)

For hooks, the pathway to recovery of self is through love, through living life in community. Living life in community requires experiencing "intimate otherness." Entering into intimate otherness becomes possible through practicing love of self.

Despite studying and teaching in elite predominantly White institutions of higher education, where hooks experienced "otherness" and "hostility" toward spirituality, she remained steadfast in feeding her spirit: "I can testify to the meaningfulness of spiritual practice and that such a practice sustains and nurtures progressive teaching, progressive politics, and enhances the struggle for liberation" (2003, pp. 162, 164). When students asked her how she had sustained herself in the same institutions of higher education, she told them her truth: "I was compelled to give them an honest account of the sustaining power of spirituality in my life. Honestly naming spirituality as a force strengthening my capacity to resist enabled me to stand within centers of dominator culture and courageously offer alternatives" (2003, p. 181). hooks invited students to cultivate an inner life, to quiet their minds, to connect with their hearts, and to affirm their whole selves. In doing so, hooks offered students spiritually sustaining pedagogies that could help heal and protect their spirits from injurious colonial pedagogies.

hooks visited Toronto in 2004. She was an invited guest of the Spirit Matters: Wisdom Traditions and the "Great Work" gathering organized by the former Transformative Learning Centre at the Ontario Institute for Studies in Education, University of Toronto. When I learned hooks would be there, I volunteered to assist with the conference, including to record and transcribe her session. hooks invited participants to sit in a circle facing one another. She then asked each participant to share their names and what drew them to the session. Most of the session was spent that way. hooks acknowledged that participants had attended to listen to her teachings, but she felt it was more important to create a sense of community, and that was her teaching. The following evening, I attended her talk "Love: Connecting Self and Community," at the Bloor Street United Church. Afterward, she stayed to sign books. When I reached her, she greeted me by my name. hooks had remembered me from the day before. That encounter has stayed with me.

hooks planted a seed of possibilities for integrating spirituality in higher education. Django Paris and H. Samy Alim's *Culturally Sustaining Pedagogies: Teaching and Learning for Justice in a Changing World* (2017) provided the language for the seed to grow into *spiritually sustaining pedagogies*. Paris and Alim define the concept of culturally sustaining pedagogies as "teaching that perpetuates and fosters linguistic, literate, and cultural pluralism as part of schooling for positive social transformation" (p. 1). They explain, "Culturally sustaining pedagogies exist wherever education sustains the lifeways of communities who have been and continue to be damaged and erased through schooling" (p. 1). Culturally sustaining pedagogies disrupt schooling as a project of the settler-colonial state: "[B]y proposing schooling as a site for sustaining the cultural ways of being of communities of color rather than eradicating them, culturally sustaining pedagogies is responding to the many ways that schools continue to function as part of the colonial project" (p. 2). Through culturally sustaining pedagogies, they "seek to disrupt anti-Indigeneity, anti-Blackness, and related anti-Brownness (e.g., from anti-Latinidad to Islamophobia) and model minority myths so foundational to schooling in the United States and so many other nation-states" (p. 2). Such teaching gestures toward the sacred, encoded in linguistic, literate, and cultural pluralism. Culturally sustaining pedagogies can be enacted in higher education. Like hooks, Paris and Alim offer pedagogies that sustain the lifeways of communities and disrupt colonial pedagogies in educational institutions that advance settler states.

The Multi-Faith Centre for Spiritual Study and Practice

The Multi-Faith Centre for Spiritual Study and Practice was created within the secular mandate of the University of Toronto, partly in response to student mobilizing for the needs of students from minoritized faith communities not reflected in Judeo-Christian institutions, knowledge systems, and practices. Designed by Moriyama & Teshima Architects, the physical building includes spaces featuring different expressions of light. The spaces are flexible and multipurpose to accommodate religious and spiritual practice, as well as interfaith exploration and engagement. The building opened in 2007. Upon its opening, the Multi-Faith Centre received funding to encourage youth to engage in interfaith projects.

Interfaith projects can enact colonial pedagogies. In her critical ethnography of the political subjectivities and mobilizations of Muslim American youth living in the San Francisco Bay area, Sunaina Marr Maira (2016) observes how interfaith engagement has been used by the United States and its institutions to define the limits of "good citizenship" for Muslim American youth:

> The US state supports and promotes interfaith projects that steer youth away from critical political engagement with Middle East politics and funnels them into depoliticized spaces focused on religious and cultural identity talk.
> . . . .

> Intercultural and interfaith dialogue has achieved a preeminent role in the post-9/11 political field as the legitimate frame for discussing political questions, erasing issues of sovereignty, colonialism, and dispossession. (pp. 101–102)

Maira acknowledges not all young people who engage in campus- or community-based interfaith programs are willing participants in such erasures. Some young people insist on and persist in critical interfaith grassroots organizing. Many of the students interning at the Multi-Faith Centre were already involved in social movement organizing, including Palestinian solidarity work. They approached interfaith work cautiously and critically. I recall one conversation among interns who were short-listing films for a series that explored the intersection of spirituality and justice. One intern who had spent a summer in Gaza suggested a film featuring the perspectives of Israeli and Palestinian children. Another intern who was involved in Palestinian solidarity work on campus challenged the proposed selection. This intern argued the film falsely equalized power relations between Palestinians and Israelis and normalized Israeli occupation of Palestine.

Maira imagines alternatives to depoliticized interfaith engagement with Robin D. G. Kelley's (1999) concept of "poly-cultural affiliation," further developed by Vijay Prashad (2001)—"ways of generating solidarity by engaging in political struggle based on overlapping cultural processes and intersecting histories, rather than on discrete identity categories or multicultural fictions of cultural authenticity" (Maira, 2016, p. 259). Maira continues, "This notion resonates with the adage that identity should emerge from one's politics, rather than politics from one's identity." (2016, p. 259). For me, conceptualizations of polycultural affiliations proposed by Kelley, Prashad, and Maira align with hooks's articulation of community as praxis guided by love and Paris and Alim's culturally sustaining pedagogies. Such conceptualizations of being with and for one another necessitate working together in ways that are not supported by depoliticized paradigms of interfaith engagement.

Activating Space and Spirit

I elaborate on select cocurricular programs I introduced through the Multi-Faith Centre. I describe the programs as *activations* of space and spirit. The activations were inspired and guided by the critical praxis of visionary Black, Indigenous, and racialized scholars, educators, and artists. The activations were free and open to the public. They involved,

* carefully selecting and arranging beautiful central spaces on campus, with particular attention to accessibility;

- warmly welcoming participants into protective and affirming healing spaces;
- providing abundant sustenance for different dietary needs;
- centering the knowledges and ways of knowing communities subjected to colonization and oppression;
- inviting in beloved ones in the ancestral and physical realms;
- evoking personal and collective memories, creating new memories; and
- gently encouraging new relational encounters and inviting mutual vulnerability and responsibility.

Love is an ancient generative energy associated with the heart, the physical center of the body, and the home of the soul. Scientific insights about the heart can further elucidate what it means to activate space and spirit. An electromagnetic organ emanating electricity and magnetism, the heart's electromagnetic field is five thousand times stronger than that of the brain (Dale, 2009). The heart contains neural cells, identical to cells in the brain (Dale, 2009; HeartMath Institute, 2019). These cells can feel, learn, and remember. Energy and information flow between the heart and the brain through cells (Dale, 2009; HeartMath Institute, 2019). The heart receives and processes information from the world outside of the body in which it resides. According to the HeartMath Institute, information about a person's emotional state is encoded into the heart's magnetic field and is communicated throughout the body and into the external environment. The heart's electromagnetic field can transmit signals between people. Such scientific insights into the beating heart point to what is possible in gatherings of people. In such gatherings it becomes possible for hearts to communicate with one another, to access different knowledges and energetic planes from cellular to astral. The activations were at once ephemeral and timeless, made possible through expanding and deepening relationship with

- Timaj Garad—Ethiopian diasporic multidisciplinary artist
- Jasmine Gui—Singaporean diasporic interdisciplinary artist
- Alexis Pauline Gumbs—queer Black feminist love evangelist
- Hawa Y. Mire—Somali diasporic storyteller and writer
- Karyn Recollet—assistant professor, Gender and Women's Studies, University of Toronto
- Brown Girls Yoga—grassroots yoga teachers' collective

Activation 1: Reimagine Everything

Grace Lee Boggs, born on June 27, 1915, in Providence, Rhode Island, transitioned on October 5, 2015, in Detroit, Michigan. Following the news of her transition, I returned to "On Revolution: A Conversation between Grace Lee Boggs and Angela Davis," which took place on March 2, 2012, at the Pauley Ballroom, University of California Berkeley, as part of the "27th Empowering Women of Color Conference, a Holistic Approach: Justice, Access, and Healing." Davis introduced Boggs. Davis provided an account of the Black radical tradition, situating herself and Boggs within it: "I came to revolutionary struggle through the Black freedom movement. And I say this in vast appreciation of the contributions that Grace Lee Boggs and her late husband James Boggs made to the Black radical tradition." Davis reflected on the contributions of non-Black racialized women to the Black radical tradition: "I think it's important that we acknowledge that this was not simply by people of African descent but by people of many racial, ethnic national backgrounds and especially women of color." Davis emphasized the leadership of youth and of those "not afraid to identify with the boldness, imaginativeness and courage of young people" and returned to Boggs's teachings on the transformative power of the imagination: "And I really agree with the point that Boggs always makes that we have to move beyond the stage of merely protesting the oppressions in this world and we have to begin to imagine what a fundamentally transformed society looks like, not only what it would look like, what it would feel like?" (Boggs & Davis, 2012).

The themes of living life in community, intergenerational relational ethics, and the transformative power of the imagination are threaded throughout the conversation between Davis and Boggs. In her opening remarks, Boggs described herself as follows:

> I am a very old woman. I was born in 1915 in what was later known as the First World War, two years after the Russian Revolution. And because I was born to Chinese immigrant parents and because I was born female—I learned very quickly that the world needed changing. But what I also learned as I grew older was that how we change the world and how we think about changing the world has to change. (Boggs & Davis, 2012)

At the time of this conversation, Boggs had already lived for nearly a century. Boggs was still evolving when she declared it was time "to reimagine everything":

> The time has come for us to reimagine everything. We have to reimagine work and go away from labor. We have to reimagine revolution and get beyond protest. We have to think not only about change in our institutions, but changes in ourselves.... It's up to us to reimagine the alternatives and not just protest them and expect them to do better.... How do we reimagine education? How do we reimagine community? How do we reimagine family? How do we reimagine sexual identity? How do we reimagine everything, in the light of a change that is so far reaching and that is our responsibility to make? We can't expect them

to make it. We have to do the reimagining ourselves. We have to think beyond capitalist categories. We have to reimagine. (Boggs & Davis, 2012)

Boggs believed the human capability to "create the world anew" was rooted in the soul. When the moderator asked Boggs to explain the concept of "growing our souls in community by building community." Boggs responded,

> I first used the concept of growing our souls about 10 years ago. Radicals don't usually talk about souls—but I think we have to. What I mean by souls is the capacity to create the world anew, which each of us has. How do we talk about that with one another? It's not only important to act, it's important to talk because when you talk you begin to create new ideas and new languages. We've all been damaged by this system—it's not only the capitalists who are the scoundrels, the villains; we are all part of it. And we all have to change what we say, what we do, what we think, what we imagine. (Boggs & Davis, 2012)

The notion of growing our souls in community by building community resonated with Davis, too: "If we are to move toward revolutionary approaches we have to relearn and I say relearn because I think somewhere deep inside we have to recognize that we are connected to each other and every single being on the planet" (Boggs & Davis, 2012).

I pondered Boggs's call "to reimagine everything." As I read and reread Boggs's words, my own imagination was captivated. Every week, I met with the brilliant and engaged group of then students, organizers, and artists, who were interning at the Multi-Faith Centre. At our weekly meetings, we discussed religion, spirituality, justice, and what it means to live a life in spirit. We read and discussed writing and actions of visionary Black, Indigenous, and racialized scholars, educators, and activists, including Bree Newsome's June 27, 2015, act of civil disobedience—ascending a flag pole to take down the confederate flag from South Carolina statehouse grounds while reciting the Lord's Prayer and Psalm 27. At our first meeting following Boggs's transition, I shared an excerpt from the conversation between Boggs and Davis that focused on Boggs's call "to reimagine everything." Boggs's ideas resonated with them. I then proposed the glimmer of an idea for a series of workshops responding to Boggs's call. The idea was met with an affirming response, and some of the student interns immediately offered to contribute to the series as cocurators and workshop facilitators. In that moment, the workshop series Reimagine Everything was born.

Jasmine Gui and Timaj Garad, both Toronto-based teaching artists, responded to Boggs's call to "reimagine everything." Following their participation in the workshop series, I invited them to develop their own programs through the Multi-Faith Centre.

Gui was among the graduate students interning at the Multi-Faith Centre during the 2015–2016 academic year. She was already an established writer and arts advocate. Gui founded Project 40—an interdisciplinary, Asian-artist community based in Toronto. She responded to the call with a workshop titled "Embracing Anger with Grace":

> Boggs as I understand it, puts everything into perspective. It gives me the capacity to hope even in brokenness, but also the courage to imagine past the brokenness into the whole. This has always been, for me, the motivation for social justice. . . . Anger means I am invested. It means strong conviction, and deep grief. This, for me, is what social justice means. Anger is considered a negative emotion to be avoided. Particularly in our dialogues of faith, particularly for women. How can we reimagine our own anger and embrace it in Boggs as part of the journey toward something better? (Gui, 2016)

Gui's workshop was designed to provoke thought among participants about their relationship with anger and to work through anger in a tangible way. The workshop took place in a light-filled room with tables and chairs organized into small groups. Each table had a set of art supplies—stitched booklets, crayons, magazines, textiles, scissors, and glue. Gui began the workshop by sharing her own evolving relationship with anger. She then offered a series of prompts, inviting participants to creatively express (using words and images) their learnings about anger, manifestations of anger, and sources of anger. To mark a shift in relating to anger, Gui invited participants to turn their booklets upside down and creatively express the hurt underlying their anger, connections between anger and what they deeply care about, and what is worthy of their anger.

A year later, I commissioned Gui to develop a four-week program. She envisioned a writing and zine-making program called "Medi(t)ations", for people who self-identify as women and Black, Indigenous, and/or racialized. The workshop series offered guided exploration of the intersection of gender, race, and spirituality through the writing of women from Black, Indigenous, and racialized communities. Participants individually and collectively experimented, drafted, and workshopped creative-writing pieces. Participants compiled and hand-stitched their zines.

Yasmine Kherfi, then an undergraduate student interning at the Multi-Faith Centre, invited me to attend an event where local poets would be performing. I met Garad after her performance. When I shared with Garad Boggs's call to "reimagine everything," she responded with a workshop titled "Poetic Heart Work: The Therapeutic Power of Performance Poetry":

> Much of my work documents a personal journey of unlearning and growth, which has led me to believe poetry is a conduit not only for ideas, but the heart work it takes to unearth our deepest truths and become our truest selves. This

performance and talk will highlight the capacity of the performing arts, particularly spoken word poetry, to bring individuals and communities to a higher state of mental and emotional wellness. The stigma of mental illness will have us believing that stories about mental illness are too melancholy, inappropriate, and will only make us look weak if told, which is why I believe speaking our pain is not only cathartic, life-affirming, and inspiring, but a radical act necessary for the dismantling of systems of oppression. When we begin to heal from the multitude of silenced trauma repressed with us, we open ourselves to inspire others to do the same—speaking our pain is the first step in the catalyst to doing so. (Garad, 2016)

Garad's workshop took place on a winter's evening, in a warmly lit multipurpose room with windows allowing participants to look into the darkening sky beyond. The smaller tables were arranged into one long table, and participants were seated around it. A snack-and-refreshments table was off to the side. Garad shared her experience with poetry—how reading, writing, and performing poetry supported her regeneration. Garad then performed two poems she had written. She offered participants a series of multisensory writing prompts, which participants used to create autobiographical poems. Some participants accepted Garad's invitation to share their poems with the rest of the group.

Later that year, I commissioned Garad to develop a four-week program. She envisioned a workshop series expanding and deepening Poetic Heart Work. She designed the program to cultivate well-being by engaging participants in creative-writing and performance practices anchored in unconditional love of self. Each session explored an aspect of wellness—body, mind, emotion, and spirit—and the necessity of seeing oneself and others fully by engaging holistically toward well-being. The purpose of the series was to call participants to explore their stories and resiliency related to those stories while providing a space to deconstruct their realities and reconstruct their futures (Garad, 2016). In this series, Garad used poetry and performance as tools for self-examination intended to awaken the deep, innate capacity to heal by connecting with our purpose through our stories, including the community care and social transformation that often occurs when we share those stories with others (2016).

Both Gui and Garad responded to Boggs's call boldly, imaginatively, and courageously. As young racialized women teaching artists working through radical women of color feminisms, they offered their gifts to support others in becoming whole.

Activation 2: Learning to Mother Ourselves

After reading *Revolutionary Mothering: Love on the Front Lines* (2016), an anthology edited by Alexis Pauline Gumbs, China Martens, and Mai'a Williams, I reached out to Gumbs, with whom I was already in community, to begin exploring the possibility of her creating a learning experience based on the book's key teachings. The anthology is part of a legacy of revolutionary anthologies—*The Black Woman: An Anthology* (Bambara, 1970), *Home Girls: A Black Feminist Anthology* (Smith, 1983), *This Bridge Called My Back: Writings by Radical Women of Color* (Moraga & Anzaldúa, 1981), and the women of color–led reproductive-justice movement: "We are flamboyantly activating the legacy of radical personal testimonies and theories of women of color feminists of the 1970s and 80s in order to make the radical practice of mothering visible as a key to our collective liberation" (Gumbs, 2016, p. 9). Gumbs describes the inspiration for the anthology: "The practice of mothering that inspired us to create this book is older than feminism; it is older and more futuristic than the category 'woman.' We are investigating and amplifying the nuances of practices that have existed as long as there have been people of different ages with different superpowers invested in each other's existence" (p. 9). She asserts, "In order to collectively figure out how to sustain and support our evolving species, in order to participate in and demand a society where people help to create each other instead of too often destroying each other, we need to look at the practice of creating, nurturing, affirming, and supporting life that we call mothering" (p. 9). The anthology offers the following expansive understanding of "mothering": "Maybe when we say 'mothering' in this book, we really mean the 'creative spirit' or 'love itself'" (p. 10).

Conversations with Gumbs expanded to include coconspirators Hawa Y. Mire and Karyn Recollet and evolved into Learning to Mother Ourselves: A Storytelling Cypher—an interactive learning experience. Both Mire and Recollet had been part of a series of public conversations (or cyphers) that I cocurated titled Hip Hop for a Different Future: Decolonization, Spirituality, and Social Transformation, in honor of Black and Indigenous peoples, historical and present-day work to dismantle White supremacy and settler colonialism, and to recenter ways of being whole (Eidoo & Blight, 2019). Intergenerational relationality, collective care, and healing were prominent themes in Hip Hop for a Different Future, particularly in the contributions Mire and Recollet made.

Gumbs traveled from Durham, North Carolina, to Toronto on the morning of October 26, 2016. Later that day, just prior to the gathering, Gumbs met with Mire and Recollet to consolidate plans. Recollet's daughter joined the meeting, with a box of crayons and coloring books. The gathering itself was held in one of the large ornate rooms at Hart House. The dais held three armchairs and a coffee table. It was situated against the south-facing wall of the large rectangular room and marked the focal point of the room. The seats were arranged in a semi-circle in front of the dais, with an aisle in the middle. On the right side of the room were long, leather sofas for those who needed more comfortable seating and an arts-and-crafts station for children. On the left side of the room were a fireplace and tables with an abundance of food and drink. The lights were dimmed and the fireplace lit. A luminous projection of a collage featured June Jordan, made by Gumbs for her Black Feminist Breathing Chorus. Solange's album *A Seat at the Table* (2016) played softly. With attention to detail, we hoped to make love powerful.

I invited participants to engage in the life-affirming practice of making one another visible by greeting one another. Because children were present, I invited them to speak their names and shared an excerpt from Jordan's 1977 speech "Children's Literature: The Creative Spirit," which was published in *Revolutionary Mothering*. Gumbs explains the significance of Jordan's speech for the anthology: "Much of the intergenerational vision that we practice and celebrate in this collection can be described through June Jordan's declaration in 1977 that 'Love is Lifeforce.' Jordan poetically and urgently articulates the importance of intergenerational relationship to the faith of human kind" (2016, p. 9). I read the following excerpt from Jordan's speech to the participants:

> I want to say to children that I love you and that you are beautiful and amazing regardless whether you are—and also precisely because you are—Black or female or poor or small or an only child or the son of parents divorced: you are beautiful and amazing: and when you love yourself truly then you will become like a swan release in the grace of natural and spontaneous purpose.
>
> And I want to say to children let us look at hunger, at famine around the world, and let us consider together, you at five years of age, and me at forty-one-how we can, how we must eliminate this genocide, this terror.
>
> And I want to say to children let us look at tiger lilies blooming to their own astonishment, and learn to cherish their own form and orderliness and freedom for our own. And I want to say to children, tell me what you think and what you see and what you dream so that I may hope to honor you. And I want these things for children, because I want these things for myself, and for all of us, because unless we embody these attitudes and precepts as the governing rules of our love, and our political commitment to survive, we will love in vain, and we will certainly not survive. I believe that the creative spirit is nothing less than love made manifest. And I deeply hope that we can make love powerful because, otherwise, there will be no reason for hope. (as quoted in Gumbs et al., 2016, p. 18)

The art-and-crafts station was supported by then students interning at the Multi-Faith Centre—Farrah Mustafa, Seema Shafei, and Motaharei Nabavi, who had volunteered to take care of children visiting the station. Children were seen and heard—meeting and playing with one another, wandering on and off the dais, venturing into the arts to create or color something, returning to their caregivers, reaching out for food. Children were in the space, taking up space.

Gumbs, Mire, and Recollet invited participants to reflect on and dedicate their participation to someone who mothered them. They also invited participants to identify a breakthrough they were seeking, share with another participant, and offer a story from their own life to support the breakthrough. The invitation required participants to hold space for one another's vulnerabilities, recognize their own resources, and share with one another. Gumbs, Mire, and Recollet then took turns sharing their own writing on mothering. The words they wove together, story after story, created portals stretching time and space, bringing forth practices of mothering, ancient and futuristic. They told stories about sorrow, longing, desire, anger, joy, and love; of relationships with mother figures; of mothering to rupture White supremacy, heteropatriarchy, capitalism, and settler colonialism; of creating relationships with the land, the cosmos, the planet Earth, and other celestial bodies. After celebrating and lovingly responding to one another's writing, Gumbs, Mire, and Recollet invited participants to share key words they identified from the stories they were just told. They then shared back the words, asking participants to embody the words. Again, participants held space for one another's vulnerabilities.

The gathering closed with a cypher led by Gumbs. When I had shared my vision for an intergenerational gathering as part of the Hip Hop for a Different Future series, Gumbs suggested the cypher. Participating in a cypher is a consensual process. Participants, sitting in a circle, a sacred shape, can enter and leave the circle as they wish and take turns moving in and out of the center, exchanging stories and beats and rhymes and coconstructing new knowledges. In Learning to Mother Ourselves, participants remained seated, passing a microphone after they shared their responses to Gumbs's prompt, "We can make [blank] with [blank]":

* "We can make lemonade with lemons."
* "We can make home anywhere with love."
* "We can make pancakes, with milk, eggs, sugar, salt, flour, and fire."
* "We can build community with our neighbors."

In responding to the prompt, participants reasserted their creative spirit by exercising their imagination, creating something new with the resources they have available to them by creating possibilities for new kinds of relationships with one another. We knew we had succeeded in making love powerful when one of the children in attendance with her mother took the microphone when it reached her and ran with it across the room, singing and laughing into the microphone before she dropped it.

Activation 3: Brown Girls Yoga

Brown Girls Yoga (BGY) is a Toronto-based grassroots collective committed to making yoga accessible as a daily healing and resilience practice for Black, Indigenous, and racialized community members who presently or formerly identify as woman or girl (BGY, 2017; see also BGY, 2012). In August 2016 I invited BGY to offer free weekly drop-in yoga classes at the Multi-Faith Centre. The University of Toronto already offered meditation and yoga classes but none exclusively for Black, Indigenous, and racialized communities. I had learned about BGY years earlier through community circles after I had removed myself from a predominantly White and culturally appropriative yoga studio. Critical yoga studies scholars and critical yoga practitioners have noted White supremacy and Orientalism uphold a superficial practice of yoga—one that obscures its origins, histories, philosophies, and connections to South Asia (Wakpa, 2018; Sood, 2018). Reflecting on South Asian peoples' relationships to lands that are formerly and presently colonized, Roopa Singh (2018) delineates, "There is a pervasive misunderstanding and lack of understanding about the South Asian diasporic experience in relation to land.... [T]his includes: lands we were brought to on slave ships for indentured servitude; lands we were coerced to as a result of economic disaster following India's independence; lands of more freely chosen immigration; and so on, and in layers, so that lands can hold all of these South Asian diasporic experiences at once" (as cited in Wakpa, 2018, p. iv). Tria Blu Wakpa foregrounds relationships between yoga and land and asks, "How and why are settler colonial and/or yoga, and 'decolonizing yoga' discourses, eclipsing, and in doing so, enacting violence on-Native American, Indigenous South Asian, South Asian American, and/or South Asian diasporic peoples and practices?" (2018, p. iv). Wakpa hypothesizes, "Yoga's popularity among European Americans is in part a case of misplaced 'imperialist nostalgia' since the practice foregrounds the interconnection among body, mind, and spirit, which European Americans have attempted to destroy through assimilation of Native practices, but simultaneously long for" (p. iv). Yoga has become more accessible in the United States (and Canada) than Indigenous people's embodied practices (p. vi).

Although I did not take classes with BGY prior to their offering at the Multi-Faith Centre, I had been in correspondence and in community spaces with different members of the dynamic group over the years. BGY accepted my invitation and began offering classes in January 2017. Studied in different yogic traditions, each teacher brings her own practice and personality to each class she teaches. BGY offerings draw on Hatha and Vinyasa and incorporate breath connection, restorative poses, and meditation. BGY (2017) creates queer and trans positive spaces in which all bodies, sizes, and levels of practice are welcome. When BGY began offering classes at the Multi-Faith Centre, I attended as many classes as my schedule permitted, my first collective practice in many years. Even now it is difficult for me to put into words that adequately capture the beauty of witnessing and experiencing the weekly gatherings of participants that led to the space for personal and collective practice. For some, BGY offered their first experience with yoga. For others, BGY offered an antidote to their prior experiences in predominantly White and culturally appropriative yoga studios. The feelings participants brought with them into the space created by BYG were often palpable—excitement, curiosity, trepidation. Each BGY teacher introduced herself to each student prior to the start of the class and asked about any physical concerns. I recall one participant with mobility difficulties. She was drawn to the class but hesitant about committing to it. She was immediately put at ease with the option to participate in a chair. Each BGY teacher shared her unique presence, perspective, and practice. In her own way, each BGY teacher acknowledged her positionality in relation to yoga and its practice within the context of settler colonialism, heteropatriarchy, and capitalism and also acknowledging ways in which practices by racialized people can also perpetuate harm by conflating our lived realities and relationships with one another and yoga, which has been used to perpetuate various supremacies including White and Hindu supremacies (Sood, 2018).

BGY's presence on campus also provoked accusations of "racism," along with demands to open the classes to everyone. Most upsetting, however, was the ongoing vandalism of outreach materials in my immediate place of work, which raised concerns about personal safety, necessitated the development of a safety plan with BGY, and required unwanted engagement with campus police. BGY's presence and practice disrupted colonial pedagogies.

Meditations on Spiritually Sustaining Pedagogies

Reimagine Everything amplified the call of legendary Detroit activist Grace Lee Boggs to "reimagine everything." Boggs asked people to recognize their own humanity and to divest from dehumanizing systems and institutions. She believed in the soul and that the human capability to "reimagine the world anew" is rooted in the soul. Boggs asked people to grow their souls in community by building community. Boggs's teachings disrupt colonial pedagogies, which are designed to uphold oppressive systems of power by isolating people from self and community, diminishing their spirits, constraining their imaginations, and frightening them into submission. Through Reimagine Everything, Boggs was made visible on campus. The outreach materials for the workshop series featured the image of an elder smiling Boggs, an invitation to experiment with theories and methods for a new world. Racialized and older women tend to be rendered invisible in societies that uphold Eurocentric ideals of beauty and youth. Some students may have seen in the image of Boggs an elder, kin, and ancestor.

A laboratory for experimenting with theories and methods for reimagining the world anew, Reimagine Everything disrupted colonial pedagogies by centering the presence and critical teachings of a younger generation of scholars, artists, and activists responding to Boggs's call. Making something new with Boggs's teachings, Gui invited participants to "reimagine anger," and Garad invited participants to "reimagine healing." Both Gui and Garad engaged participants in personal reflection and creative expression. The workshops they designed and facilitated for Reimagine Everything served as foundations for future offerings. Gui offered a writing and zine-making program for self-identified women from Black, Indigenous, and racialized communities, which explored the intersection of race, gender, and spirituality. Garad offered a poetry writing and performance workshop and guided participants through exploration of mind, body, heart, and spirit. Centering the presence and critical teachings of Gui and Garad disrupts colonial pedagogies. Gui reflected, "Reimagine Everything was an intentional intervention—introducing new bodies, voices, names, and language as sites of radical resistance, unapologetic existence, and creative possibility. To reimagine you must see the limits and gaps of where you currently are and then build an agential subjectivity that you dream up" (2016).

An interactive learning journey guided by Gumbs, Mire, and Recollet, Learning to Mother Ourselves: A Storytelling Cypher centered the ancient and futuristic practice of mothering—"the creative spirit" or "love itself" (Gumbs, 2016, p. 10). The three leaders invited participants to practice mutual vulnerability and responsibility. The act of turning to another person, who might have been a complete stranger prior to that moment, to share a personal memory or struggle necessitates a mutual vulnerability and responsibility. Using storytelling and counterstorytelling, Gumbs, Mire, and Recollet disrupted colonial heteropatriarchal narratives that fetishize *mother* and challenged the idea that any one human being can meet all of the needs and desires of another. Their storytelling and counterstorytelling celebrated the practice of mothering; of growing communities into families; of fostering relationships with the land, waters, and cosmos; of raising children collectively. Gumbs, Mire, and Recollet invited participants to turn inward and to listen to embodied knowledge about the practice of mothering. From opening to closing, they guided participants through a spiraling sacred cypher. The cypher itself invited participants to exercise their creative spirits. Activating the legacy of radical personal testimonies and theories of women of color feminists of the 1970s and 1980s and beyond, Learning to Mother Ourselves called for honoring the childhoods of Black children, Indigenous children, and other racialized children as sacred and created space for them to freely be themselves.

The presence and offerings of Brown Girls Yoga disrupted colonial pedagogies of yoga. BGY's pedagogies called into question the sense of entitlement to South Asian–embodied practices and epistemological understandings of body-mind-spirit, as well as associations of yoga with Whiteness and Orientalism. BGY's presence preceded their offerings on campus, with outreach materials featuring BGY teachers' glowing images set against warm hues of yellow and purple. The outreach materials were defaced by some and adored by others. Committed to making classes financially accessible and practices emotionally and physically safe for participants in different bodies, BGY is seeding a movement and shaping expectations for what self-identified women from Black, Indigenous, and racialized communities can expect from yoga studios and teachers in the GTA.

The activations described in this chapter independently and together work to disrupt colonial pedagogies by foregrounding spiritually sustaining pedagogies. Spiritually sustaining pedagogies offer wholeness and truthfulness in formal educational institutions that function as part of a colonial project (hooks, 2003; Paris & Alim, 2017). Colonial pedagogies are injurious to the human spirit (hooks, 2003). Depoliticized interfaith projects preserve and perpetuate the colonial project and limit youth engagement in religious and cultural identity talk (Maira, 2016). Freedom, however, is based on a radical conception of community (Kelley, 1999) guided by love (hooks, 2003). Freedom requires political work that recognizes overlapping cultural processes and intersecting histories (Prashad, 2001). The activations cultivated sacred life-affirming and truth-telling spaces on campus. In those gatherings, hearts can communicate with one another and know freedom is possible.

References

Abdi, A. A. (2011). Foreword. In N. N. Wane, E. L. Manyimo, & E. J. Ritkes (Eds.), *Spirituality, education, & society: An integrated approach* (pp. xi–xiii). Rotterdam, Netherlands: Sense.

Bambara. T. C. (1970). *The Black woman: An anthology*. New York, NY: New American Library.

Boggs, G. L., & Davis, A. (2012). On revolution: A conversation between Grace Lee Boggs and Angela Davis. [Transcript, web extra only]. 27th Empowering Women of Color Conference, "a holistic approach: Justice, access, and healing," University of California Berkeley, March 2, 2012. *Making Contact International Media Project*, 2022. Accessed December 10, 2022, from https://www.heartmath.org/research/science-of-the-heart/energetic-communication/

Brown Girls Yoga. (2012). *Brown Girls Yoga*. [Facebook page]. Accessed December 10, 2022, from facebook.com/BrownGirlsYoga

Brown Girls Yoga. (2017). *Brown Girls Yoga*. [Flyer]. Multi-Faith Centre for Spiritual Study and Practice, University of Toronto, Canada.

Dale, C. (2009). *The subtle body: An encyclopedia of your energetic anatomy*. Boulder, CO: Sounds True.

Eidoo, S., & Blight, S. (2019). One dish, one spoon: Reclaiming land, life, and spirit through hip hop in Tkaronto. In A. Hudson, A. Ibrahim, & K. Recollet (Eds.), *In this together: Blackness, Indigeneity, and hip hop* (pp. 45–64). New York, NY: DIO Press.

Garad, T. (2016, February 11). Poetic heARTwork: The therapeutic power of performance poetry. [Workshop proposal]. Multi-Faith Centre for Spiritual Study and Practice, University of Toronto, Canada.

Gui, J. (2016, January 28). Embracing anger with Grace. [Workshop proposal]. Multi-Faith Centre for Spiritual Study and Practice, University of Toronto, Canada.

Gumbs, A. (2016). Introduction. In A. Gumbs, C. Martins, & M. Williams (Eds.), *Revolutionary mothering: Love on the front lines* (pp. 9–10). Oakland, CA: PM Press.

Gumbs, A., Martens, C., & Williams, M., Eds. (2016). *Revolutionary mothering: Love on the front lines*. Oakland, CA: PM Press.

HeartMath Institute. (2019). *Science of the heart*. Retrieved December 10, 2022, from https://www.heartmath.org/research/science-of-the-heart/energetic-communication/

Henry, N. L. (2019). Racial segregation of Black people in Canada. *The Canadian Encyclopedia*. Retrieved December 10, 2022, from https://www.thecanadianencyclopedia.ca/en/article/racial-segregation-of-black-people-in-canada

hooks, b. (2003). *Teaching community: A pedagogy of hope*. New York, NY: Routledge.

Jordan, J. (2016). The creative spirit—Children's literature. In A. Gumbs, C. Martins, & M. Williams (Eds.), *Revolutionary mothering: Love on the front lines* (pp. 11–18). Oakland, CA: PM Press. Originally published in 1977.

Kelley, R. D. G. (1999). People in me. *Color Lines, 1*(3), 5–7.

Maira, S. M. (2016). *The 9/11 generation: Youth, rights, and solidarity work in the war on terror*. New York: New York University Press.

Moraga, C., & Anzaldúa, G. (Eds.). (1981). *This bridge called my back: Writings by radical women of color*. Watertown, MA: Persephone Press.

Paris, D., & Alim, H. S. (2017). *Culturally sustaining pedagogies: Teaching and learning for justice in a changing world*. New York, NY: Teachers College Press.

Prashad, V. (2001). *Everybody was kung fu fighting: Afro-Asian connections and the myth of cultural purity*. Boston, MA: Beacon Press.

Singh, R. (2018). Email to Tria Blu Wakpa. In T. B. Wakpa, Decolonizing yoga? and (un)settling social justice. *Race and Yoga, 3*(1), iv.

Smith, B. (1983). *Home girls: A Black feminist anthology*. New York, NY: Kitchen Table, Women of Color Press.

Sood, S. (2018). Cultivating a yogic theology of collective healing: A yogini's journey disrupting White supremacy, Hindu fundamentalism, and casteism. *Race & Yoga, 3*(1), 12–20.

University of Toronto Truth and Reconciliation Commission Steering Committee. (2017). *Answering the call: Wecheehetowin. Final report of the Steering Committee for the University of Toronto response to Truth and Reconciliation Commission of Canada*. Retrieved December 10, 2022, from https://www.provost.utoronto.ca/wp-content/uploads/sites/155/2018/05/Final-Report-TRC.pdf

Wakpa, T. B. (2018). Decolonizing yoga? and (un)settling social justice. *Race & Yoga, 3*(1), i–xix.

8

Dear Doctoral Student of Color

Academic Advising as Anti-Colonial Womanist Pedagogy and Theory

PATRICIA KRUEGER-HENNEY

> The issue is not whether there should be standards and qualifications; there always are. The issue is who sets and will set them, and for whose benefit they function. [. . .] The specter of failing to meet institutional standards and "qualifications" inhibits the search for new models of knowledge and teaching.
>
> —Joy James

From where I stand I see . . .

That pre-tenure female professors of color and their female doctoral students of color inhabit similar epistemological spaces of professional survival in academia: both groups frequently are "presumed incompetent" by their white and male colleagues even though their academic accolades legitimize their participation and presence inside the towering structures of academia (Gutiérrez y Muhs, Niemann, Gonzalez, & Harris, 2012). The words of Joy James above are poignant in that performing successful tenure reviews and completing arduous doctoral degrees are both institutionalized practices rooted in the rituality of racist ideology of white, patriarchal, heterosexist, ableist, and misogynist settler colonialism: scrutinizing, assessing, and surveilling the non-white body and mind for her intellectual fitness and competence to represent and disseminate hegemonized standards of Western Eurocentric knowledge systems. Academia's evaluative protocols and rituals are similar to the institutionalized and high-stakes hazing practices of other exclusive communities (i.e., fraternities and sororities, sports teams, the military), as these test and push the limitations of individual prowess, stamina, and willingness to join academia's exclusive membership—no matter how large the size of long- and short-term emotional, physical, or mental toll on the body. As doctoral students, we anxiously revise and edit our drafts of dissertation chapters over and over until each dissertation committee member is pleased and no longer finds fault with them. Other times we are asked to reinvent ourselves by changing research topics as per our dissertation committee's request, or we abandon our rich and ancient traditions of storytelling about truth and power to replace it with *more-empirical* methodologies that have been already claimed by student handbooks for introducing qualitative-research approaches. As pretenure faculty members, our tenured colleagues advise (read: intimidate) us to be generous with offering our time and energy and to not say no when we are invited to participate in committees at all service levels—university, department, and program. Not wanting to lose the endorsement from our dissertation chairs or jeopardize our colleagues' trust in us or our good standings with them, female doctoral students and pretenure faculty of color decide to please, listen, follow, do as they are told, and neglect our own judgment about reaching the prize waiting for us at the end of the obstacle course. Institutionalized hazing requires supervision and bystandership by its already inducted membership. It also requires as little interference as possible from tenured faculty, staff, and graduates to remain legitimate, authoritative, reasonable.

From where I stand, as a cis-gender, pretenure female doctoral faculty of color, I live the pretenure/tenured and faculty/student dialectic mirroring some of the social dynamics similar to those of a public performance: performer and observer, antagonist and protagonist, actor and prompter, trainer and trainee, junior and senior. In other words, the physical and ideological structures of the university depend on a tenured professoriate to model and teach those who come after them about how to adhere to institutional(ized) practices as guiding standards for initiating the apprenticing scholar into admissions of degree completion, promotion, and tenure. In addition, admissions to the highest-ranking group of permanently employed university workers (i.e., full professors) necessitates competition among its workers, as well as administering all mechanisms and structures of a (academic) system predicated on differential status. Individual professional success is hinged in the welfare of the university. However, I trouble that doctoral-level and pretenure scholars—especially and disproportionately Black, Indigenous, and women of color—are asked to endure the demands of a system built on leveraging profits for the university but without giving consent to the intellectual and psychological abuse, mental illness, and humiliation these cause in their personal and collective lives.

In this chapter and in the good company of the womanist scholars in this volume, I dare to think about the curriculum—purpose, content, and directionality—of the academic advising work I do with doctoral students of color, with Black, Indigenous, and women of color, in particular. There is a wealth of written work done on the groundings of Black feminist thought (Hill Collins, 1999), embodied womanist pedagogies (Thompson, 2017), Black feminist and womanist theorizing within curriculum theorizing (Taliaferro Baszile, Edwards, & Guillory, 2016), Black womanist ethics (Cannon, 2006), and the lived experiences of women of color in academia (Berry & Mizelle, 2006), for example. But far fewer insights have been documented that closely examine the curricular possibilities for critical and womanist academic advising work with graduate students of color that intentionally are grounded in an anti–settler colonial stance, as well as in the extent to which our classed, racialized, gendered, and able-bodied positionalities determine our relationships with learning institutions that were not created for people of color but, instead, for the offspring of land- and labor-owning (white) settler families (Woodson, 1993) and through which we are expected to guide and mentor students and each other. This chapter hosts some of my beginning reflections and desires I have for anchoring academic advising of female doctoral students of color within the grounds of anti-colonial womanist pedagogy and theory.

The Logic of Settler Colonialism in Academia

Academia's admissions, graduation, and promotion practices reinforce the logic of settler colonialism by re/activating what education-researcher Leigh Patel calls "three mutually dependent components": erasure, commodification of knowledge, and enslavement (2016a, p. 33). As a continuous process, settler colonialism erases first before it replaces; it claims the land, resources, cultural practices, and goods in a desired location "in order to enable non-Indigenous peoples' rightful claim to land" (Smith, 2016, p. 68). Throughout our academic training and tenure practices, we experience this most prevalently by way of the erasure of our home knowledges and a prioritization of citations of scholarship that celebrate the individual accomplishments of professional and, generally, white and male academics. In addition, the silencing, if not absence, of Indigenous peoples and knowledges in academic achievement, admissions, and enrollment in graduate programs and professional promotion highlights the systemic erasure of Indigenous and other non-white peoples and cultures in higher education.

Secondly, settler colonialism constructs and restricts settler-slave relationships under which knowledge is commodified, owned, and managed by a few in land-owning positions. Knowledge is seized as property and can be denied to and withheld from those whose laboring bodies are privately owned and exploited for surplus production (i.e., build a robust individual record of productive and published scholarship to which academic institutions claim property rights). In academia, those who gatekeep and administer academic knowledge are promoted tenured faculty and high-level university administrators who have climbed the ladder of higher education's ranking order and are in positions of power from where they impose the same ranking system on their junior colleagues. They also have authority to declare who has not worked hard enough, not followed proper citation practices, or not produced sufficient scholarship to merit admissions to the elite of academia's permanent professoriate. Supervisors of dissertations, too, must decide to what extent students' contributions to academic knowledge are sufficiently rigorous, generalizable, and empirically valid before deserving to be inducted into membership of academia's loyal powerbrokers.

Thirdly, settler colonialism imports slave labor in chains and renders humans as chattel working in racialized positions of subjugated property and human inferiority (Spillers, 1987). Slave labor is necessary to become chattel, harvest resources of the land, and, through economic stratification and appropriation, ensure that land and property rights are reserved for a much-smaller group of settlers (Tuck & Yang, 2012). In academia, many of its professoriate are competing for the limited resources of higher status reflected in salary and reputation as measured by the numbers of publications and the obtainment of grants. Racist premises narrate the one-way benefitting relationships between researcher and researched and academics and local community members, the latter most frequently living in economically underresourced communities. At the modern university, still under the profit-seeking and private property–owning spell of settler coloniality, the individual pre-and posttenure laboring body is tied to the geographical and ideological terrains of the university by way of adhering to the processes and ethics of knowledge productions that merit induction to academia and promotion in higher education (Wilder, 2014).

Moreover, the systemically appropriated labor of scholars of color is a telling manifestation of how the university's fiscal livelihood depends on the intellectual exploitation and endurance of its always replaceable workers, namely adjunct, nontenure, and pretenure faculty, and, in particular, female workers of color, at the bottom of academia's food chain: those who are trainers and those who are in training. Female faculty and students of color frequently find themselves in extremely tight ontological spaces from where they work through contradictions between "the ever-present external obstacles of indifference and hostility" and our internalized collective commitment to non-Western European radical traditions rooted in love and respect for those who came before us, those with us, and those not yet born (James, 1993, p. 126).

While being "in but not *of* the modern university" (Harney & Moten, 2013, p. 26, emphasis added), I am intentional about referring to some of the abovementioned contours of ongoing settler coloniality in higher education while working with doctoral students as their academic adviser and course instructor. "Settler coloniality in higher education" is the umbrella term I use here to include the historical contexts of modern academic institutions that are steeped in the racist ideology of white supremacy and the economic (capitalist) relations that propel forms of private property, patriarchy, heterosexism, ableism, and xenophobia. To secure the livelihood of the doctoral program I work in, my work contract tells me that the university expects me to train students to become future stewards of knowledge systems that are rooted in the history and development of white and Western European countries. As the settler-colonial university anticipates me to release highly trained wardens and newly minted pioneers of these epistemic traditions into other spaces (most often academic), I find myself increasingly getting uncomfortable and restless with my positioning as a Brown woman who teaches and guides other Brown and Black bodies from within the university. The university expects me to teach and advise doctoral students about the one-sided groundings of academic-research ethics and practices drenched in Western European traditions (Tuck & Guishard, 2013) they will need to have to build a career in academia. This includes training students in adhering to academic institution–protecting research ethics (i.e., building research protocols required by Institutional Research Board) and teaching students about social theories from the same dominating white male and Eurocentric scholarly canon whose scope lacks race-sensitive criticality. Throughout this epistemologically molding of individualizing selves, we are required to alienate ourselves ontologically from our collective roots and communal legacies. It took me several years in academia to raise some of the questions that are bewildering me about my academic (hegemonized settler-colonial epistemic) position: What are some of the fundamental ontological tensions that inform the content of academic advising of female doctoral students of color? What theories and pedagogies help with making these tensions visible? What ought a curriculum for academically advising doctoral students of color be about in light of ongoing settler coloniality in academia?

Toward a Womanist and Anti-Colonial Stance in the University

I wrote this chapter to name and speak to a sample of instances that have been marked by academic pains and shaped by ideological obstacle courses my female doctoral students of color have endured, been paralyzed by, surrendered to, and also so fiercely fought against. I critically reflect on the purposes and intentions of my academic student advising as pedagogical work and collide my critical transnational womanist participatory and anti-colonial stance in student advising with academia's master narrative that delegitimizes community-centered wisdoms, the pedagogical values enacted by liberation movements, and the epistemological arrest (if not death) of non–Western European knowledges (Harney & Moten, 2013; Carruthers, 1999). I position academic student advising to offer possibilities for dialogic communication based on respect and recognition for each other and our collective struggles for manifestations of justice.

My graduate student–advising work is an intentionally disconnected space from academic standards and expectations and from where students and I create collaboratively on striving against aforementioned top-down relations in higher education that ossify "the nastiness in this world" (Robinson, 1983): exploitative economic structures and the social despair and suffering these produce in daily life. I prioritize building more dehierarchized relationships with students to feed mutually benefitting exchanges between us both as messengers—*as opposed to adviser and advisee*. I frequently meet students individually in spaces outside and away from the university to workshop their research designs or talk through the stories they are beginning to hear across the narratives of their research participants. I do not require students to come *to me* at the end of a long and demanding workday, as they most often occupy positions of full-time teachers, school administrators, or afterschool practitioners. Instead, students invite me into their everyday workspaces that have nourished their research desires and that will also bring to light any recommendations they will be making in their final dissertation. We have met in social studies, math, and writing classrooms. I enjoy watching my students interact one last time with their own students at the end of the school day and witnessing their approaches to teaching as they guide young people through homework assignments and mentor them through college applications. My students make time for their high school students, even in the presence of their professor. I take mental notes of what student- and desire-centered pedagogies look like that privilege students' life worlds without trying to fit them into predetermined educational molds and are guided by students' personal desires and visions they have declared for themselves. Rarely do I hear my doctoral students offer solutions that their own schools promote, including "just focus," "you got to work harder," or "you have too much going on" as part of their advice to complete the given task. Instead, they abandon narratives that rely on grit and meritocracy to encourage learning, as they are deeply aware of young people's individual circumstances. The timelines and to-do list they create with and for students honor young people's commitments to family and community relations.

In their classrooms and offices, we have covered the surfaces of floors and desktops with drafted pages of their dissertations to re/organize the content and structure of the stories they wish to tell. We place ourselves on our hands and knees, and I respond to students' requests to move and cut pages to create new paginations on the papers that deliver their expertise. Students direct me on how to be of service to them by documenting their ideas and protecting their edits in ways that mirror their desires and intentions. Together, we listen for the *almosts* and the *not-yets* in their narratives and record their sounds, especially when they think these do not mirror traditions of "academic writing" (read: white and male).

Throughout these conversations, I, too, make my own not-knowing visible to students to learn and grow under their guidance. I, too, become accessible as daughter, mother, caregiver, learner, human. But most important to me is the physical connection between their writing and the time-spaces that ignite their curiosities, passions, and frustrations that have helped them commit to a specific area of inquiry. Repeatedly, students are adamant about their dissertations needing to inform and improve their own daily educational practices and personal relationships with the students they serve and the communities they live in and do not wish for their dissertations to disappear among the dust particles on top of an unvisited bookshelf in the university's library.

This said, I continue to reimagine student academic-advising work at once to be a powerful but also an all-risk-taking curricular space for performing and instilling anti-colonial womanist ways. From my conversations with students, I have learned that anti-colonial and womanist-centered academic-advising work requires a rigorous and intentional abandoning of the internalized knowledge systems we absorbed throughout our schooling years. While this decoupling is absolutely fundamental to interrupting ongoing legacies of settler colonialism in the knowledge traditions that academia privileges and rewards, it is, nonetheless, an act of "epistemic disobedience" (Mignolo, 2015) that turns its back to epistemic master narratives. I have written elsewhere that moving ourselves into "no-places" invites different, previously underpracticed approaches to questioning and learning that are:

> rich and diverse in testimonies and lived expertise with struggles and survival [...] to facilitate a falling in love with each other (with people's radical selves that could not surface otherwise), and with the potential that a "collective not-knowing" holds for reimagining and striving for something new. (Krueger-Henney, 2016, p. 59)

In other words, to learn how to embrace, embody, and enact anti-colonial womanist ways necessitates an unlearning, and this cannot happen in what is commonly referred to as "safe space" that is built on conventions that embrace the permanence of ownership-driven manifestations of status quo and does not battle against the roots of white supremacy and coloniality. Academic spaces are inherently unsafe. Hence, academic advising that enacts anti-colonial womanism is not interested in creating safe spaces; neither does it want nor need safe spaces. I have been listening closely to the words of Patel, who has made an invaluable statement for outlining anti-colonial womanism as pedagogy and theory for academic advising work. By positioning academia as structurally and ideologically intertwined with the settler colonialism of the United States, Patel argues that "learning is a fugitive act" and

> Learning as resistance within a context that creates and contains Black and Brown student bodies and accumulates property rights for a few, cannot be sufficiently described without addressing the intermittent departures from those structures. (2016b, p. 400)

Anti-colonial womanist pedagogies and theorizing are unhinged from standardized curricular instructions and rubrics and unfold in opposition to master, homogenized narratives about people's histories and lived experiences. Anti-colonial, womanist ways of being in and knowing about our world are unpredictable, unsettling, daring, nonlinear, communal, at times dangerous when we risk our admissions to and promotions (and our livelihoods!) within settler-colonial institutions. I contend that anti-colonial, womanist ways for being with each other in and knowing about our world are an undeniable lifesaving force to reckon with!

On the remaining pages of this chapter, I write a letter in the form of a reflective stream of thoughts I wish to dedicate to my female doctoral students of color. In this letter I recall and think through some of the specific academic-advising conversations, moments, and connections I have had with them. The aforementioned social and ideological deconstructions of settler colonialism are fundamental to my commitments, troubles, and articulations of my advising work that stands in the service of the daily unfolding of an anti-colonial womanist politic in academia.

My use of "you," "I," "we," and "us" is deliberate. I also conflate them in order to point to an ontological intimacy between my students and me. Nonetheless, I am not blind to the power my position as a university worker holds over their academic success. This is the difference between "you" and "I." The "we" and "us," however, hinge in white supremacy and systemically silence and erase us as women of color in doctoral programs and tenured university faculty. With the "we" and "us" and "our," I forefront these structures and their circuitous, dispossessing configurations to connect us at once to a collectivized knowledge of other women of color in academia everywhere around the world (Fine & Ruglis, 2009). The letter's narrative, then, is both biographic of and dialogic with our collective selves; the "you" is always and already inscribed in "I" and "us."

With a collectivized "us," I intend to highlight the dearth of our bodies in academia and the knowledges and subjectivities we embody. According to the National Center for Education Statistics:

> Of all full-time faculty in degree-granting postsecondary institutions in fall 2016, 41 percent were White males; 35 percent were White females; 6 percent were

Asian/Pacific Islander males; 4 percent were Asian/Pacific Islander females; 3 percent each were Black males, Black females, and Hispanic males; and 2 percent were Hispanic females. Those who were American Indian/Alaska Native and those who were of two or more races each made up 1 percent or less of full-time faculty in these institutions. (US Department of Education, 2018)

Similarly, of the 178,547 doctoral students who completed a degree in the 2014–2015 academic year, only 21 percent were women of color (US Department of Education, 2016). Various factors contribute to the low numbers of non-white female doctoral students and faculty members of color in academic spaces, including a lack of mentorship and support services for female doctoral students, racist and xenophobic campus environments, and lack of opportunities to access resources that are vital to practice scholarly skills. Amid the scarcity of our bodies in academia's racist and dispossessing spaces, I assume, in my letter, an intellectual and emotional closeness with my female students of color to emphasize that the racist settler-colonial university has created social realities we share. In *The Undercommons: Fugitive Planning and Black Study* (2013), Stefano Harney and Fred Moten describe this closeness to be a process, a historicized product: "Though forced to touch and be touched, to sense and be sensed in that space of no space, through refused sentiment, history and home, we feel (for) each other" (p. 98). As female doctoral students and pretenure faculty of color, our physical proximity is the result of our shared position at the bottom of academia's racist, capitalist ranking system: a cadre of replaceable, exploitable, manageable laborers.

Dear Doctoral Student: A Stream of Thoughts about Us

I do not know how else to be in this world as my sense of self is always in direct relationship with you. And through the forces of our bodies, rage, courageous tears, joys, and truth-telling power, we give re/birth to our anti-colonial, transnational, womanist selves. It is in the carefully crafted and quiet spaces behind closed doors where we shatter settler-colonialism logics in higher education and instill in each other's hearts an unyielding beat that upholds our humanity. We hold our breath while we also remind each other of how our willful breathing is our collective disruption "to the epistemology, the theology-philosophy, that produces a world, a set of protocols, wherein black flesh cannot easily breathe" (Crawley, 2017, p. 3).

I am not claiming that my academic advising leads to the systemic decolonization of land, labor, people. But I contend that our conversations plant seeds for an epistemologically and ontologically unsettling of conventions that reveal the colonial ghosts inside contemporary social structures by way of an earnest naming of what we do *not* know about each other and about the world. I seek to replace Eurocentric pillars with Black and Brown, feminist, antiracist, collaborative, and community-centered texts on which we lay down our insights and conclusions. Our anti-colonial stances are further strengthened by ousting ongoing systems of mind control and the ways we explain our relationality to the mundaneness of our institutional lives. I am beginning to see how much of our conversations about your academic progress and task completion shatters the settler-colonial grounds of the university. I see our words and hopes standing in the service of anti-colonial womanism holding because they compose messages of epistemic fugitivity and pedagogies of hope, joy, transnational solidarities, and an unapologetic dedication to our social survival outside our current restrictive, violently anti-Black, racist, commodifying, private property–seeking, exploitative social realities. Most significantly, and by wholeheartedly embracing Joyce King's call to dismantle "epistemological nihilation" (2017), anti-colonial, womanist advising work sparks knowledge mobilization toward epistemological sovereignty and the freedom and courage to govern over our own production and maintenance of knowledge systems without interference from white and male colleagues.

Any specific moments of our conversation that I remember here appear like beads of mantras carefully strung together in no particular order. I have repeatedly "worn" these with a stubborn will, to remove the haze draped over my eyes in moments when I am not able to recognize how academia is isolating me from my communities and dissecting my professional performances into three distinct floor routines: teaching, service, and research. Make no mistake, our productivity feeds all tentacles of the permanently hungry academic-industrial complex. Every conversation with students has been deeply personal and professional; we do not (re)imagine ourselves as scattered bits and pieces of ourselves. The splitting of our personal and professional selves is academia's most prized venom as it "implies that well-roundedness is a pathology, the equivalent of academic arrested development, and it condemns our real black women's lives as at best inconsequential precisely because we find this well-roundedness unavoidable and vital" (Phillips & McCaskill, 1995, p. 1015). Every day, and during each advising conversation, we weave together a vast and fearless tapestry of rationales and impact we are expected to leave behind.

An Invitation to Anti-Colonial Womanist Student Academic Advising

This right here, the bond between you and me, is not new. We are extensions of struggles that began centuries ago, everywhere. I dream of us being power circuit-breaking warriors in these academic spaces that lack reverberations of our ancestors' legacies. But here we are in admiration for each other without being in collaboration with each other. This is the tragedy of our genius. The systemic distancing and hierarchizing between my tenure track–chase and your all-but-dissertation status are unsettling me for many reasons, as documented practices for doctoral advisee-adviser relationships usually do not illuminate some of the ethical tensions I have encountered since I stepped into the role of being a university worker. Our relationship is political, and this makes us political subjects. We are each other's most reliable and dependable compass, and it guides any advice I may have for you.

Look, you are writing your dissertation proposal, seeking permission to produce knowledge from a social institution that is tainted with unethical, if not violent (research) traditions across time-spaces etched into the histories of our commodified bodies (Skloot, 2011). Unsure of how to determine your market worth, you have changed your research focus two times during the last six months. But more important, you have shown that you are not sentimental about letting go of versions of yourself that only matter to academia's gaze. And you continue to reinvent yourself over and over again until your performance is flawless. Please stop. Which version of yourself do you want to and can you, must you live with?

Last week you spoke to me with angry tears about wanting to honor the betrayal and disappointment you absorbed from your participatory and community-centered coresearchers; academia thirsts for knowledge productions that perpetuate the damage done to our communities (Tuck, 2009), instead of privileging the hard work of our research participants as expert knowledge holders about the structural mechanisms that regurgitate deficit labels of being culturally impoverished (Kelley, 1997) and perpetually helplessness (Goffman, 2015). Seldom do we learn in schools about how our communities have *always* fought systemic racism and economic structures of exploitation (Au, Brown, & Calderón, 2016, emphasis added). The young people we research will fight hard and refuse to be fed alive to the forces of damage-centered discourses that demand you to remain objective about the banalities of white supremacy and the epistemological negation of the wisdom that communities of color possess (King, 2017). You have also fought hard against the violence of dominant knowledge paradigms that want to freeze us into silenced and catatonic bystanders. You are alive and, thus, wise to recognize how academia's dispossessing protocols implicate us all. There are no insider or outsider options for doing research about people, their lives, their land, and the profound relationalities among people, their lives, and land.

Inside the window-less space of my office, together, we often wonder, crave, and demand: How do researchers avoid the pathologizing dangers of telling single-sided stories about people's complex lives (Adichie, 2009)? What do we gain from conducting research that demands us to disentangle ourselves from the lived lives of people who entrust us with documenting who they are, what they fear, and also what they are ashamed of? You ask, what counts as evidence? And I wonder, what futurities can y/our research advocate for from within the epistemological spaces of hegemonized research logics?

We could potentially become collaborators, accomplices, in world-changing scientific inquiry, but we first learn about how to be suspicious of each other. While I drill you to fit your research desires into the mold of heavily prescribed dissertation protocols we inherited from the coloniality of generalizable research designs (Patel, 2016a), you, in similar spirit, run internet searches on the productivity, relevance, and my preparedness for what I am doing to you. Our bodies are trapped by the same racist and merit-driven knowledge brokers that measure the impact of our intellectual labor and the extent to which we participate in protecting Western European whiteness as the primary and perhaps only photographic lens through which we can see and become visible to each other (Wynter, 2003). Truth is, our visibility is juxtaposed by our social invisibility at large. This is what makes my advising work at times unbearable, painful, impossible, and extremely fictitious.

Academia also demands from me to instill in you discipline-specific skills, in particular, "proper" citation practices. Who and what we cite tend to regurgitate genealogies of the white settler-colonial state and, along with it, numerous codes of ethics it has violated. Foregrounding the accomplishment and advancement of whiteness secures the absence of melanin-rich expertise, brilliance, genius. However, whiteness as commodified and privately owned property is the primary mode through which we are asked to circulate our intellectual work. It is through my liberating attempts to move our relationship outside the jurisdiction of academia's white Eurocentric gaze and from where I can only dream of unscripting protocols for us about who we are to each other and what we are capable of doing. I ask you, does academia deserve our stories about strategizing and surviving?

The violence through which academia reigns over us is always physical. The white settler-colonial university feeds off of our bodies and maximizes on our assumed able-bodied-ness. Yet, our Black and Brown bodies are looked at and feared as the crazies in need of taming; the living savages to be watched, questioned, doubted, dominated, socially disinvested, studied, fixed, and overcome. We disguise our despair and anger with daytime performances that please and assure our white colleagues. The objectification of our non-whiteness will always nourish tidal waves of coloniality for as long as we are positioned to lick our own wounds and operate despite the pain and paralysis these structural assaults unleash onto us. We think thrice about ways to respond and offer feedback and recommendations using language they can hear and understand. Under settler-colonial ideology, our physical and mental injuries are evidence for their authenticity. Our objectification guarantees coloniality's longevity.

We cannot forget at what costs we earn our degrees and promotions as doctoral students and teaching university faculty. Our lineages are blood stained. We bring our hopes to the university and invest ourselves in leading efforts of institutional changes we expect to see after mobilizing some of the university's resources. But Robin Kelley (2016) reminds us that we cannot be sentimental about the university being a place for social transformation. Public learning institutions have always been sites of cultural genocide and social control (Sojoyner, 2016); the curriculum of knowledge production injects docility into our Black and Brown backbones. While in this doctoral program and, similarly, in a tenure-track position, we are on training grounds for an epistemologically reconditioning of our hearts, bodies, and minds.

You are soon to join the new cadre of university workers and in charge of advancing social sciences research. And you, too, are expected to be productive with minting future university workers. Your writer's block may signify both resistance and willful determination to make sense out of these contradictions: on one hand, you are the first in your family to obtain a doctoral degree. And that fills us both with pride and hope. On the other hand, this degree will also epistemologically and ontologically distance you from the places you call home and the people you love. We had many meetings during which you asked me to feed you spoonsful of stamina and what you thought was my own lived wisdom about how to push through this historical but yet life-threatening labyrinth in which we are both incessantly running around.

You already know how you fit the student profile that the university brags about being committed to: you are a product of a local K–12 public school system chronically injured by systemic underfunding. My white colleagues admire you for your resilience, for your drive, and passion to surviving despite the many traps designed to fail and destroy you and the many others who look like you, sound like you, think like you. While in this program, you have continued to teach some of the city's most underserved and educationally denied. Yet, your accomplishments will be known through damage-centered perspectives that Indigenous scholar Eve Tuck (2009) cautioned us about. What must we do so that your doctoral degree is not positioned to be the savior that lifts you out of the materially dilapidated conditions of life and places you into the (false) ideological spaces of intellectual elitism?

Then there is me. My work as a faculty person deeply implicates me in this white settler-colonial logic the university sanctions. Perhaps similar to you, I live through everyday crises fed by an irresolute but yet hopeful state of mind. My contract positions me to service a manufactured dependence on the university for social mobility. I am entrusted with instilling "scientific skills" in you and other students who are preferably historically underrepresented in higher education and

Dear Doctoral Student of Color

who have overcome personal hardships. The university banks on us doing miracle work. Academic institutions love collecting stories about their accomplishments of saving people who work hard despite the paralyzing material conditions they come from—as long as they can demonstrate how hard they have worked to make something out of themselves. I don't believe in miracles.

During annual admissions season, my work embodies this bridge between identifying those who show potential and promise to be trained in maintaining dominant logics of scientific knowledge production in autopilot. I am your epistemological sculptor, your ultrasound technician, who ensures that your internal and external conceptualizations of social phenomena are in unison with the meritocratic mission of social science scholarship. I am here to feed you legitimized cultural capital that will allow you to excel, survive, and flaunt your expert knowledge. I am expected to act on behalf of this white settler-colonial institution while also sustaining scrutinizing investigations of my own value to academia.

I find reassurance in what Tuck and K. Wayne Yang have called "research refusal" (2014). My student-advising practices willfully resist voluntary fertilization of hegemonized academic relations. Tuck and Yang write, "Refusal, and stances of refusal in research, are attempts to place limits on conquest and the colonization of knowledge by marking what is off limits, what is not up for grabs or discussion, what is sacred, and what can't be known" (225). My refusal to participate in the coloniality in academia manifests in a series of deliberate moving and pausing I encourage you to make with me. These often start with you reading over and over again a few pressing comments as feedback on drafts of your dissertation writing: my handwritten notes often read "monolithic; please offer a more nuanced explanation" or "this is a generalization about people's lives." Your work is our collective construction site where we excavate to resuscitate our silenced roots and our multifaceted realities. My comments are my nudging to remind us both of the importance of not participating in easy-to-tell stories about our and other people's lived lives with the self-serving methodological tools we have inherited from knowledge systems built on atrocities committed through systemic dispossession and death. The rage and joy our conversations feed me are my invitation to you to join me in interrupting social science research and refusing to participate in the silencing of all forms of structural racism always embedded in the stories academia tells us about us and our communities.

Many times, our conversations take place off campus. We meet at a local coffee shop or in my living room to shed away our protective layers and feel emotionally and physically freed from the ideological violence we endure while on campus to talk about reimaginations of ourselves and our social, materialized worlds. I passionately believe that truth-telling writings by us, about us, and for us can only be mind-altering when we separate our narratives from tropes and canons. We eat meals together, are each other's witness to our hesitations, and are accomplices in creating mirrors and reflections for each other. And while we give voice to our dreams and make fearless declarations of hope and desire, our children play together in the other room.

To Be Continued. I Love You

Anti-colonial womanist work in student academic advising is tainted by some level of cruelty I am committing against students and myself. On one hand, I am asking you to lift your fears and be excited about politicizing our relationships with academia and recognize that our lives can be, and already are, different. Through our cocreations of transformative and liberating visions of and for each other, I wish to infect you with a radical optimism about all the changes to come. But, on the other hand, and according to Lauren Berlant (2011), this is a "cruel optimism" that both guides our desires and becomes an obstacle to our flourishing within the constraining social conditions around us. Speaking our minds and standing up against oppressive structures have shown to be brave endeavors, at times even quite dangerous, and we could potentially never see the successful completion of our dissertations or tenure reviews. Yet, everything about our futurity is at stake if we do not dare to dream and love openly, generously.

With a village of people behind you, who readied you to be here and in the right-now, and who will continue to throw you lifelines stronger than material goods, I invite you to take a leap of faith beyond the writing of your dissertation. But make no mistake, I will join the celebrations of you and the acknowledgments of the sacrifices you and your loved ones have made for you to reach this historical moment for all of us. This leap, however, necessitates our willful abandonment of sentimental attachments to defaulted normatives. It is not an elegant leap but, rather, a clumsy and injury-prone stepping into fully embracing anti-colonial transnational womanisms while not knowing whether or not we will always land on our feet. The grounds we stand on still lack sufficient fertility, but the season is coming, it is near. I remain energized by the possibility of weaving together our readings of the world so that we can be strategic and deliberate about building practices for recovery, reciprocity, and regeneration that benefit us mutually and collectively. In this awkward leap toward our anti-colonial, transnational womanist ways of being in tune with the world, I am asking: what in-between spaces in the master's house *must* we build together and occupy to be with each other—emotionally, intellectually, historically, materially—despite his narrative that tells us we do not belong here? It is this kind of out-of-sync-ness that anti-colonial womanist love for each other demands from us and that drives and defines my commitment to advising you.

I am desiring our collective liberation from the ongoing tyranny of the anti-Black, racist, heterosexist, ableist, patriarchal, white, settler-colonial state we encounter at the university and everywhere else. I hold on dearly to what Crystal Laura tells us: "Love acts are driven by the notion that every human being deserves to live fully and freely in the world, and that each of us is an expert on the qualities of our own experiences" (2013, p. 291). You are not a miracle. While it has taken you, us, an extraordinary amount of effort to fight ourselves into these spaces, our relationship to the historicity of our futurity is not chimeric. We belong here, in living flesh.

Finally, and in summary, perhaps, every time we meet, you show me how anti-colonial womanism as pedagogy and theory resides within your daily thinking and writing. Specifically, you teach me about how inserting ourselves into the exclusive spaces of academia needs to be fueled by three courageous practices that are interwoven with all the thinking and talking and writing we do as anti-colonial womanist pedagogues and theorists and that shatter the systemic erasure, commodification of knowledge, and enslavement work of the white settler university: self-introspection to scrutinize the (single-sided) knowledge we have been exposed to and have internalized about ourselves and our communities; self-reflection to name our expertise in our lived experiences with legacies of settler colonialism in academia and elsewhere in everyday life; and enacting proclamations of ourselves and our knowledges as legitimate and irreplaceable (Sumner, 2018).

You have my heart-felt admiration and respect. I am yours, always and truly.

References

Adichie, C. N. (2009, July). *Chimamanda Ngozi Adichie: The danger of a single story* [Video file]. Retrieved from https://www.ted.com/talks/

Au, W., Brown, A. L., & Calderón, D. (2016). *Reclaiming the multicultural roots of US curriculum: Communities of color and official knowledge in education*. New York, NY: Teachers College Press.

Berlant, L. G. (2011). *Cruel optimism*. Durham, NC: Duke University Press.

Berry, T. R., & Mizelle, N. D. (2006). *From oppression to grace: Women of color and their dilemmas in the academy*. Herndon, VA: Stylus.

Cannon, K. (2006). *Black womanist ethics*. Eugene, OR: Wipf and Stock.

Carruthers, J. (1999). *Intellectual warfare*. Chicago, IL: Third World Press.

Crawley, A. T. (2017). *Blackpentecostal breath: The aesthetics of possibility*. New York, NY: Fordham University Press.

Fine, M., & Ruglis, J. (2009). Circuits and consequences of dispossession: The racialized realignment of the public sphere for US youth. *Transforming Anthropology, 17*(1), 20–33.

Goffman, A. (2015). *On the run: Fugitive life in an American city.* New York, NY: Picador.

Gutiérrez y Muhs, G., Niemann, Y. F., Gonzalez, C. G., & Harris, A. P. (2012). *Presumed incompetent: The intersections of race and class for women in academia.* Logan: Utah State University Press.

Harney, S. M., & Moten, F. (2013). *The undercommons: Fugitive planning and Black study.* Brooklyn, NY: Minor Compositions.

Hill Collins, P. (1999). *Black feminist thought: Knowledge, consciousness, and the politics of empowerment.* New York, NY: Routledge.

James, J.(1993). Teaching theory, talking community. In J. James & R. Farmer (Eds.), *Spirit, space & survival: African American women in (white) academe* (pp. 118–135). New York, NY: Routledge.

Kelley, R. D. G. (1997). *Yo' mama's dysfunctional! Fighting the culture wars in urban America.* Boston, MA: Beacon.

Kelley, R. D. G. (2016). Black study, Black struggle. *Boston Review, 7.*

King, J. E. (2017). 2015 AERA presidential address: Morally engaged research/ers: Dismantling epistemological nihilation in the age of impunity. *Educational Researcher, 46*(5), 211–222.

Krueger-Henney, P. (2016). What are we listening for? (Participatory action) research and embodied social listening to the permanence of anti-black racism in education. *International Journal of Critical Pedagogy, 7*(3), 49–66.

Laura, C. T. (2013). Intimate inquiry: Love as "data" in qualitative research. *Cultural Studies↔Critical Methodologies, 13*(4), 289–292.

Mignolo, W. D. (2015). Sylvia Wynter: What does it mean to be human? In K. McKittrick (Ed.), *Sylvia Wynter: On being human as praxis* (pp. 106–123). Durham, NC: Duke University Press.

Patel, L. (2016a). *Decolonizing educational research: From ownership to answerability.* New York, NY: Routledge.

Patel, L. (2016b). Pedagogies of resistance and survivance: Learning as marronage. *Equity & Excellence in Education, 49*(4), 397–401.

Phillips, L., & McCaskill, B. (1995). Who's schooling who? Black women and the bringing of the everyday into academe, or why we started "the womanist." *Signs: Journal of Women in Culture and Society, 20*(4), 1007–1018.

Robinson, C. J. (1983). *Black Marxism: The making of the Black radical tradition.* Chapel Hill: University of North Carolina Press.

Skloot, R. (2011). *The immortal life of Henrietta Lacks.* New York, NY: Broadway Books.

Smith, A. (2016). Heteropatriarchy and the three pillars of white supremacy: Rethinking women of color organizing. In INCITE! (Ed.), *Color of violence: The INCITE! anthology* (pp. 66–73). Durham, NC: Duke University Press.

Sojoyner, D. M. (2016). *First strike: Educational enclosures in Black Los Angeles.* Minneapolis: University of Minnesota Press.

Spillers, H. J. (1987). Mama's baby, papa's maybe: An American grammar book. *Diacritics, 17*(2), 64–81.

Sumner, K. A. (2018). *Native daughter: A lived experience of desegregation* (Doctoral dissertation). University of Massachusetts Boston.

Taliaferro Baszile, D., Edwards, K. T., & Guillory, N. A. (2016). *Race, gender, and curriculum: Theorizing working in womanish ways.* Lanham, MD: Lexington.

Thompson, B. (2017). *Teaching with tenderness: Toward an embodied practice.* Chicago: University of Illinois Press.

Tuck, E. (2009). Suspending damage: A letter to communities. *Harvard Educational Review, 79*(3), 409–428.

Tuck, E., & Guishard, M. (2013). Uncollapsing ethics: Racialized sciencism, settler coloniality, and an ethical framework of decolonial participatory action research. In T. Kress, Curry S. Malott, & Brad J. Portfilio (Eds.), *Challenging status quo retrenchment: New directions in critical qualitative research* (pp. 3–27). Charlotte, NC: Information Age.

Tuck, E., & Yang, K. W. (2012). Decolonization is not a metaphor. *Decolonization, Indigeneity, Education & Society 1*(1). Retrieved November 4, 2018, from https://jps.library.utoronto.ca/index.php/des/article/view/18630

Tuck, E., & Yang, K. W. (2014). R-Words: Refusing research. In D. Paris & M. T. Winn (Eds.), *Humanizing research: Decolonizing qualitative inquiry with youth and communities* (pp. 223–247). Thousand Oaks, CA: SAGE.

US Department of Education. National Center for Education Statistics. (2016). "Degrees and other formal awards conferred." Higher Education General Information Survey (HEGIS), Surveys, 1976–77 and 1980–81; "Completions survey." Integrated Postsecondary Education Data System, IPEDS-C:90–99); "Completions component." IPEDS Fall 2000 through Fall 2015. Retrieved from https://nces.ed.gov/programs/digest/d16/tables/dt16_324.20.asp

US Department of Education. National Center for Education Statistics. (2018). *The condition of education 2018* (NCES 2018–144), Characteristics of Postsecondary Faculty. Retrieved from https://nces.ed.gov/fastfacts/display.asp?id=61

Wilder, C. S. (2014). *Ebony and ivy: Race, slavery, and the troubled history of America's universities.* New York, NY: Bloomsbury.

Woodson, C. G. (1993). *The mis-education of the negro.* Trenton, NJ: Africa World.

Wynter, S. (2003). Unsettling the coloniality of being/power/truth/freedom: Towards the human, after man, its overrepresentation—An argument. *CR: The New Centennial Review, 3*(3), 257–337.

Contributors

SILVIA GARCÍA AGUILÁR is a *promotora* specialist in healing practices with Healing the Soul—Curando el Alma—Na' Sanna'e Ini'e in the Mixteco/Indigena community and conducts outreach and research within the community. She works for Mixteco/Indigena Community Organizing Project's (MICOP) Every Woman Counts project and as an interpreter in Oxnard, California, school districts. Before moving to the United States, she lived in San Martin Peras, Oaxaca, with her grandparents and became interested in how her grandmother cured people. She has certification in Usui/Holy Fire Reiki 1 and 2 and is studying to become a Reiki master. Selected publications include *Co-decolonizing Research Methods: Toward Research Sustaining Indigenous and "Other" Community Engaged Ways of Knowing* (2021) and *Black, African American, and Migrant Indigenous Women in Leadership: Voices and Practices Informing Critical HRD* (2022), both with the collective.

KHALILAH ALI is an assistant professor of education foundations, secondary methods, and clinical experiences at Spelman College. A social-cultural theoretician of education, Ali's current research focuses on literacy and Black women teacher identity. She is working on a manuscript that examines the ways in which Black women culture workers who are teachers and/or adult allies for youth in schools or in out-of-school (OST) contexts construct radical Black artist-educator-activists identities as expressed through hip-hop, spoken word, visual art, or performative texts. By observing the dialogic evident in the classroom or educative communal event, her research attempts to discover the hidden and overt meanings of those social interactions and their importance in fostering literacy communities.

ADRIANA DIEGO is a garden coordinator at Community Roots Garden and a field specialist at Abundant Table Farm. She is an Oxnard Native who works in a range of community organizer/collective capacities toward social and Indigenous justice. She was a research assistant and evaluation coordinator with Healing the Soul—Curando el Alma—Na' Sanna'e Ini'e and has served as project coordinator and supervisor for Mixteco/Indigena Community Organizing Project's (MICOP) Conexión con Mis Compañeras. Diego has certification in Usui/Holy Fire Reiki 1 and 2 and is studying to become a Reiki master. She is also a founder of and volunteers for the Oxnard Heirloom Seed Library. Selected publications include *Co-decolonizing Research Methods: Toward Research Sustaining Indigenous and "Other" Community Engaged Ways of Knowing* (2021) and *Black, African American, and Migrant Indigenous Women in Leadership: Voices and Practices Informing Critical HRD* (2022), both with the collective.

LECONTÉ J. DILL is an associate professor in the Department of African American and African Studies at Michigan State University. In her work as a community-accountable scholar, educator, creative writer, and artist, she listens to and shows up for urban Black girls and works to rigorously document and amplify their experiences of safety, resilience, resistance, and wellness. Dill's scholarly and creative works have been published in a diverse array of spaces, such as *Feminist Anthropology, The Feminist Wire, Poetry Magazine, Health Promotion Practice,* and *Mom Egg Review.*

SAMEENA EIDOO is an award-winning educator and an assistant professor in the Department of Curriculum, Teaching, and Learning, Ontario Institute for Studies in Education, University of Toronto. She is the author of *Shaping Muslim Futures: Youth Visions and Activist Praxis* (2021).

GENEVIEVE FLORES-HARO serves as the associate director for the Mixteco/Indigena Community Organizing Project (MICOP), overseeing the organization's policy priorities, special events, and communications. She currently serves as board president for Ventura County's local LGBTQ organization Diversity Collective and for the Planned Parenthood Central Coast Action Fund and is a founding member and board president of the 805 UndocuFund. She also supervises MICOP programs specific to health access and advocacy, families with children ages 0 to 5, unaccompanied minors, mental health, and domestic violence. In 2021 she was appointed to the Ventura County Behavioral Health Advisory Board and represents MICOP on the Ventura County Public Safety Racial Equity Advisory Group. She is also an alternate for disability, access, and functional needs on the Ventura County Emergency

Planning Council. During the COVID-19 pandemic, her focus was on advocating for farmworker labor rights, mask distributions (for both healthcare workers and farmworkers), language access, and safety-net programs for undocumented Californians. In 2018 she was awarded a Women of the Year Award for her work during the Thomas Fire. Selected publications include *Co-decolonizing Research Methods: Toward Research Sustaining Indigenous and "Other" Community Engaged Ways of Knowing* (2021) and *Black, African American, and Migrant Indigenous Women in Leadership: Voices and Practices Informing Critical HRD* (2022), both with the collective.

JILLIAN FORD is an associate professor of social studies education at Kennesaw State University. As a queer Black abolitionist teacher, scholar, and community member, she values individual and collective well-being. Ford honors the land on which she lives and works, which is the unceded territory of the Muscogee (Creek) Nation. Ever aware of the enslaved caretakers of this land, she is learning to grow vegetables as a means of ancestral connection. Her work has been published in *Journal of Curriculum Theorizing* and *Journal of Lesbian Studies*, in addition to several edited volumes.

LEENA N. HER is currently director of Academic Support Services at Calbright College, an adult learner–serving institution within the California Community College system. She has been an educator for over twenty years. As an educator, she is focused on developing programs and resources to disrupt inequitable access to schooling for immigrant and BIPOC students.

NATHALIA E. JARAMILLO is professor of interdisciplinary studies at Kennesaw State University, Atlanta, Georgia. She has lectured throughout Latin America and in Spain, Finland, Turkey, Greece, and Portugal. A selection of her coauthored and single-authored work has been translated into Spanish, Portuguese, Greek, and Turkish. Her work is interdisciplinary and examines questions around culture, politics, gender, and epistemology, utilizing the frameworks of decolonial and feminist thought. She is the author of *Immigration and the Challenge of Education* (2012) and coeditor of *Epistemologies of Ignorance in Education* (2011) and has written extensively in the fields of critical educational thought and politics of education.

PATRICIA KRUEGER-HENNEY is an associate professor in the urban education, leadership, and policy studies doctoral program at the University of Massachusetts Boston. Before entering academia, she taught social sciences in high schools and organized with multiple youth communities around issues of (in)justice. Her research responds to the power and wisdom of young people. Her publications include articles in *Curriculum Inquiry* and *Girlhood Studies*, both in 2019, and a chapter, "Trapped inside a Poisoned Maze: Mapping Young People's Geographies of Disposability in

Neoliberal Times of School Disinvestment," in *Critically Researching Youth*, edited by Shirley R. Steinberg and Awad Ibrahim (2016).

LUISA LEÓN SALAZÁR is a promotora specialist for Healing the Soul—Curando el Alma—Na' Sanna'e Ini'e. She also works as a promotora specialist with el proyecto Voz de la Mujer Indígena at Mixteco/Indigena Community Organizing Project (MICOP). She conducts outreach for Voz and research within the Curando el Alma community. She is originally from Guadalupe Morelos, Oaxaca, Mexico, and her knowledge of Indigenous medicine comes from her mother. León Salazár specializes in energetic and Indigenous healing practices. She has certification in Usui/Holy Fire Reiki 1 and 2 and is studying to become a Reiki master. Selected publications include *Co-decolonizing Research Methods: Toward Research Sustaining Indigenous and "Other" Community Engaged Ways of Knowing* (2021) and *Black, African American, and Migrant Indigenous Women in Leadership: Voices and Practices Informing Critical HRD* (2022), both with the collective.

CLAUDIA LOZÁNO is a promotora specialist for Healing the Soul—Curando el Alma—Na' Sanna'e Ini'e in Mixteco/Indígena and is a community development coordinator for the nonprofit organization Community Action of Ventura County. She specializes in energetic Indigenous healing practices and conducts outreach and research within the community. She attributes her love of nature to her grandparents, and in nature and the wisdom of her ancestors she has found peace and strength. She has certification in Usui/Holy Fire Reiki 1 and 2 and is studying to become a Reiki master. Selected publications include *Co-decolonizing Research Methods: Toward Research Sustaining Indigenous and "Other" Community Engaged Ways of Knowing* (2021) and *Black, African American, and Migrant Indigenous Women in Leadership: Voices and Practices Informing Critical HRD* (2022), both with the collective.

LILIANA MANRIQUEZ is an Oxnard Native, raised by two Mexican immigrant parents. She is a research assistant and evaluation coordinator for Mixteco/Indigena Community Organizing Project's (MICOP) Healing the Soul—Curando el Alma—Na' Sanna'e Ini'e, where she is utilizing her degrees in psychology and Mexican American studies to help better the people in her community. Manriquez also is a project coordinator for Proyecto Acceso with MICOP. She has been a teaching assistant, community organizer, and student outreach for higher education. Her goal is to do work that makes an impact to the people in underserved and underrepresented communities; and, most important, she values the impact of her family. Selected publications include *Co-decolonizing Research Methods: Toward Research Sustaining Indigenous and "Other" Community Engaged Ways of Knowing* (2021) and *Black, African*

American, and Migrant Indigenous Women in Leadership: Voices and Practices Informing Critical HRD (2022), both with the collective.

ANGELA MALONE CARTWRIGHT is the director of Diversity Initiatives and Community Engagement in the Division of Diversity, Equity, and Inclusion at West Virginia University. Malone Cartwright taught secondary social studies and elementary social studies and literacy, was principal lecturer for academic development at the University of Sunderland in London, and was tenured associate faculty in Midwestern State University's West College of Education. Her articles have been published in *Teachers College Record, Educational Foundations,* and *International Journal of Education and Social Science,* and her chapters have appeared in multiple edited volumes. Cartwright has also coedited three volumes, and one is forthcoming.

ALBERTA SALAZÁR is a *mamá* and pillar of the local Mixteco community and a *promotora* specialist for Healing the Soul—Curando el Alma—Na' Sanna'e Ini'e. She is the head ethnobotanist/herbalist specializing in the curative use and application of medicinal plants, herbs, and gardening as related to energetic and Indigenous healing practices. Originally from San Francisco de Higos, Oaxaca, Mexico, she observed her mother and other women healing their town using herbs and other Indigenous medicines. She was a teacher for the Mixteco/Indigena Community Organizing Project (MICOP) and *promotora* of a number of MICOP projects, including childcare. She has certification in Usui/Holy Fire Reiki 1 and 2 and is studying to become a Reiki master. Selected publications include *Co-decolonizing Research Methods: Toward Research Sustaining Indigenous and "Other" Community Engaged Ways of Knowing* (2021) and *Black, African American, and Migrant Indigenous Women in Leadership: Voices and Practices Informing Critical HRD* (2022), both with the collective.

LORRI J. SANTAMARÍA is the director of faculty development and inclusive excellence at California Lutheran University. She is a former director and principal investigator for the collective Healing the Soul—Curando el Alma—Na' Sanna'e Ini'e and director for Proyecto ACCESO at the Mixteco/Indigena Community Organizing Project (MICOP). She was a professor of multilingual and multicultural education and educational leadership in the School of Education at California State University, San Marcos, and at the University of Auckland in New Zealand. With over fifty scholarly books and publications, her research interests are centered around critical aspects of social justice and equity, decoloniality, Indigeneity, Indigenous healing, and diversity as a resource. Her focus is on international culturally responsive/sustainable educational leadership, spiritual activism, and antiracist research practices. In 2017 she was granted the Jeffrey V. Bennett Award for Outstanding International Research for the University Council of Educational Administration. Selected publications include

Co-decolonizing Research Methods: Toward Research Sustaining Indigenous and "Other" Community Engaged Ways of Knowing (2021) and *Black, African American, and Migrant Indigenous Women in Leadership: Voices and Practices Informing Critical HRD* (2022), both with the collective; and *Culturally Responsive Leadership in Higher Education* (2015) and *Applied Leadership in Education* (2012), both with Andrés Santamaría.

Index

Note: Page numbers in *italics* denote figures.

Abdi, Ali, 69
Alim, H. Samuel, 87, 102, 136–37, 138
Aluli-Meyer, Manulani, 97, 100
Anarcha, 120, 129n4
Ancient Immortals, 14–15
anger, 142, 146, 149, 163
anti-communism, 53
Antonio-Damian, Pancho, 97
Anzaldúa, Gloria, 3, 9, 40, 88, 90, 94, 106, 108, 113
Arvin, M., 80
Asad, T., 80–81
Atlanta, Georgia, 15, 121
Atlanta University Center (AUC), 121
"At Risk" (Dill), 115
Avery, Billye Y., 122

Baartman, Saartjie, 20
Bakare-Yusuf, Bibi, 24
Bambara, Toni Cade, 35
Bamboo among the Oaks (Moua), 61, 64, 65
Bell, Barbara, 122
Beloved (Morrison), 128–29n3
Benjamin, Regina, 123
Berlant, Lauren, 166
Bethune, Mary McLeod, 120

Betsey, 120, 129n4
Bhabha, Homi K., 54–55, 64, 105
Black femininity, 13, 14, 19–22, 29n2
Black Indigenous and women of color (BIP[W]OC), 85, 87, 90–91, 101, 102, 104–7, 108n2
Black Panther Party, 123
Black Woman, The (Bambara), 144
Black women, 13–14, 119–20, 123, 126, 129; archetypal images, 15, ethics, 93; as expendable commodities, 22; perspectives of, 28, teachers, 45. *See also* Black femininity; violence: medical
Bland, Sandra, 13, 16, 27, 28–29n1
Bodies That Matter (Butler), 18
Boggs, Grace Lee, 3, 5, 139–43, 148–49
Bonilla, Yarimar, 122
Boyd, Rekia, 13
breath, 41–42
Brown Girls Yoga (BGY), 139, 147–48, 150
Brown, Ruth Nicole, 129n5

Calling in the Soul (Symonds), 56
Cancer Journals, The (Lorde), 41
Cannon, Katie G., 93
capitalism, 2, 19, 34, 77, 88
Catholicism, 74, 94
Central Intelligence Agency, 53

Index

de Certeau, Michel, 52
Cherokee Nation, 37
"Children's Literature: The Creative Spirit" (Jordan), 145
Christianity, 3, 29n5, 93, 135, 137
#CiteBlackWomen, 123, 129n9
civilizing mission, 3–4
Claiming Place (Vang, Nibbs, and Vang), 61
Clarke, Cheryl L., 88
Clifton, Lucille, 124–25
Collins, Patricia Hill, 3, 14, 15, 20, 96, 108
colonialism, definition, 34. *See also* settler colonialism
coloniality, 1–3, 19, 34, 36–40, 42, 45, 155, 158, 163
Combahee River Collective (CRC), 3, 88–89, 90–91, 94, 105, 120
conocimiento, 40
consciousness, 40, 42, 44; Black, 17; colonial, 4, 28; ecological, 39; Mixtec, 98
conquest, 1–3, 9, 34, 36, 54, 78, 98, 165
Cooper, Anna Julia, 120
Cooper, Robert, 56
Crawley, Ashon T., 41
Crenshaw, Kimberlé Williams, 86, 90, 108
critical literacy, 64
compulsory education, 72
critical race theory (CRT), 123
crunk, definition, 121
Crunk Feminist Collective, 121, 122
Culturally Sustaining Pedagogies (Paris and Alim), 136–37
curanderas, 91, 92, 94, 98, 100, 103
curriculum, 69, 127, 154; American exceptionalism, 36; colonial, 37, 39, 41; Eurocentric, 33; hidden, 13–29; passim; higher education, 156, 164; K–12, 77, 79

Dalton, Brenda, 122
Davis, Angela Y., 41, 140–41
decolonial theory, 37
Decolonizing Educational Research (Patel), 36
Dei, George, 76
Deloria, Vine, Jr., 70, 71, 72, 80
Diagnostic and Statistical Manual of Mental Disorders, 4th ed., 37
Diallo, Dazon Dixon, 122
Diego, Adriana, 87
Dillard, Cynthia, 3, 5, 42–43, 72, 78, 119

dissertation production, 115–16, 153, 155, 157–58, 162–63, 165, 166
division of labor, psychosocial, 19
Donnelly, Nancy D., 54, 56–57, 64
Dreeben, Robert, 4
Duffy, John M., 60

educational attainment of Hmong children, 55
Eisler, Riane, 76
Elders, M. Jocelyn, 123
energy transmutation, 43–44
Enlightenment, 69–70, 71, 72, 73–80
epidemiology, 121, 129n6
epistemology, 34, 39, 52, 65, 69, 71, 75, 97; feminist, 70; Mixtec/Indigenous feminist, 99, 104; non-Western, 73, 79–81, 155; spaces, 152; violent, 73
Eurocentrism, 20, 29n5, 33, 79, 86, 96, 149, 153, 156, 161, 163

Fadiman, Anne, 57–59, 64
Fanon, Frantz, 33, 59
feminism, 27; anti-colonial, 79–81; BIP[W]OC, 90–91; Black, 22, 27, 33–35, 42–43, 88, 96, 118–20, 123, 127–28, 154; of Color, 33; whitestream, 79
feminist, Indigenous, Mixteco, migrant research epistemology (FIMME), 97–100, 104
Flores-Haro, Genevieve, 87
Floyd, George, 100
Forman, Ruth, 123, 129n8
Foucault, Michel, 52, 76
Frazier, Demita, 88

Gaines, Koryyn, 13
Garad, Timaj, 139, 141–43, 149
García Aguilár, Silvia, 87
genocide, 2, 3, 34, 35–36, 72, 98, 145, 164
gentrification, 118, 126, 128n1
Goodie M.O.B., 126
grand narrative, 33, 36, 79
Grande, Sandy, 3, 4, 37, 79, 80
Griffin, R. A., 106
Grosfoguel, Ramón, 65, 66, 96
Gui, Jasmine, 139, 141–43, 149
Gumbs, Alexis Pauline, 40, 45, 139, 143–46, 149
Guy-Sheftall, Beverly, 122

Index

Harjo, Joy, 49
Harjo, Laura, 34
Harney, Stefano, 160
Harper, Frances E. W., 120
Harris, Charles Teenie, 126
Hawkins, David R., 43
Healing the Soul Collective, 104–5
heart, 16, 27, 42, 75, 135, 136, 139, 142, 149, 150, 160, 164
HeartMath Institute, 139, 142, 143
Herrera, Timothy M., 97
hip-hop, 14–15, 28, 122
historically Black colleges and universities (HBCUs), 121, 122, 128
Hmong American Writers' Circle, 64, 65
Hmong culture, 55
Hmong diaspora, 52–53
Hmong kinship structure, 53–54
Hmong women, 55; agency, 54, 58, 60, 61; assimilated, 55, 61–63; authentic, 56–59; motherhood as womanhood, 60, 61; refugee, 55, 59–61
holistic education, 70, 72, 76
Home Girls (Smith), 144
Honeywood, Varnette P., 126
hooks, bell, 38, 70–71, 75, 81, 90, 100, 108, 134, 135–37, 138
How Do I Begin? (Hmong American Writers' Circle), 61, 64–65
Huber, L. P., 106
Hughes, Langston, 124
Hurston, Zora Neale, 93, 106, 108

"I Come From" poems, 125–26
"I Give You Back" (Harjo), 49
"I Used to Love H.I.M." (Ali), 15
Indian Removal Act (1830), 36
individualism, 36, 39, 70, 105
inner light, 44–45
intersectionality, 16, 86, 90, 118, 123, 142, 149

Jackson, Andrew, 36, 37
Jackson, Fleda Mask, 122
Jackson, P. W., 17
James, Joy, 152
Jay-Z, 122
Jenkins, William "Bill," 121–22
Jezebel, 15, 20
Jones, Camara P., 123

Jordan, June, 104, 125, 145
Joseph, Gloria, 41

Kaomea, Julie, 76
Keating, AnaLouise, 39
Kelley, Robin D. G., 138, 164
Kherfi, Yasmine, 142
Killing Rage, The (hooks), 38
King, Joyce, 161
knowledge, 1–2, 4, 8, 43, 54, 70–71, 76, 89, 95, 98, 120, 139, 149, 158, 161–62; bodily, 38, 41; commodification, 154–55, 167; cultural, 5, 72, 73, 76; decolonization, 65; feminist, 5; Hmong, 57, 64; Indigenous, 76, 77, 88–90, 93–95, 97, 134, 154; Mixtec, 91, 93, 97, 98, 100; non-Western, 157; production, ix, 52, 54, 81, 89, 96, 97, 107, 119, 155, 162, 164–65; spiritual/religious, 4, 43; Western, x, 38, 80, 86, 153. *See also* Eurocentrism
Koltyk, Jo Ann, 53

"La Güera" (Moraga), 35
"Lament for Dark People" (Hughes), 124
Laos, 53, 56, 58, 60
Latehomecomer, The (K. K. Yang), 61
Lawrence, Jacob, 126
Lecrae, 122
Lefever, Harry, 122
"Lemonade Stand" (Ali), 15
León Salazár, Luisa, 87
"Light in the Dark / Luz en lo Escuro" (Anzaldúa), 113
Lil Jon, 122
limpia, 93–94
Lorde, Audre, 35, 41, 88, 106, 108, 118
love, 2, 4, 35, 45, 72, 94, 138–39, 143–46, 149, 155, 166–67; self-, 35, 104, 126, 136, 141
Lozáno, Claudia, 87
Lucy, 120, 129n4
Luxocracy, 44–45
lynching, 24–25

Mabud, Shaikh, 76
Maira, Sunaina Marr, 137–38
Manriquez, Liliana, 87
Mansa, Nana, II, 5
Maparyan, Layli, 39, 40, 43–44
Marsh, Roya 126
master-servant relationship, 56, 154–55

Index

Maxwell, Annette, 88
Medical Apartheid (Washington), 22, 117–18
mental health, 35, 38, 85, 87, 90, 92, 94–95, 172;
 DSM IV definition, 37
mental illness, 33, 35, 37, 117, 143, 154
meritocracy, 36, 157, 165
metaphysics, 43, 44
methodology, 16–17, 62, 76, 123; feminist, 90;
 participatory narrative analysis, 125; spiritual, 71; womanist, 27
Mire, Hawa Y., 139, 144, 146, 149
misogynoir, 19, 24
Mixteca feminist theory, 91
Mixteco/Indígena community, 85, 87, 89–90,
 92–94, 100–101, 104–7
Mixteco/Indígena Community Organizing
 Project (MICOP), 87–88
modernity, 19, 34, 61, 73–75
Mohanty, Chandra, 3, 54, 96, 104
moore, jessica Care, 126
Moore, Opal, 122
Moore, Thomas, 72
Moraga, Cherríe, 3, 35, 88, 90, 94, 106, 108
Morrill, A., 80
Morrison, Toni, 119, 128–29n3
Moten, Fred, 160
Moua, Mai Neng, 64
multiculturalism, 80, 138
Multi-Faith Centre for Spiritual Study and
 Practice, 135, 137–38, 141
Museum of Man, 20
Muslim, 8, 76, 137
Mustafa, Farrah, 145

Nabavi, Motaharei, 145
National Association for the Advancement of
 Colored People (NAACP), 24
National Black Women's Health Project, 123
neurodivergent, 13, 28–29n1
Newsome, Bree, 141

Odums, Brandan "BMike," 126
Okazawa-Rey, Margo, 88
ontology, ix, 1, 6, 18, 39, 42, 78–79, 81, 124–25,
 155, 156, 159–60, 164
Orientalism, 77, 78–79, 147, 150
Osha, S., 20, 29n5
O'Sullivan, Edmund, 72

*Other Side of the Asian American Success Story,
 The* (Walker-Moffat), 60

Palmer, Parker, 72, 81
Paris, Django, 87, 102, 136–37, 138
Patel, Leigh, 36, 87, 105, 154, 158–59
patriarchy, 34
pedagogy of collegiality, 124
Perez, Emma, 63, 64
Phillips, Mona Taylor, 122
Playing with Fire (Anupamlata et al.), 89
poetry, 16, 20, 27, 52, 64, 115–16, 124–26, 127,
 129n8, 142–43
police, 14, 15, 16, 24, 27, 28–29n1
post-oppositionality, ix–x
Prashad, Vijay, 138
praxis, x, 8, 19, 80, 88–89, 91, 120–23, 138;
 Black feminist, 35, 120; decolonizing,
 118–20, 124, 128
promotora, 87, 95, 101, 103, 105
public health critical race praxis (PHCRP),
 122–23, 129n7. *See also* praxis

racial capitalism, 34
Recollet, Karyn, 139, 144, 146, 149
Red Pedagogy (Grande), 37
Reiki, 94
Reimagine Everything, 139–42, 148–49
religion, 44, 73–76, 80–81, 93
rememory, 19, 118–20, 127, 128–29n3
resilience, 99, 116, 128n1, 147, 164
Revolutionary Mothering (Gumbs, Martens,
 and Williams), 143–45
Rhi, Iliana Yunuen, 97
Rickaby, Joseph, 74
risk, 2, 7, 75, 115–18, 119, 120, 126
Ritskes, Eric J., 75, 76
Rosa, Jonathan, 122

Said, Edward, 77, 78–79
Salazár, Doña Alberta, 87
Sangtin grassroots women's collective, 89, 108
Sangtin Writers Collective, 3, 89, 91, 96, 102,
 104
Santamaría, Lorri J., 87
Santamaría Graff, Cristina, 87
Sapphires, 13, 16
Satcher, David, 122

Index

Scholasticism, 74–75
self-love. *See* love: self-
settler colonialism, 34, 144, 154–56, 158–59, 167
Shafei, Seema, 145
Shahjahan, Riyad, 70, 71, 74
Sheppard, Phillis, 38–39
Sims, Marion, 22–23, 27, 129n4
Singh, Roopa, 147
SisterLove, 123
Sloan, Douglas, 75
Smith, Barbara, 88
Smith, Beverly, 88, 120
Smith, Christen, 129n9
Solórzano, D. G., 106
South Africa, 20
South Asia, 147
Spence, Cynthia Neale, 122
Spillers, Hortense, 18–19
Spiral to the Stars (Harjo), 34
Spirit Catches You and You Fall Down, The (Fadiman), 57
Spirituality, Education, & Society (Abdi), 69
subjectification, 55
Symonds, Patricia, 56

Taylor, Breonna, 101, 108
Taylor, Janelle S., 59
Taylor, Keeanga-Yamahtta, 88
Terrell, Mary Church, 120
Thailand, 53, 56, 60
This Bridge Called My Back (Moraga and Anzaldúa), 35, 144
Transformation Now! Toward a Post-Oppositional Politics of Change (Keating), x
Trawick, Cynthia, 122
Troutman, Adewale, 122
Truth, Sojourner, 120
Tubman, Harriet, 88, 120
Tuck, Eve, 80, 89, 106, 117, 118, 124, 164, 165
Tuhiwai Smith, Linda, 2, 4, 77, 78, 87, 103
Turner, Mary, 24
turner, sheila, 126
Tuskegee Syphilis Study, 121

ubuntu, 5
Undercommons, The (Harney and Moten), 160
Undrowned (Gumbs), 40
universal truth, 70, 73
University of Toronto, 134–36
US Supreme Court, 37

Vang, Burlee, 65
Vietnam, 53
violence, 16, 17–20, 34–36, 73, 118, 147, 162, 163, 165; medical, 22, 24–25; state, 28, 33, 128n1
Virgen de Guadalupe, 93

Wade, Bruce, 122
Wakpa, Tria Blu, 147
Walker, Alice, 11, 71, 72
Walker, Rebecca, 90
Walker-Moffat, Wendy, 60–61
Wane, Njoki N., 75, 76
Washington, Harriet, 22, 117
Weems, Mary, 126
Weisinger, Jean, 41
wellness, 33, 37–38, 42, 117–20, 126–27, 128, 143
Wells-Barnett, Ida B. 120
whiteness, 25, 33, 150, 163
White supremacy, 22, 25, 87, 146, 147, 156, 158, 159, 162
Williams, Fabian, 16, 18, 21, 23, 25, 26
Wind Is Spirit, The (Joseph), 41
womanism, 27, 33, 34, 38–39, 42, 43, 119; anti-colonial, 158–59, 161, 166, 167; worldview, 34
Womanist Idea, The (Maparyan), 39, 44
Woods, Jamila, 126
Wretched of the Earth (Fanon), 33
WritersCorps San Francisco, 125
Writing from These Roots (Duffy), 60

Yancey, Antronette "Toni," 123
Yang, K. Wayne, 89, 165
Yosso, T. J., 106
Young, Robert J. C., 77

TRANSFORMATIONS: WOMANIST, FEMINIST,
AND INDIGENOUS STUDIES

Teaching with Tenderness: Toward an Embodied Practice   *Becky Thompson*
Building Womanist Coalitions: Writing and Teaching in the Spirit of Love
    Edited by Gary L. Lemons
Hungry Translations: Relearning the World through Radical Vulnerability   *Richa Nagar,*
    in journeys with Sangtin Kisan Mazdoor Sangathan and Parakh Theatre
Shared Selves: Latinx Memoir and Ethical Alternatives to Humanism   *Suzanne Bost*
Shapeshifting Subjects: Gloria Anzaldúa's Naguala and Border Arte   *Kelli D. Zaytoun*
Queering Mesoamerica Diasporas: Remembering Xicana Indígena Ancestries   *Susy J. Zepeda*
Virgin Crossing Borders: Feminist Resistance and Solidarity in Translation   *Emek Ergun*
Disrupting Colonial Pedagogies: Theories and Transgressions   *Edited by Jillian Ford*
    and Nathalia E. Jaramillo

The University of Illinois Press
is a founding member of the
Association of University Presses.

———————————————

University of Illinois Press
1325 South Oak Street
Champaign, IL 61820–6903
www.press.uillinois.edu